Honoured Members

HOCKEY HALL *of* FAME

HONOURED MEMBERS
A Fenn Publishing Book / First Published in 2003

Fenn Publishing Company Ltd.
Bolton, Ontario, Canada

Distributed in Canada by H.B. Fenn and Company Ltd.
Bolton, Ontario, Canada, L7E 1W2
www.hbfenn.com

All images courtesy of the Hockey Hall of Fame from the following collections:
Foreword photo courtesy of Bobby Orr: vi
Dave Sandford/HHOF: vii, 201, 208, 210, 214, 226
Doug MacLellan/HHOF: 6, 186, 190, 192, 217
Frank Prazak/HHOF: 43, 77, 78, 93, 97, 107, 112, 116, 120, 126, 130, 137, 140, 144, 145, 146, 157, 161, 164
Fred Keenan/HHOF: 129
Graphic Artists/HHOF: 74, 96, 98, 99, 108, 110, 113, 114, 120, 121, 122, 125, 128, 130, 136, 142, 146, 148, 150, 153, 156, 162, 165, 168, 169, 177, 178
Hockey Hall of Fame Archives: 2, 3, 4, 5, 8, 9, 10, 11, 12, 13, 16, 18, 19, 20, 22, 23, 24, 26, 27, 28, 29, 30, 31, 32, 34, 36, 37, 38, 40, 41, 42, 44, 45, 46, 48, 49, 50, 51, 52, 54, 55, 56, 57, 58, 59, 60, 61, 62, 64, 65, 66, 68, 69, 70, 71, 72, 80, 82, 84, 86, 88, 90, 92, 94, 97, 100, 103, 106, 107, 108, 118, 126, 150, 154, 158, 165, 168, 170, 177, 183, 184, 189, 192, 194, 196, 198, 206
IIHF/HHOF: 195, 227, 228
Imperial Oil-Turofsky/HHOF: 2, 12, 14, 16, 26, 27, 29, 32, 34, 40, 41, 43, 44, 49, 57, 64, 65, 66, 69, 71, 74, 75, 76, 77, 80, 84, 85, 89, 92, 98, 100, 102, 100, 103, 104, 110, 111, 117, 121, 124, 125, 126, 132, 133, 138, 153, 154, 166, 170, 174, 181, 187, 192, 204
James McCarthy/HHOF: 89,156
James Rice/HHOF: 9, 19, 27, 36, 64, 68, 74
London Life-Portnoy/HHOF: 128, 136, 141, 144, 148, 149, 152, 160, 173, 181, 187, 188, 194, 195, 204
Matthew Manor/HHOF: viii
Mecca/HHOF: 186, 218
Miles Nadal/HHOF: 208
O-Pee-Chee/HHOF: 124, 128, 172, 180, 218, 221
Paul Bereswill/HHOF: 164, 172, 176, 178, 182, 183, 190, 198, 200, 201, 202, 205, 209, 210, 212, 213, 216, 217, 220, 221, 222, 224, 225
Ralph Bacon/HHOF: 11, 134

National Library of Canada Cataloguing in Publication

Honoured members: the Hockey Hall of Fame.

ISBN 1-55168-239-7

1. Hockey players—Biography. 2. Hockey—History.

GV848.5.A1H66 2003   796.962'092'2   C2003-902104-1

Printed in Canada

Honoured Members

HOCKEY HALL *of* FAME

Fenn Publishing Company Ltd.
Bolton, Ontario

Contents

Hockey has been my passion for as long as I can remember. From the moment you pick up a hockey stick, you dream about one day playing in the National Hockey League. But you don't dare think about being inducted into the Hockey Hall of Fame. To have the opportunity to play hockey as a professional athlete was a dream come true. To be further honoured with a place in this hallowed Hall has been both gratifying and extremely humbling.

Honoured Members is about men who shared with me the same dreams of achieving at the highest levels of our game. Whether they were Players, Officials or Builders, the stories you will read all represent the lifelong efforts of some very gifted and passionate individuals. This book is a tribute to the perseverance and sacrifice demonstrated by hockey's greatest names that, in the end, make them the 'Honoured Members.'

Bobby Orr

Foreword

Introduction

As you turn the pages of this celebratory book, there are hockey games being played in locations around the world. Some will be games played by elite athletes at hockey's most scrutinized level; most will be of the grassroots variety played on streets, frozen lakes, or in hometown rinks with players young and old. But there is a common bond that unites all hockey games – passion. It is a passion for the sheer love of playing the sport; passion for competition amongst friends; passion for the camaraderie that binds the players of this wonderful game together.

Each of the players eloquently depicted in this book possessed the same dreams as you, me, and those young hockey players down the street chasing their beat-up tennis ball. The difference is that opportunity, God-given talent, and hard work allowed these players to reach a level that makes them the greatest players ever to take part in the game. The Honoured Members of the Hockey Hall of Fame have been selected by a panel of peers through the decades to represent an elite level of Players, Builders, and Officials. Whether they are identified as forwards, referees, or general managers, these distinguished men are intrinsically bound together through their passion for the greatest game in the world.

The Hockey Hall of Fame is the virtual home for these Honoured Members. In 2003, the Hockey Hall of Fame celebrated its tenth anniversary at BCE Place, located at the corner of Yonge and Front Streets in downtown Toronto. The Hockey Hall of Fame exists in a majestically restored bank building that has become a cathedral for these icons of hockey and a theatrical setting for the induction of the greatest Players, Builders, and Officials in hockey's history.

We at the Hockey Hall of Fame strive to preserve the legacy of our game with the same passion that these Honoured Members displayed during their distinguished careers. I hope *Honoured Members* is an enjoyable book for you, but maybe more importantly, I hope that it inspires you through the players' passion for the greatest game in the world.

Sincerely,

Bill Hay
Chairman and CEO
Hockey Hall of Fame

1945

April 30, 1945: The International Hockey Hall of Fame is Born

Captain James T. Sutherland spent his life in hockey. Yes, he played the game—but more importantly, he celebrated it. In 1903, when he was just 33, he declared his hometown of Kingston, Ontario the birthplace of hockey. This was a singular claim, but Sutherland had done some research on the subject; not many historians for other cities had done more. Besides, in 1886, students of Queen's College and the cadets of Royal Military College played a game in Kingston, and Sutherland knew of no other organized contest that predated this for sophistication of play and rules employed.

Sutherland was a shoe salesman by trade, but he was also a referee. In 1910, he became a member of the Ontario Hockey Association's executive, a position he held for most of the rest of his life. He also fought for Canada in World War I (1914–18). But Sutherland is best known in hockey circles for his unparalleled efforts to honour the game's great men by inaugurating a Hockey Hall of Fame. In 1938, Major League Baseball had selected Cooperstown, New York as the site for the Baseball Hall of Fame (at the time, Cooperstown was recognized as the place where baseball began), and Sutherland almost immediately set out to make Kingston the home to hockey's equivalent museum.

The war raged, though, and raising money for a hockey building was low on everyone's list of priorities. But by 1943 Sutherland's intense enthusiasm and unrelenting pursuit of a Hockey Hall of Fame led to an agreement between the Canadian Amateur Hockey Association and the National Hockey League that a hall should be built in Kingston, the purpose of which was—to use Sutherland's own words—"to perpetuate the memories of the men who have done so much to develop nationally and internationally Canada's great winter sport."

By this time, groups from Halifax and Montreal had laid greater claims to being the birthplace of hockey, but neither city had a supporter as influential and magnanimous as Sutherland. Furthermore, Sutherland had been a collector of all things hockey for nearly half a century. He could have opened a museum just by using the memorabilia in his own house.

Initially, the International Hockey Hall of Fame had two mandates: first, to honour the great players of the past; second, to raise funds toward the building of a suitable museum to celebrate in perpetuity their lives. Toward the latter goal, Sutherland donated $1,000 and enlisted Mayor Stuart Crawford of Kingston to raise the rest of the necessary money. Toward the former, the Hall inducted nine Players on April 30, 1945: Hobey Baker, Chuck Gardiner, Eddie Gerard, Frank McGee, Howie Morenz, Tommy Phillips, Harvey Pulford, Hod Stuart, and Georges Vézina. Additionally, two Builders were also honoured: Lord Stanley and Sir Montagu Allan.

NORTH (MGR.) MACCOLL KILNER BRYAN LEE FITZPATRICK (COACH)
WINANTS KUHN BAKER (CAPT.) PATTERSON EMMONS
COWAN CARTER

Hobey Baker

b. Wissahickon, Pennsylvania, January 15, 1892
d. Toul, France, December 21, 1918

During his four years at Princeton University, Baker quickly established himself as the best hockey player ever produced by the United States. He was the fastest skater on the team, the best stickhandler, and the most skilled competitor. He played hard but was renowned for fair and gentlemanly conduct. He studied history, politics, and economics, and his exploits on the football

field were as famous as those on the ice. He graduated in 1914 and played one season of amateur hockey with the great St. Nicholas club of New York. Then he became an army man, joining the Lafayette Escadrille and working his way to lieutenant and then, in 1917, commanding officer. (For Baker, flying was much the same as skating full speed.) On December 21, 1918, he was called home, and decided to take one last flight in a No. 7 Spad. The plane crashed and Baker died. Years later, the Hobey Baker Award was established by the National Collegiate Athletic Association to be given annually to the best college hockey played in the United States.

The epitaph on Hobey Baker's headstone speaks to the respect and admiration he earned while a member of the U.S. military: "You who seemed winged, even as a lad,/With that swift look of those who know the sky,/It was no blundering fate that stooped and bade/You break your wings, and fall to earth and die./I think some day you may have flown too high,/So that immortals saw you and were glad,/Watching the beauty of your spirits flame,/Until they loved and called you, and you came."

Chuck Gardiner

b. Edinburgh, Scotland, December 31, 1904
d. Winnipeg, Manitoba, June 13, 1934

In seven seasons of hockey with Chicago in the NHL (1927–34), Gardiner did not miss a single game. He won the Vézina Trophy twice and played in the 1934 Ace Bailey Benefit Game at Maple

Leaf Gardens (pictured here), and although the Hawks were never a good team during his years, Gardiner was always the best. His last season was his ultimate. He led the league with 10 shutouts, and the fact that his team scored the fewest goals in the NHL did not stop him from taking them to the Stanley Cup. In eight playoff games, Gardiner allowed just a dozen goals.

He returned home to Winnipeg, where an infection escalated to uremic convulsions and a brain hemorrhage. Gardiner died in hospital in the prime of his life, a Stanley Cup champion.

GARDINER DEAD AT 33

Marvin McCarthy of the *Chicago Herald-American* eulogized the great goalie Chuck Gardiner upon learning of his untimely demise: "Another valiant warrior lies at eternal ease in the shadow of professional ice hockey's symbol of courage, the Georges Vézina Trophy for keepers of the goal. Chuck Gardiner is dead. Curly-headed Chuck, holy terror of the ice, young Blind Fury personified, who times galore has startled and thrilled us with headlong rushes into the very thing that I'm afraid played a part in his death—the hurtling puck.

"No onslaught that stout Chuck ever faced was so sudden or stunning as Death's swift charge that laid him low. Early Wednesday afternoon on June 13, Chicago hockey fans learned that Gardiner was ill at his home in Winnipeg. A few hours later, the last red light had flashed for Chuck.

"The best goalie in all hockey, who could stop rubber bullets, was powerless before his charge, and Death had scored a goal."

Eddie Gerard

b. Ottawa, Ontario, February 22, 1890
d. Ottawa, Ontario, August 7, 1937

The number 2 who played his entire career in Ottawa won a Stanley Cup with Toronto in 1922 under unique circumstances. The St. Pats lost a man to injury and were allowed to name a replacement. They chose Gerard and the St. Pats went on to win the Cup. It wasn't the first time for Gerard. He had been on two championship teams with the Senators—winning in 1920 and 1921—and he went on to win with the Senators again in 1923. Gerard started his career as a forward and in later years moved back to defence. Back in 1917–18, the first year of the NHL, he had been a playing coach with the Senators; after retiring in 1923, he moved full-time into coaching. From 1924 until 1935, he was a bench boss almost continuously, notably with the Maroons and the Americans. In 1925–26, he led the English Montrealers to a Stanley Cup, his first and only championship as a coach.

Frank McGee

b. Ottawa, Ontario, November 4, 1882
d. Courcelette, France, September 16, 1916

While playing for the Ottawa Aberdeens in the first years of the 1900s, McGee was struck in the eye by a lifted puck and lost sight in that eye. He continued to play hockey and became one of the game's greatest goal scorers, notably in Stanley Cup challenge play. McGee played on the famed Ottawa Silver Seven that vanquished challenger after challenger to win the Cup every year from 1902 to 1906. His defining moment came on January 16, 1905 when he scored 14 goals against the Dawson City team that had trekked from the Northwest Territories to Ottawa to try to wrest the Cup from the Silver Seven. McGee scored eight of those goals in under nine minutes.

Howie Morenz

b. Mitchell, Ontario, June 21, 1902
d. Montreal, Quebec, March 8, 1937

He was called the Stratford Streak because during his junior days in that city, Morenz electrified fans with his speed as no one had before. When he got to the NHL, he was the principle reason to go to a game. Morenz played most of his career with the

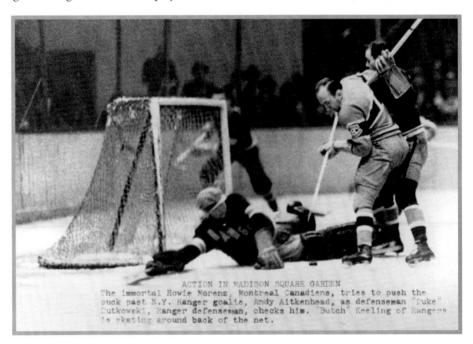

ACTION IN MADISON SQUARE GARDEN
The immortal Howie Morenz, Montreal Canadiens, tries to push the puck past N.Y. Ranger goalie, Andy Aitkenhead, as defenseman "Duke" Dutkowski, Ranger defenseman, checks him. "Butch" Keeling of Rangers is skating around back of the net.

Canadiens, starting in 1923. He skated like the wind, scored with amazing regularity, and was the first superstar of the league, bringing people out of their seats when he gathered the puck in his own end. He won three Stanley Cups and led the NHL in scoring with 33 goals in 1927–28. But his career ended on January 28, 1937 when he was checked by Earl Seibert behind the Chicago net. He fell, and his skate blade got caught in the wood boards, shattering his leg. Just a few weeks later, Morenz died, never having left hospital. Because his career was irrevocably over with that check, his friends said that he died of a broken heart.

1945

The funeral for Howie Morenz at the Forum in Montreal was one of that city's greatest and saddest moments as thousands of fans paid tribute to their hero.

On Friday, March 12, 1937, the Montreal Forum had more people in it than at any other time during its hockey association with Montreal. But the occasion was not a Stanley Cup game; it was the funeral of Howie Morenz. Reverend Malcolm Campbell presided over a congregation that came to pay their last respects to the greatest hockey player of the era. Morenz lay in wake at centre ice, his casket surrounded by floral tributes, a police guard, and a guard of honour that included teammates Johnny Gagnon, Pit Lepine, and Armand Mondou. Over the course of the day, tens of thousands paid their respects, and the line outside the Forum ran on and on into the night streets of Montreal. Howie Morenz was no more.

Tommy Phillips

b. Rat Portage (Kenora), Ontario, May 22, 1883
d. Toronto, Ontario, November 30, 1923

As a developing hockey player in the early 1900s, Phillips showed great skating ability and had a backhand of unequalled speed and accuracy. He played his early hockey in Montreal, but his career was defined by his time with his hometown Kenora Thistles from 1905 to 1907. He led the charge in that first year against the Ottawa Silver Seven to challenge for the Cup, but Ottawa was too strong a team. Two years later, though, the Thistles travelled to Montreal to play the Wanderers in a two-game, total-goals challenge. Phillips scored all four goals in a 4-2 win in the first contest, and

Kenora won the second game 8-6 to win the Stanley Cup. To this day, Kenora is the smallest town to win the sacred silverware. Out west, Phillips was often called the greatest player in the game (much like Frank McGee in the east).

Harvey Pulford

b. Toronto, Ontario, April 22, 1875
d. Ottawa, Ontario, October 31, 1940

Pulford played his entire amateur and professional hockey career in Ottawa, beginning in 1893 and spanning some 15 seasons. His career culminated with the Silver Seven with whom he won a series of Stanley Cup challenges to earn championship honours in 1903, 1904, and 1905. A defenceman, he shunned the accepted practice of lifting the puck, and instead carried the puck up ice, thus becoming a pioneer of the rushing defenceman style of play. Pulford became a referee after retiring as a player, but he was perhaps best known as an all-round athlete and a champion in everything he undertook—from boxing to football to lacrosse to rowing.

Hod Stuart

b. Ottawa, Ontario, 1879
d. Bay of Quinte, Ontario, June 23, 1907

An outstanding and complete player, Stuart could skate and shoot and pass with the best of his peers. He played amateur hockey in Ottawa and Quebec before going to Pittsburgh in 1902 to play professionally. In 1906 he returned to Canada to play for the Montreal Wanderers, a team that had tried to lure him many times previously. Stuart was a member of the team in March 1907 when the Redbands defeated Kenora to win the Stanley Cup. On vacation that summer, he dove from a deck into shallow waters, breaking his neck. His death shocked the hockey world. The next winter, the Wanderers played a memorial game on January 2, 1908 against the best players from the rest of the East Coast Amateur Hockey Association. It was the first "all-star game" in hockey history.

Georges Vézina

b. Chicoutimi, Quebec, January 21, 1887
d. Chicoutimi, Quebec, March 27, 1926

From the time he entered the net of the Montreal Canadiens in the National Hockey Association in 1910 until the time he left the goal, deathly ill, during a game on November 28, 1925, Vézina did not miss a single game for the Club de Hockey. He won two Stanley Cups with the team, one in 1915–16 in the National Hockey Association and the other in 1923–24 in the NHL. He was cool as a cucumber in goal— which is how he got the moniker Chicoutimi Cucumber—and his stand-up style of goaltending made him without question the pre-eminent stopper of his generation. He left the crease during the first game of the 1925–26 season, and a few weeks later died of tuberculosis, at home. To perpetuate his memory, the NHL introduced the Vézina Trophy, emblematic of the best goalie in the NHL, based first on goals allowed and, more recently, votes.

Sir Montagu Allan

b. Montreal, Quebec, 1860
d. Montreal, Quebec, September, 1951

By 1908, the Stanley Cup was no longer a purely amateur trophy. The proliferation of pro leagues in the east ensured that the best teams in the country were made of paid players. As a result, William Northey of Montreal convinced Sir Montagu Allan, a sportsman and wealthy financier, to donate a trophy that would be emblematic of amateur supremacy in Canada. Thus was born the Allan Cup, won first by Queen's University.

Lord Stanley of Preston

b. London, England, January 15, 1841
d. London, England, June 14, 1908

LORD STANLEY – DONATED THE STANLEY CUP, EMBLEMATIC OF WORLD PROFESSIONAL HOCKEY SUPREMACY.

Lord Stanley arrived in Ottawa in 1888 with virtually no knowledge of or association with Canada's winter game. But as he assumed duties as Canada's governor-general, he quickly discovered the pleasure of the sport

1945

and the social and physical benefits of both watching and playing. During his final year in office, he decided that, in order for Canada to celebrate the best team in the land, a trophy was needed. To that end, he commissioned a silversmith in England to design a cup that would be awarded each year to that team, and on March 18, 1892, at a dinner in Ottawa, Stanley made his intentions clear through a letter that Lord Kilcoursie read on his behalf: "I have for some time been thinking that it would be a good thing if there were a challenge cup, which should be held from year to year by the champion hockey team in the Dominion. There does not appear to be any such outward sign of a championship at present, and considering the general interest which matches now elicit, and the importance of having the game played fairly and under rules generally recognized, I am

willing to give a cup which shall be held from year to year by the winning team." Almost from the moment the cup first arrived in Ottawa, everyone called it the Stanley Cup—and it has been called such ever since.

The Stanley Cup

Upon his departure from Canada, Lord Stanley appointed two trustees of the trophy, Sheriff John Sweetland and P. D. Ross. From then on, the Cup has been maintained by two trustees. When one trustee dies, he wills a successor to ensure continuity of the trusteeship. Today, the two men responsible for carrying out Lord Stanley's wishes are Brian O'Neill and Scotty Morrison.

The original Stanley Cup bowl in all its simplicity and glory.

1947

February 12, 1947: Dit Clapper Night

On February 6, 1947, Dit Clapper announced that he was going to play his final game six nights later. Mayor Stuart Crawford, president of the Hall of Fame in Kingston, immediately announced that on February 12, Clapper would be inducted straight into the Hall, thus becoming the first living player so honoured. Clapper was coaching the Bruins at the time, but he played a total of six games in 1946–47. His retirement as a player marked the end of 20 years' continuous service with one team; Clapper was the first NHLer who could make such a claim. In pre-game ceremonies, Clapper received a Hall of Fame scroll from Captain James T. Sutherland and a sterling silver tea service from the six NHL teams (pictured on the next page). His number 5 was immediately retired by the club. Clapper continued as Boston coach until the end of the 1948–49 season.

1947

Aubrey "Dit" Clapper

b. Newmarket, Ontario, February 9, 1907
d. Peterborough, Ontario, January 21, 1978

Dit Clapper grew up near Peterborough and developed into a top-flight prospect in Toronto. He signed in 1926 with the Boston Tigers and a year later, at age 19, he was ready for the Bruins and the NHL. Clapper was a defenceman, but the B's moved him to the wing because he had such a terrific shot. He had his greatest success on the Dynamite Line with Cooney Weiland and Dutch Gainor, winning three Cups with the team (1929, 1939, and 1941). In 1929–30, he scored a career high of 41 goals. When the great Eddie Shore retired in 1938, coach Art Ross moved Clapper back to right defence—and he was named to three successive First All-Star Teams as a blueliner.

One of the many gifts Dit Clapper received the night of February 12, 1947, when he became the first living player to be inducted into the International Hockey Hall of Fame.

On February 25, 1947, the selection committee for the International Hockey Hall of Fame added 13 new names to the honour roll—six Players and seven Builders. Russell Bowie, Aurel Joliat, Frank Nighbor, Lester Patrick, Eddie Shore, and Cyclone Taylor were the newest Player additions; Frank Calder, William Hewitt, Francis Nelson, William Northey, John Ross Robertson, Claude Robinson, and Captain James Sutherland were the Builders. In October 1947, the Allan Cup champions Montreal Royals played the Toronto Maple Leafs in a benefit game in Kingston, with the money from that game going to the Hall of Fame Building Fund. The previous year, the Rangers and Bruins in the NHL, and the senior Ottawa Senators and a local Kingston team all played for the same purposes. By this time, the Building Fund was in excess of $50,000.

Russell Bowie

b. Montreal, Quebec, August 24, 1880
d. Montreal, Quebec, April 8, 1959

He was considered the finest stickhandler of his era, but throughout his career, Bowie steadfastly remained an amateur player with the Montreal Victorias—despite annual efforts by other teams to make

him a well-paid professional. Bowie's goal scoring was the stuff of legend. He once had 10 goals in a single game, and during his decade with the Vics he averaged almost three goals a game. He led the league in scoring five times and won one Stanley Cup, in 1899, as a rookie. His career came to an end when he suffered a serious break of his collarbone.

Aurel Joliat

b. Ottawa, Ontario, August 29, 1901

d. Ottawa, Ontario, June 2, 1986

Goalies said his shot couldn't break a pane of glass, but Joliat got around this weakness by becoming the most deft player around the net, famous for deking goalies and putting the puck gently into the open cage. The "Little Giant" weighed perhaps 138 pounds soaking wet, but he was among the greatest scorers of his era. He joined the Canadiens in 1922 and the team soon became known as the Flying Frenchmen for its speed, skill, and scoring ability. Montreal acquired him by trading Newsy Lalonde. The trade was a testament to the high value the team placed on the youngster who had not yet played a game in the NHL. Joliat played 16 seasons with the Canadiens, winning three Stanley Cups and, in 1933–34, being named winner of the Hart Trophy. He was not as flashy as Howie Morenz and he lacked the outward fire of Johnny Gagnon, teammates both, but Joliat was as great a threat to score as any player on the Montreal teams.

April 17, 1947

Aurel Joliat was formally inducted into the International Hockey Hall of Fame in a moving ceremony on April 17, 1947 at the Montreal Forum, before game five of the Toronto-Montreal finals. Captain James T. Sutherland and Mayor Stuart Crawford were on hand to present the scroll to Joliat, who received a standing ovation from 12,000 fans.

Frank Nighbor

b. Pembroke, Ontario, January 26, 1893

d. Pembroke, Ontario, April 13, 1966

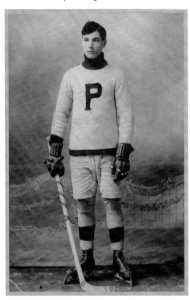

The "Pembroke Peach" accomplished more than almost any player in the early years of the NHL. For starters, Nighbor won five Stanley Cups, the first in 1914–15 with the Vancouver Millionaires, and the other four in the NHL in the 1920s with the Ottawa Senators. He won two Lady Byng Trophies and in 1924 was the inaugural winner of the Hart Trophy. Nighbor was a goal scorer, but his greater claim to fame was the poke check. He was the master without compare: his darting stab at the puck thwarted one opponent rush after another and he created many a scoring chance off the counterattack. He was also renowned as a "60-minute player," a forward who played the entire game without rest. By the time he retired in 1930, Nighbor had left an indelible mark on the game.

Lester Patrick

b. Drummondville, Quebec, December 30, 1883

d. Victoria, British Columbia, June 1, 1960

The extraordinary career of the Silver Fox started with consecutive Stanley Cup victories in 1905 and 1906 with the Montreal Wanderers and didn't end until shortly before his death more than half a century later. As a player, Patrick was a

1947

defenceman who liked to rush the puck instead of lifting it into enemy territory. He and brother Frank moved to the west with their father to work in the lumber business, and in 1911 they convinced him to build two arenas with artificial ice, the first two in Canada. With rinks in Vancouver and Victoria, the brothers started their own league, one that was innovative and forward-looking, one that sought to entice the best players from the east, and one in which they themselves could also play. This became the Pacific Coast Hockey Association. Patrick retired in 1926 and began an equally long association with the Rangers, first as a coach for 12 years and then as a general manager. The name Patrick continues to be an important part of the game. Lester had two sons, Lynn and Muzz, who played in the NHL, and his grandsons Craig and Glenn also played. Craig remains the general manager of Pittsburgh, a Patrick connection to hockey that began with the Wanderers almost a full century ago.

A 44-Year-Old Goalie

On April 7, 1928, Lester Patrick stood behind the bench to coach his Rangers in game two of the Stanley Cup finals in Montreal. But early in the second period of the scoreless game,

his goalie, Lorne Chabot, was hit in the face by a shot and couldn't continue. Patrick decided to go in net and named Odie Cleghorn as coach for the rest of the night. Miraculously, Patrick led the Rangers to a stunning 2-1 victory in overtime. He had never played goal before, and he certainly never played again. The Rangers went on to win the Cup with Joe Miller in goal, becoming the first American NHL team to win Lord Stanley's cherished donation.

Eddie Shore

b. Fort Qu'Appelle, Saskatchewan, November 25, 1902
d. Springfield, Massachusetts, March 16, 1985

The same day that Boston newspapers trumpeted the induction of Dit Clapper into the International Hockey Hall of Fame—the first living player so honoured—stories were also published at the outrage of not including Eddie Shore in the honours. He had been retired several years (the Clapper naming was a special celebration to coincide with Clapper's own retirement) and was acknowledged by one and all to be the finest player in Boston Bruins history. By the end of the month, Shore's name was part of the complete list of inductees for 1947, and he took his rightful place in the pantheon of hockey greats.

There was only one Eddie Shore, and of those who crossed paths with him, half are thankful, half are rueful. Mercurial, brilliant, violent, enigmatic, Shore was the greatest defenceman in the history of hockey until 1966, the year Bobby Orr first graced the NHL. Shore kept the Bruins franchise alive. He could score goals and intimidate opponents from the blue line, and his presence alone raised the quality of team play. In the 1930s, he was a First Team All-Star seven times, and he is the only NHL defenceman to win the Hart Trophy four times. His brilliant play was always offset by spasms of violence, most notably on the night of December 12, 1933 when he nearly killed Ace Bailey in a game at the Garden. He was called "Mr. Hockey" long before Gordie Howe, and when he retired, the Bruins retired his number 2 as a tribute.

An Owner's Nightmare

Some players called him a tough but brilliant coach. Others called him far worse. Toward the end of his career, Eddie Shore played for both the Bruins and the Springfield Indians of the American Hockey League, the team he bought. As an owner, he was as successful and controversial as he had been when playing (in this photo he poses in front of the Indians' arena). He won Calder Cups with the Indians, but he was so vilified that, one season, the players went on strike and refused to play for him. Shore worked his own way, and that wasn't always everyone's way. Even so, there's no denying that he was a champion.

Fred "Cyclone" Taylor

b. Tara, Ontario, June 23, 1883

d. Vancouver, British Columbia, June 10, 1979

Although Taylor never played in the NHL, his skills were so tremendous that to ignore them would have been foolhardy. It was common knowledge that he could skate backwards faster

FRED TAYLOR IN ACTION

than almost any other player could skate forwards. Taylor spent the vast majority of his career out west. He had won a Stanley Cup with Ottawa in 1909 and won a second with the Vancouver Millionaires in 1914–15. A perennial All-Star, he led the Pacific Coast Hockey Association in goal

scoring three times and led in points five times. In a game on March 9, 1910, his abilities became legend. The *Renfrew Journal* offered this account of a goal he scored: "Perhaps one of the most sensational features was the fulfilling by Fred Taylor of his promise to score a goal on Ottawa backwards. Taylor got the puck on a pass and skating down in his usual fine fashion, he turned, and going backwards, he skated a piece and then sent the shot home in the Ottawa nets with skill and swiftness."

Not many people know who Fred Taylor was, but everyone knows the name Cyclone Taylor. While watching Taylor play for Ottawa in a game against the Montreal Wanderers on January 11, 1908, Earl Grey, Canada's governor-general, proclaimed that Taylor was "a cyclone if ever I saw one." The *Ottawa Free Press* picked up on this and reported: "In Portage la Prairie they called him a tornado. In Houghton, Michigan, he was known as a whirlwind. From now on, he'll be known as Cyclone Taylor."

Perhaps there has never been a funnier, more insightful remark than that made by Babe Pratt in reference to Cyclone Taylor. Pratt became a goodwill ambassador of sorts for the Vancouver Canucks when they joined the NHL, and Taylor dropped the puck at the first home game for the team. When asked by a reporter how many goals Taylor might score in the watered-down NHL of the modern era, Pratt replied, "about 20." This stunned the reporter. "But Babe!" he cried. "Cyclone Taylor could do it all! He was the greatest player of his day!"

"I know," deadpanned Pratt. "But the man's 90 years old."

1947

Frank Calder

b. Bristol, England, November 17, 1877
d. Montreal, Quebec, February 4, 1943

In 1907, Calder became the sports editor for the *Montreal Herald* and quickly established a reputation for being tough and fair, intelligent and ethical. He earned the admiration of many hockey men, and in 1915 he was named secretary of the National Hockey Association. Two years later, when the NHA folded and re-emerged as the NHL, Calder was named president. For the next quarter-century, he took the league and hockey to a higher level, ruling with foresight and a keen sense for the game, even though he had never played it. The Calder Trophy was named in his honour, and after his sudden passing following a heart attack, it became known as the Calder Memorial Trophy.

William Hewitt

b. Cobourg, Ontario, May 15, 1975
d. Toronto, Ontario, September 8, 1966

While his son, Foster, became an icon to everyone who followed hockey, William Archibald Hewitt was a hero in the backrooms. He acted as secretary of the Ontario Hockey Association from 1903 to 1961. He and Claude Robinson helped form the Canadian Amateur Hockey Association in 1914. He took Canada's Olympic hockey team to Antwerp in 1920 and helped establish CAHA rules as the official rules of international hockey. He was, in short, an integral part of the development and popularization of the game.

Francis Nelson

b. unknown
d. Balboa, Panama, April 15, 1932

While working as the sports editor of the *Toronto Globe*, Nelson earned the praise of John Ross Robertson, president of the Ontario Hockey Association. In 1903, Robertson hired Nelson as his vice president, a position Nelson held for three years. He then became the OHA governor to the Amateur Athletic Union of Canada and later was made a lifetime member of the OHA.

William Northey

b. Leeds, Quebec, April 29, 1872
d. Montreal, Quebec, April 9, 1963

Although Northey helped with the construction of the Westmount Arena in 1897, he was better known a few years later as the man who built the Montreal Forum. He ensured it was

William Northey receives his Hall of Fame plaque from NHL president Clarence Campbell.

a structure with no interior columns to block sightlines and that it had a suitable capacity (almost 10,000). Northey was involved in amateur and professional hockey all his life. In 1908, he convinced Sir Montagu Allan to donate a trophy for amateur champions in Canada to replace the Stanley Cup, which was becoming more and more a pro trophy. As a result, Northey was the first trustee of the Allan Cup. He later teamed with Claude Robinson to establish the Canadian Amateur Hockey Association and he was integral in changing hockey from a seven-man sport to six a side.

John Ross Robertson

b. Toronto, Ontario,
*   December 28, 1841*
d. Toronto, Ontario,
*   May 31, 1918*

He was a writer and a promoter of Canada's youth, but in a hockey context Robertson made an important contribution. He met with the Ontario Hockey Association in 1898, and out of that collaboration he donated three trophies for annual competition in Canada. There was one trophy each for senior, intermediate, and junior level hockey—to encourage athletics at all ages of growth for kids.

Claude Robinson

b. Harriston, Ontario,
*   December 17, 1881*
d. Vancouver, British Columbia,
*   June 27, 1976*

Robinson was associated with the Victorias in Winnipeg, the city of his youth, for both an Allan Cup and Stanley Cup victory. His defining moment, though, came on December 4, 1914 at

the Chateau Laurier hotel in Ottawa, when he suggested that Canada's hockey program be shaped under one umbrella organization that would oversee all amateur hockey. Thus, the birth of the Canadian Amateur Hockey Association. He became its first secretary and later its first lifetime member.

Captain James T. Sutherland

b. Kingston, Ontario, October 10, 1870
d. Kingston, Ontario, September 30, 1955

JAMES T. SUTHERLAND
KINGSTON
Past President and Life Member, O.H.A.

Coach, referee, president, Sutherland was first and foremost a man who championed hockey for its myriad contributions to Canadian society. He was one of the first to try to pinpoint the birthplace of the game, and he was the sole driving force in trying to establish a Hockey Hall of Fame to house the artifacts and memories of the game's great stars. Thanks to him, Kingston was chosen host city for a possible Hall of Fame building, and under his guidance, the Hall began inducting players and executives beginning in 1945. Sutherland served as Ontario Hockey Association president from 1915 to 1917 and Canadian Amateur Hockey Association president from 1919 to 1921.

1949

December 2, 1949: Celebrating Hockey's Early Stars

In 1949, there were still many great players who had not yet been inducted into the International Hockey Hall of Fame, in large part because of a complex system of voting. The new president of the hall of fame was now James Garvin, and a Board of Governors (a group of 16) presided over the voting. Each served for a term of five years and each could nominate up to three men (though they could only deem a maximum of two men worthy of induction). Notification of the nominations had to be made 60 days before the group was to meet. Upon meeting, each governor filled in a ballot with up to 10 names for consideration. For a player to be inducted, he must appear on 75 percent of the ballots (or, 12 of the 16). In 1949, only the names of Dan Bain and Art Ross passed the strict procedure; no one could dispute their worthiness.

1949

Dan Bain

b. Belleville, Ontario, February 14, 1874
d. Winnipeg, Manitoba, August 15, 1962

Bain was named Canada's athlete of the last half of the 19th century. He excelled at many sports, but his specialty was hockey. He played his entire career with the Winnipeg Victorias and to this day is considered Manitoba's finest hockey player. In 1896, he scored the winning goal in a 2-0 victory over the Montreal Victorias to give Winnipeg the Stanley Cup. Although the 'Peg lost challenges in 1896 and 1899, Bain brought glory to his city again in 1901 by scoring the winner over the Montreal Shamrocks. He won his third and final Cup the following year, at which time he retired.

The announcement that Bain and Ross were to be inducted into the hall of fame occurred on October 21, 1949, but Art Ross was formally inducted in a special ceremony at centre ice on December 2, 1949, prior to a Boston game. Ross was presented his scroll by president James Garvin, and then–NHL president Clarence Campbell gave him a sterling silver tray with the emblems of the six teams engraved on it. After the game, a special dinner was held at the Hotel Statler, and there Ross was showered with more gifts and kind speeches for his tremendous contributions to the game.

Art Ross

b. Naughton, Ontario, January 13, 1886
d. Boston, Massachusetts, August 5, 1964

As a player, Ross was brilliant and much admired. He was credited with introducing a "kitty bar the door" style of play to preserve a lead, and he won two Stanley Cups, one with the Kenora Thistles in 1907 and another with the Montreal

Wanderers a year later. Despite a 12-year career, Ross played only one year in the NHL, his last and its first. He started with the Wanderers, but when the arena burned down he retired and became a hockey executive, though not before first establishing himself as the best referee in the new league. In 1924, when Charles Adams brought hockey to Boston, he hired Ross as general manager. It was the start of an association with the team that lasted almost until the day Ross died some 30 years later. He brought three Cups to Boston, formed the Bruins' great Dynamite and Kraut Lines, and developed virtually every great player the team knew.

A Great Innovator

Few men had the practical impact on the game that Art Ross did. He designed the puck that became standard issue in the NHL for decades, and his goal net was also widely used, because for the first time the puck stayed inside, rather than whipping in and out. When the league had to find a solution to differentiating the red line from blue lines on television, it was Ross who came up with the simple solution: make the red line striped. To honour his lifelong devotion to the game, the league introduced the Art Ross Trophy in 1947 to be given to the scoring champion each year (which he presents, below, for the first time in 1948, to Elmer Lach).

1950

June 27, 1950: Stanley Cup Heroes

In the summer of 1950, International Hockey Hall of Fame president James Garvin announced that nine men had been elected into the museum: Scotty Davidson, Graham Drinkwater, Mike Grant, Si Griffis, Newsy Lalonde, Joe Malone, George Richardson, and Harry Trihey as Players, and Frank Patrick as a Builder.

Scotty Davidson

b. Kingston, Ontario, March 6, 1891
d. France, June 6, 1915

He was a hockey hero turned war hero. A junior with the Frontenacs, Davidson turned pro with the Toronto Blueshirts in 1912. Two years later, he led the team to its first Stanley Cup, and soon after he was one of the first pro hockey players to enlist in the war. His name is on the Vimy Memorial, a testament to his valorous life. Davidson was killed in World War I by German machine gun fire while trying to save an officer in the aftermath of a raid.

Graham Drinkwater

b. Montreal, Quebec, February 22, 1875
d. Montreal, Quebec, September 25, 1946

It is likely that Drinkwater was inspired to play hockey while at McGill University when, in 1893, the local Montreal Amateur Athletic Association won the first Stanley Cup. Drinkwater played for the junior AAA and in 1895 joined the city rivals Victorias, winning his first Cup that same year. The team lost the great chalice the next year and then won three successive years, ensuring Drinkwater's place in hockey's early history.

Mike Grant

b. Montreal, Quebec, January 1874
d. Montreal, Quebec, August 20, 1955

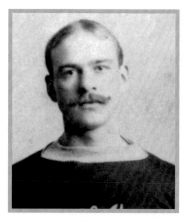

Grant captained the Montreal Victorias to four early Stanley Cups, in 1895, 1896, 1897, and 1898. He was known as a cover point who could rush the puck at a time when this was not common practice. After retiring in 1902, Grant became a referee and later still a goodwill ambassador for hockey, travelling through the United States and promoting the great Canadian winter game.

Si Griffis

b. Onaga, Kansas, September 22, 1883
d. Vancouver, British Columbia, July 9, 1950

As a boy, Griffis moved from the United States, first to St. Catharines and then to Rat Portage (later Kenora) where he became a hockey player starting in 1900. He played cover point and had blazing speed. He became a hometown hero in 1906 when he led the Thistles to an improbable Stanley Cup victory. He then decided to move to Vancouver, but the citizens of Rat Portage offered him a house if he stayed. He declined, and they gave him a purse of gold as a token of their appreciation. In 1915, Griffis captained the Millionaires to a Cup, and he retired four years later.

Newsy Lalonde

b. Cornwall, Ontario, October 31, 1887
d. Montreal, Quebec, November 21, 1970

By the time he retired in the 1920s, Newsy Lalonde had scored more goals as a pro than any other player. He skated in the Federal league and International league and then founded more established footing in the National Hockey Association and NHL, where he twice led the league in points while playing for the Montreal Canadiens. In all, he was a scoring champion in five different leagues, and he was the first member of the Canadiens to wear number 4, in 1910. He came by his nickname honestly—he worked for a newspaper in his youth—but as a hockey player he was a legend. His only Cup came with the Canadiens in 1915–16 and he once scored nine goals in a game while playing for Renfrew.

Joe Malone

b. Quebec City, Quebec,
February 28, 1890
d. Montreal, Quebec,
May 15, 1969

True, there is something magical and poetic about saying "50 in 50," in reference to Maurice Richard's great season of 1944-45. Joe Malone's "44 in 22" doesn't have quite the same ring, but two goals a game is the greater feat. In the NHL's first season, 1917–18, Malone set a record that stood for a quarter-century when he scored 44 goals for the Montreal Canadiens. Two years later, he set another record yet to be equalled when he scored seven goals in a single game against Toronto. He had won two Cups with Quebec, in 1912 and 1913, and his six NHL years were also for the record books: in 126 career games, he scored 143 times, a goals-to-game average that will never be matched.

George Richardson

b. Kingston, Ontario,
September 14, 1886
d. Wulverghem, Belgium,
February 9, 1916

Richardson was considered a great hockey player on many counts. He was a fine stickhandler and a powerful skater, and he possessed a hard shot. His finest amateur years came with Queen's University, for which he played three years, winning the Allan Cup in 1909. He went on to play senior hockey with the 14th Regiment of Kingston, but his life was cut short when he was killed in action during World War I.

1950

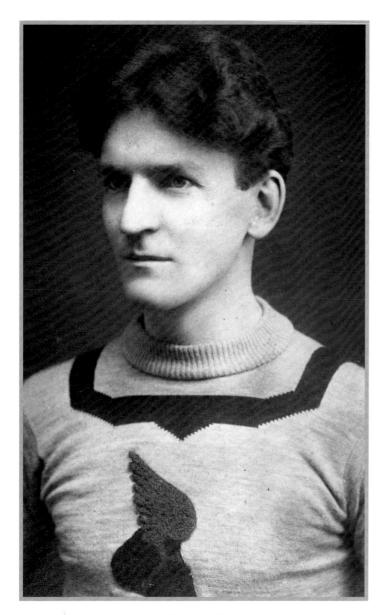

Harry Trihey

b. Montreal, Quebec, December 25, 1877
d. Montreal, Quebec, December 9, 1942

Lawyer, athlete, gentleman, and patriot, Lieutenant Colonel Harry Trihey fulfilled his hockey ambitions with the Montreal Shamrocks, winning the Stanley Cup in 1899 and 1900 as its rover and captain. His career with the team lasted but five years, at which time he became associated with the Canadian Amateur Hockey League and practised law in Montreal. In wartime, Trihey established the 199th Battalion of the Duchess of Connaught's Own Irish Canadian Rangers, which he led to battle overseas.

Frank Patrick

b. Ottawa, Ontario, December 21, 1885
d. Vancouver, British Columbia, June 29, 1960

Patrick never played in the NHL, though he did have an extensive career in Montreal and in the Pacific Coast league that he and his brother, Lester, established. He won a Cup with Vancouver in 1914–15. More important, though, he made a remarkable contribution to the development of the game. No fewer than 22 rules in the NHL can be credited to Frank Patrick. He initiated forward passing, unlimited substitution of players during a game, and use of numbers on players' sweaters. It was he who brought the blue line to the game and his system of playoffs became the norm in many pro sports. He introduced the penalty shot and permitted kicking the puck (except to score), and he was the man to initiate the practice of crediting players with assists on goals. Patrick's ideas revolutionized the game and was salient to its progress in the early days of pro hockey.

1952

August 19, 1952: Catching Up on the Past

The 16 governors of the International Hockey Hall of Fame inducted six new men into the pantheon of greats: Dickie Boon, Bill Cook, Moose Goheen, Moose Johnson, Mickey MacKay, and Nels Stewart. MacKay was the only deceased of the group and Goheen was the second American, after Hobey Baker, to be inducted (although Si Griffis was born in the U.S., he was Canadian). Cook, coach of the Rangers, was the only one of the six still active in the game.

Dickie Boon

b. Montreal, Quebec, January 10, 1878

d. Montreal, Quebec, May 3, 1961

For Dickie Boon, Montreal was home; he gave to the city as much as it gave him. The cover point, who—amazingly—never weighed more than 115 pounds as a player, was an indomitable spirit for the Montreal Amateur Athletic Association. In fact, the Montreal AAA won the Stanley Cup in 1902 and in so doing, became known as the "Little Men of Iron." As one of these "Little Men," Boon used his speed and quickness to avoid most of the physical play of the day. In 1904, he switched teams to play the last two years of his hockey life with the Montreal Wanderers, a team he helped form along with James Strachan, among others. After retiring, Boon remained the team's manager for a decade, winning four more Stanley Cups.

Bill Cook

b. Brantford, Ontario, October 6, 1896

d. Kingston, Ontario, May 5, 1986

An original Rangers forward, Cook was one of the greatest players to wear the Broadway Blueshirt. He played in the NHL exclusively with the New Yorkers, from the time they entered the league in 1926 until the time he retired in 1937. Cook twice won the scoring championship and was a member of three First All-Star Teams during this time. He also led the Rangers to their first two Stanley Cup victories, in 1928 and 1933, thanks in large measure to Cook and brother Bun with Frank Boucher. Cook later coached the Rangers from 1951 to 1953.

Francis "Moose" Goheen

b. White Bear Lake, Minnesota, February 9, 1894

d. White Bear Lake, Minnesota, November 13, 1979

Goheen played the vast majority of his career with the St. Paul Saints, an amateur team that won the McNaughton Cup and were national champions in the United States from 1920 to 1923. He also played for his country at the 1920 Olympics, winning a silver medal to Canada's gold, and he was called the most skilled American hockey player of all time. He refused all overtures to turn pro, preferring to keep his job with the Northern States Power Commission in Minnesota and play amateur hockey. Goheen played both forward and defence and had extraordinary stamina.

Ernie "Moose" Johnson

b. Montreal, Quebec, February 26, 1886

d. White Rock, British Columbia, March 24, 1963

Few players of any era can rival Johnson's career for longevity and success. He started pro hockey in 1905 with the Wanderers and over the next five years won the Cup four times. He moved west to play in the Pacific Coast league, and brought success with him, this time to Portland in 1915–16 when the team lost in the Cup

Moose Johnson was renowned for his long stick which gave him a reach of an incredible 99"!

finals to the Canadiens. Johnson was a big man who had the longest reach in the history of the game: fully 99 inches, thanks to his long hockey stick (in the days before restrictions were in place). He played defence his whole career, one that stretched until 1931, 26 years after he first began. He had a successful career, despite having lost some fingers on his right hand from an electrical accident in his youth.

Mickey MacKay

b. Chesley, Ontario, May 21, 1894
d. Ymir, British Columbia, May 21, 1940

MacKay could do many things well. He was an expert poke checker and he could deke an opponent to either side. He was tough as nails and a gifted scorer. He was a quick skater who possessed quick reflexes. MacKay turned pro in 1914 with the Vancouver Millionaires. He won the Cup in his first season and spent 12 years altogether in Vancouver in the Pacific Coast Hockey Association. He came to the NHL in 1926 with Chicago, at age 33, and for four years he played in the best league in the east. MacKay was a perennial All-Star in the west, and the east first took notice of him in the Cup finals against Toronto when many a critic called him the best player in the series.

Nels Stewart

b. Montreal, Quebec, December 29, 1900
d. Wasaga Beach, Ontario, August 21, 1957

By the time he retired in 1940, Nels Stewart was the all-time leading goal scorer and point maker in NHL history. As a rookie with the Montreal Maroons in 1925–26, he led the NHL in scoring with 34 goals and 42 points. That year, he also won the only Stanley Cup of his career. Soon after, he worked in combination with Babe Siebert and Hooley Smith to form the S-Line, one of the finest scoring units of the era. His scoring earned him the nickname Ole Poison and he won the Hart Trophy twice, in 1925–26 (as a rookie) and 1929–30. His goal scoring record wasn't broken until more than a decade later when Maurice Richard scored his 325th career goal.

Three of hockey's all-time greats—Charlie Conacher, Edouard "Newsy" Lalonde, and Nels Stewart—pose for the camera during a break in the action between the Montreal Maroon Oldtimers and the Ontario Old Timers at the Montreal Forum.

1958

April 27, 1958: The Hall's Spirit Moves from Kingston to Toronto

Without question 1958 was a watershed year for hockey history. The International Hockey Hall of Fame was stationed in Kingston, thanks to the great work of Captain James T. Sutherland, but only $65,000 had been raised toward the building of a permanent home there—some $200,000 short of the funds necessary. It seems that when Sutherland died in 1955, the hopes for realizing the Kingston project also died.

By February 1958, the Canadian National Exhibition in Toronto and the NHL made an agreement to open a new hall in the Exhibition's Canadian Sports Hall of Fame, in time for the Canada's oldest annual pre-Labour Day exhibition. The plans called for the hall to be open for the full three weeks of the Exhibition and, if well received, to stay open year-round. Sure enough, on August 20, 1958, the Hockey Hall of Fame museum opened with the help of Prime Minister John Diefenbaker. Over the run of the CNE, some 350,000 people visited the hall, making patently clear the necessity to keep the exhibit open. The hall consisted of all NHL trophies, select memorabilia, and drawings by artist Irma Coucill of every honoured member.

Meanwhile, the Hall executive was being reshaped. The new selection committee consisted of nine men: Lester Patrick, Red Dutton, Al Pickard, George Dudley, Milt Dunnell, Marcel Desjardins, Baz O'Meara, Danny Gallivan, and Walter Brown. They had plenty of work to do in that no new Players had been inducted since 1952. In all, they inducted 15 Players and six Builders, the largest honour roll in the Hall's 13-year history. The Players included Frank Boucher, King Clancy, Sprague Cleghorn, Alec Connell, Red Dutton, Frank Foyston, Frank Fredrickson, Herb Gardiner, George Hay, Dick Irvin, Ching Johnson, Duke Keats, Hugh Lehman, George McNamara, and Paddy Moran. The Builders were George Dudley, James Norris, Al Pickard, Senator Donat Raymond, Conn Smythe, and Lloyd Turner.

1958

Frank Boucher

b. Ottawa, Ontario,
October 7, 1901
d. Kemptville, Ontario,
December 12, 1977

The line of Bill and Bun Cook on the wings with Frank Boucher in the middle was the greatest Rangers line in the first decades of the team's existence. In all, Boucher led the NHL in assists three times while feeding the puck to his wingmen, but his defining characteristic was his sportsmanship. He won the Lady Byng Trophy seven times in an eight-year period (1927–35), a feat that so impressed its donor, Lady Byng, that she finally gave Boucher the trophy and had another made for the NHL. Although Boucher began his career with the Ottawa Senators in 1921–22 before heading west for four seasons, he was a lifetime member of the Blueshirts. After 12 years as a player, he became a coach and then manager, winning two Cups as a centreman (1928 and 1933) and another as bench boss (1940).

"King" Clancy

b. Ottawa, Ontario, February 25, 1903
d. Toronto, Ontario, November 8, 1986

There is not a soul in the history of hockey who can claim to have done as much—at as many levels—for as many years as King Clancy. As a player, he started out with Ottawa, joining the Senators in 1921. He stayed in his hometown for nine years, winning two Stanley Cups and establishing himself as one of the best defencemen in the league. He is the only man to play all six positions in one game, a feat he accomplished in the Stanley Cup playoffs against Vancouver in 1923. Small, he was more tenacious than any man and fought men much larger in the name of helping his mates. He was a fine skater and playmaker, and he was universally admired. The Senators, though, were frequently in financial purgatory and sold

their star players on an annual basis. In 1931, Clancy was purchased by Conn Smythe in Toronto for the exorbitant price of $35,000, and for most of the next 55 years, Clancy became synonymous with the blue and white maple leaf. He won his third Cup in 1931–32 with the Leafs and was the team's most popular player. After retiring, he became a referee in the league for a dozen years, sharing the kudos with Bill Chadwick as the best in the business. He also coached the Leafs and Maroons and he was an assistant general manager and goodwill ambassador for Toronto for the rest of his life. Upon his death, the Leafs donated a trophy in his name to be given annually to the player who makes a humanitarian contribution off the ice. Clancy is the only man to play in, referee, and coach an All-Star Game.

Becoming a Leaf

Conn Smythe was a gambler and racetrack lover, and one day he placed a sizeable wager on a horse named Rare Jewel. It paid big money, and Smythe, the owner of the Leafs, now had the funds ($35,000) necessary to purchase Clancy from Ottawa. Clancy voiced great enthusiasm for moving to the rival Leafs. Smythe took the deal to the board of directors, and they too enthusiastically endorsed the trade. And so, on October 11, 1930, the Leafs sent Eric Pettinger and a cheque for $35,000 to Ottawa for King Clancy.

March 17, 1934, St. Patrick's Day, was a special one for Clancy and the Leafs. The King was honoured for his contributions to the game, and in a fancy pre-game ceremony, he was wheeled out in a royal sleigh wearing green all over, including his face (as pictured below). He even wore a special green sweater,

but after the first period the referee told him to change into his Leafs tunic to avoid confusion. He was king for a lifetime at centre ice and king in the hearts of his fans and admirers.

Clancy was a respected referee in the NHL for more than a decade. He was known as a player's ref because of his career with the Senators and Leafs, and he was good at taking a jibe and giving one in equal measure. (In the picture below he explains things to the Boston bench.)

Sprague Cleghorn

b. Montreal, Quebec, March 11, 1890
d. Montreal, Quebec, July 11, 1956

In a span of five years (1919–24), Cleghorn won the Stanley Cup with three different teams, Ottawa in 1919–20, Toronto in 1921–22, and Montreal in 1923–24. He was a scoring sensation from the blue line, but he was also one of the dirtiest, most vicious players in NHL history. He could score goals at one moment, and at the next send someone off on a stretcher with his stick work. Cleghorn began his career in 1910 in the National Hockey Association with Renfrew and retired some 18 years later. His 83 goals by an NHL defenceman were second only to Harry Cameron's 88 on the all-time list in 1928.

Alec Connell

b. Ottawa, Ontario, February 8, 1899
d. Ottawa, Ontario, May 10, 1958

Recognizable for wearing a black cap while tending the nets, Connell set a record likely never to be broken. Midway through the 1927–28 season with Ottawa, he recorded six successive shutouts and was not scored upon for 446:09 of playing time. He joined the Senators in 1924 and played every game for six straight years. In 1925–26, he allowed just 42 goals in 36 games, and in three of his first four years he led the NHL in shutouts. By the time he retired in 1937, Connell had 81 shutouts in only 417 games played and a career goals-against average of just 1.91.

Mervyn "Red" Dutton

b. Russell, Manitoba, July 4, 1896
d. Calgary, Alberta, March 15, 1987

In his 10 years in the NHL, Dutton played for two defunct teams. From 1926 to 1930 he played for the Montreal Maroons and from 1930 to 1936 he led the New York Americans. Dutton was a ferocious and fearless defenceman. And though, for two seasons, he spent more minutes in the penalty box than any other player, he was a leader without compare. Dutton was also a great champion of New York's "other" team, and after retiring became general manager of the Amerks. He was grief stricken when the franchise folded, and on becoming NHL president in 1943, one condition he asked of the governors was that he be allowed to resuscitate the Amazing Amerks once the war ended.

Frank Foyston

b. Minesing, Ontario, February 2, 1891
d. Seattle, Washington, January 19, 1966

It was only when the Victoria Cougars were sold in 1926 that Foyston went to Detroit and played in the NHL. He started his career in Toronto, with the Blueshirts of the National Hockey Association, winning the Stanley Cup in 1914. After another season in the east, he moved to the Pacific Coast Hockey Association and spent the formative years of his career in Seattle. He helped the Metropolitans win the Cup in 1917 and played in the finals two years later against the Canadiens, a series that had to be abandoned because of the influenza epidemic. Foyston won a third Cup with the Cougars in 1925 before ending up in Detroit for two seasons. Although awkward-looking on the ice, he was an accomplished scorer.

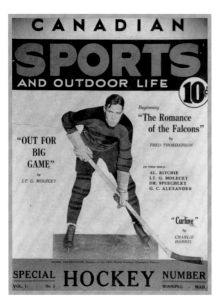

Frank Fredrickson

b. Winnipeg, Manitoba, June 11, 1895
d. Toronto, Ontario, May 28, 1979

Between two stints in World War I and World War II, Frank Fredrickson was an accomplished hockey star. He began with the Winnipeg Falcons soon after returning from military service, captaining the team to the 1920 Allan Cup and then Olympic gold in Antwerp, Belgium. He turned pro in the Pacific Coast Hockey Association with Victoria, helping the Cougars win the Cup in

1925. Two years later, he made his NHL debut with Detroit. He spent his last five years in the league with Boston and Pittsburgh before returning to Detroit at the end of his career.

Herb Gardiner

b. Winnipeg, Manitoba, May 8, 1891
d. Philadelphia, Pennsylvania,
January 11, 1972

Incredibly, Herb Gardiner did not play much serious hockey until he turned pro with the Calgary Wanderers in 1918 at age 27. He remained in that city for eight years, not making his NHL debut until 1926 with Montreal, when he was 35 years old. The rookie won the Hart Trophy and played just two more years in the NHL before settling in to a coaching career in the Can-Am league with Philadelphia, his home for the rest of his life.

George Hay

b. Listowel, Ontario, January 10, 1898
d. Stratford, Ontario, July 13, 1975

The small Hay weighed in at only 155 pounds at the height of his powers, yet he was a resilient and determined player during a 15-year career. After an honourable discharge from the army in 1919, Hay played out west with Regina and Portland before joining Chicago in 1926. He was so impressive that first year that most critics and coaches considered him the best left winger in the league, though he was traded to Detroit the next year. Hay finished his career with that team, playing for the Cougars, Falcons, and Red Wings, the three successive names of Detroit's NHL entry.

Dick Irvin

b. Limestone Ridge, Ontario,
July 19, 1892
d. Montreal, Quebec, May 16, 1957

There were two celebrated careers to the life and times of James Dickenson Irvin. In the first, he was a star centre, first in Winnipeg where he helped the Monarchs to an Allan Cup in 1915. After a three-year hiatus in the army, Irvin picked up his sticks and skates and resumed his career in Regina and Portland before landing in the NHL with Chicago in 1926. He had an outstanding rookie season, but early the next year he was checked hard by Red Dutton and hit his head on the ice. Irvin missed the rest of that season and was ineffective the next. He chose to retire rather than risk more serious, even fatal, injury. It was for his playing career that he was inducted into the Hockey Hall of Fame.

A Great Member of the Coaching Fraternity

After retiring as a player, Irvin was hired by Toronto's general manager Conn Smythe to coach the Leafs. He bossed the bench from 1930 to 1940, taking the team to the Cup finals on seven occasions. (In the photo below he patrols the Montreal bench.) Irvin left to coach Montreal and remained there for 15 years. He finished his career where he began, in Chicago, but failing health forced him to retire. In all, Irvin won four Cups as a coach and went to the finals a record 15 times.

Ivan "Ching" Johnson

b. Winnipeg, Manitoba, December 7, 1898
d. Takoma Park, Maryland, June 16, 1979

"Colourful" is the epithet most frequently used for Ivan "Ching" Johnson, thanks largely to his size (210 pounds) and great strength. He played pro in the United States until 1926 when he joined the NHL's Rangers and, over the course of the next decade, helped bring two Stanley Cups to Broadway. He closed out his career in 1937–38 with the rival Americans. Because he suffered a number of injuries during his career, Johnson played just 436 NHL games in all.

Gordon "Duke" Keats

b. Montreal, Quebec, March 21, 1895
d. Victoria, British Columbia, January 16, 1972

No player earned greater recognition and respect simply for his art of stickhandling, a skill by no means common in hockey's formative years. Keats played for Toronto in the National Hockey Association before the war, but when the fighting started, he joined the Sportsmen's Battery and headed overseas. Upon returning, he moved to the west and helped establish the West Coast Hockey League, coming east only in 1926 to play for the Boston Bruins. Keats played three years in the NHL and ended his career in the minors with Tulsa.

1958

Hugh Lehman

b. Pembroke, Ontario, October 27, 1885

d. Toronto, Ontario, April 8, 1961

Goaltenders of hockey's early years generally did not have long careers, but Lehman stopped his first puck in the pro ranks in 1906 and was still stopping them 22 years later—a phenomenal testament to longevity. He started with the Canadian Soo and later became a fixture in the Pacific Coast Hockey Association. Lehman backstopped the Vancouver Millionaires to a Stanley Cup in 1914–15 during his 12-year stay in that city. He was known for rushing the puck, sometimes as far up as centre ice. When the league folded in 1926, Lehman moved to the NHL with Chicago, finishing his career with a year-and-a-half stint in the Windy City.

George McNamara

b. Penetanguishene, Ontario, August 26, 1886

d. Miami, Florida, March 10, 1952

George and brother Howard McNamara were affectionately called the Dynamite Twins when they partnered on the blue line. George played with the Canadian Soo in 1906 at the start of his pro career but he spent most of his time in Toronto. He played for the Blueshirts in 1913–14 when they won the Stanley Cup and he finished his career with the 228th Battalion in 1917–18 before heading off to war. He later coached the Canadian Soo to the Allan Cup in 1924.

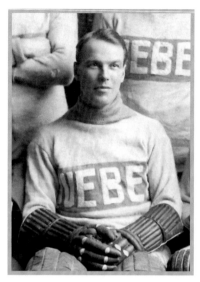

"Paddy" Moran

b. Quebec City, Quebec, March 11, 1877

d. Quebec City, Quebec, January 14, 1966

With the exception of the 1909-10 season, Moran spent his entire playing career guarding the goal in his native Quebec with the Bulldogs. He started there in 1905 and in 1912 and 1913 backstopped the team to consecutive Stanley Cup wins. A strictly stand-up goalie, he retired in 1917 when the National Hockey Association disbanded to make way for the NHL.

George Dudley

b. Midland, Ontario, April 19, 1894

d. Midland, Ontario, May 8, 1960

Upon learning of the death of George Dudley, Conn Smythe stated simply: "They say there is always someone to take your place. No one will take his place." A lawyer by education, Dudley became a member of the Canadian Amateur Hockey Association executive in 1925, becoming president for a two-year term in 1940. He also worked as secretary treasurer and was treasurer for many years. Dudley was president of the International Ice Hockey Federation and oversaw the participation of countries at the 1960 Olympics in Squaw Valley. In all, he was associated with hockey for half a century.

James Norris

b. St. Catharines, Quebec, December 10, 1879

d. Chicago, Illinois, December 4, 1952

He may have made a vast fortune in grain and real estate, but the true passion of Norris's life was hockey. From the time he bought the Detroit Red Wings in 1933 until his death, he was as active an owner as any in the pro ranks. He also had interests in Madison Square Garden and in Chicago, but it was primarily with the Wings and the Olympia that Norris was associated. Under his ownership, the team won the Cup in 1936 and 1937, and again in 1950 and 1952, shortly before his death.

James Norris (foreground, dark coat) was the first and most successful owner in Detroit history.

Al Pickard

b. Exeter, Ontario, January 2, 1895

d. Exeter, Ontario, April 7, 1975

It was for his work in the amateur ranks of hockey in Canada that Pickard took his place of honour in the Hockey Hall of Fame. He first made his mark in Regina where he ran the local YMCA and the Regina Parks League and then moved up as an executive with the Saskatchewan Amateur Hockey Association, serving as

president from 1941 to 1942. He became a member of the Canadian Amateur Hockey Association, first as an executive and later as president, and he was awarded a lifetime membership for his service to that organization. Pickard also served as a member of the selection committee for the Hockey Hall of Fame for a number of years.

Senator Donat Raymond

b. St. Stanislas de Kostka, Quebec, January 3, 1880

d. Montreal, Quebec, June 5, 1963

He owned hotels, became a Senator, and made large sums of money as a financier, but everyone in Montreal remembers Donat Raymond as the man who spearheaded the building of the Forum. Raymond recognized that an arena was essential

for the development of the game, and when the Westmount Arena burned to the ground in 1918, he decided to do something to remedy the situation. Raymond became president of the Canadian Arena Company and the Forum was built in 1924 under his guidance—at the time, it was the greatest hockey rink built. When the Molson family bought the team and building in 1957, Raymond was named chairman of the board. Through the years, he remained keenly interested in the running of the team, from player acquisitions and development to the details of building operations and management.

Conn Smythe

b. Toronto, Ontario, February 1, 1895
d. Toronto, Ontario, November 18, 1980

The contributions made to hockey by Conn Smythe are, quite simply, inestimable. Under his guidance, Toronto became the hockey capital of the world and the Gardens the place where innovation originated (from the study of video to the tracking of individual ice time, from Plexiglas to painted ice to television broadcasts). His pro career began inauspiciously: after less than a year on the job, he was fired as general manager of the Rangers. He returned to Toronto, and with financial support bought the Toronto St. Pats, renaming them the Maple Leafs. He financed the construction of the Gardens during the height of the Depression; he hired Foster Hewitt to carry Leafs games to the homes of everyone in Canada; and he brought the city seven Stanley Cups during his reign as owner and general manager (below he hams it up with coach Dick Irvin in 1931).

Smythe was a fiercely proud Canadian, a man who gave his life to God, King, and hockey, in that order. He fought in World War I, and when fighting began in 1939, he was quick to act.

Smythe formed the Sportsmen's Battery and encouraged NHLers, particularly his Leafs, to enlist. He went overseas and was badly wounded, and when he came home, he spent a year recuperating. Pictured right with his son, Stafford, Conn rejected the league's offer to become the new NHL president, preferring to regain his health and re-establish control of the Leafs, the team he founded and nurtured.

Showman and Genius

Smythe knew the importance of showmanship and promotion to making hockey successful. His name was in the paper every day of the season, and he went out of his way to be a colourful and emotional owner. His public feuding, notably with Art Ross in Boston, helped sell tickets and generate interest in the game, and he was known on occasion to run out onto the ice to deal with opposing players or officials in person. He was a shrewd judge of talent and a character as well.

Lloyd Turner

b. Elmvale, Ontario, August 9, 1884
d. Calgary, Alberta, April 7, 1976

No name in Calgary hockey history has greater meaning than Turner's. He moved west to pursue a baseball career but then became sidetracked by a passion for the ice game and a goal to improve the fate of Calgarians of all ages. It was Turner who built the Corral, which was used by the Tigers in the pro ranks and helped that team challenge for the Stanley Cup in 1924. Turner later helped restructure the West Coast Hockey League and was the only reason many Allan Cup games were held in Alberta in the 1930s. His foresight and generosity of spirit were important not just to pros, but also to the thousands of local kids' teams that got to use his arenas.

1959

September 5, 1959: Visitors Crowd the Temporary Hall

Momentum from the spectacular success of 1958's makeshift Hockey Hall of Fame at the Canadian National Exhibition carried through to the succeeding hockey season. By February, National Hockey League president Clarence Campbell had agreed that talks to build a permanent hockey home on CNE grounds were necessary, and in the coming months plans were drawn up. Later in the year, on September 5, the Hall inducted three new members: Jack Adams, Cy Denneny, and Tiny Thompson. The announcement came during a special luncheon on "Hockey Day" at the CNE at which 30 of the 34 previously Honoured Members were in attendance. The Selection Committee included George Dudley, Milt Dunnell, Red Dutton, Danny Gallivan, Baz O'Meara, Al Pickard, Lester Patrick, and Bobby Hewitson. Walter Brown was ill and could not attend, and Marcel Desjardins was in Europe and had to send his nominations by telegram.

Jack Adams

b. Fort William, Ontario,
June 14, 1895
d. Detroit, Michigan, May 1, 1968

Adams was the first man to have both a great playing career and executive career. He turned pro in 1917 with the Toronto Arenas, winning the Cup in his first season, 1917–18. After one more year, he moved out west to play in the Patricks' Pacific Coast Hockey Association with Vancouver, and returned to Toronto in 1922. In his final five seasons he developed into a fine scorer in the NHL, winning his second Cup in 1926–27, his one and only season with Ottawa, and his last as a player.

Motor City Saviour

Jack Adams moved right from playing to coaching, signing with Detroit in 1927 as bench boss after having just retired as a

forward with Ottawa. This was to be the start of a lifelong association with the Red Wings, one that saw him win seven Stanley Cups as coach and general manager, 12 league titles, and a record seven successive first-place finishes (1948–55). Despite the victories and successes, Adams maintained that his greatest accomplishment was recognizing one player's special talent and getting him to play for the Wings. His name? Gordie Howe. (Above Adams celebrates with two of his troops.)

Cy Denneny

b. Farran's Point, Ontario, December 23, 1891
d. Ottawa, Ontario, October 12, 1970

After turning pro in 1915 with Toronto in the National Hockey Association, Denneny ended up with Ottawa by the time the NHL began operations in 1917. He played all of his 12 seasons with the Senators, save the last, which was with Boston.

During that time, Denneny became the top scorer in the league, winning the points parade in 1923–24 and finishing second six times. By the time he retired, Denneny had totalled 333 points in just 328 games. He had also won an amazing five Stanley Cups, four with the Senators and the last with those Bruins in 1928–29. In 1923, he fired the Cup-winning goal against Edmonton. Denneny was the first man to play with a curved stick.

"Tiny" Thompson

b. Sandon, British Columbia, May 31, 1905
d. Calgary, Alberta, February 11, 1981

In 12 years of NHL play, Thompson made his mark in the crease as few goalies did before or since. He started with Boston in 1928–29, and in his rookie season he led the league with 26 wins and allowed just three goals in five playoff games. The Bruins won the Cup thanks to him, and although it proved to be his only triumph, his career was always brilliant (below he stops a Montreal rush during a game on November 26, 1937). He missed only eleven games over his career, playing in nine complete seasons. He led the league in shutouts four times and won the Vézina Trophy four times. Thompson played his entire career with the Bruins except the last two seasons when he dressed for Detroit. He also played in the six-overtimes game at Maple Leaf Gardens in 1933 when the Leafs prevailed 1-0 on a goal by Ken Doraty.

1960

September 8, 1960: Construction for a Permanent Home Begins

Plans continued apace to build a permanent Hall of Fame at the Exhibition grounds in Toronto, and National Hockey League president Clarence Campbell confirmed that the league was willing to provide full funding for the $300,000 facility. In the summer, Cyclone Taylor and numerous hockey luminaries were on hand in Toronto for the official sod-turning ceremony. Taylor was joined by Foster Hewitt, Conn Smythe, Mayor Nathan Phillips, Frank Selke, Clarence Campbell, Bruce Norris, Walter Brown, and Robert LeBel.

Meanwhile, Frank Selke and Cyclone Taylor were named to the Selection Committee, joining Red Dutton, Al Pickard, Danny Gallivan, Marcel Desjardins, Walter Brown, Milt Dunnell, James Dunn, and Baz O'Meara. Selke came on board as the chairman. The committee then elected six men to the hall, three Players (George Boucher, Sylvio Mantha, and Jack Walker) and three Builders (Charles Adams, General John Kilpatrick, and Selke himself).

1960

George Boucher

b. Ottawa, Ontario, August 19, 1896

d. Ottawa, Ontario, October 17, 1960

One of the famed Boucher brothers of Ottawa, George was considered a top defenceman during the early years of the NHL. He played forward in his youth, but when he moved back to the blueline, he became a partner to many a great blueliner, notably those of the Ottawa Senators. Boucher won four Stanley Cups with the team in the 1920s, playing with the likes of Sprague Cleghorn and King Clancy. In later years, he suffered from throat cancer and he was presented his Hockey Hall of Fame award while in hospital. He died just a few weeks later.

Sylvio Mantha

b. Montreal, Quebec, April 4, 1902

d. Montreal, Quebec, August 7, 1974

Mantha played all but four of his 542 career NHL games with the Canadiens. He won his first of three Stanley Cups while a rookie, in 1923–24, a season in which he started as a forward and shifted to defence—where he remained the rest of his playing days. Mantha was a scoring blueliner and a gifted stickhandler. Twice he hit double digits in goals and twice he was named to the league's Second All-Star Team. He finished his career in 1937 with a brief stay in Boston.

Sylvio Mantha receives his miniature plaque from NHL president Clarence Campbell during induction ceremonies in 1961.

Jack Walker

b. Silver Mountain, Ontario, November 28, 1888

d. Seattle, Washington, February 16, 1950

The master of the hook check, Walker played pro hockey until he was 44 years old. He started in Port Arthur and moved down to Toronto in 1913, where he played in the National Hockey Association for the Blueshirts, winning a Cup in his first full season with the team. Two years later, Walker headed west to

Seattle, the city that was to become his home after playing days. He led the Metropolitans to a Cup in 1917 and won another with Victoria eight years later. When the Cougars and the Western Hockey League folded, Walker finally made his NHL entrance, now 38 years old. He played two seasons for Detroit before moving back to Seattle to finish his career.

Charles Adams

b. Newport, Vermont,
October 18, 1876

d. Boston, Massachusetts,
October 2, 1947

The life of Charles Adams and the fortunes of the NHL changed in the early spring of 1924. That was when Adams watched the Stanley Cup finals and fell in love with the game, the playoffs, and the great trophy. That summer he started the Boston Bruins, and thanks to his efforts, the NHL grew its American roots. Two years later, he bought the entire Western Hockey League so that players from those teams could be made available to new NHL teams, notably New York, Chicago, and Detroit—teams that started as a direct result of his purchase. Adams then sought to build a new arena for his Bruins, and the Boston Garden opened in November 1928. He was a visionary and pioneer, a wealthy businessman who realized his ambitions and dreams through hockey. His son, Weston, later took control of the team.

General John Reed Kilpatrick

b. New York, New York, June 15, 1889

d. New York, New York, May 7, 1960

A savvy businessman and a proud American who fought in both World Wars, Kilpatrick became president of Madison Square Garden in 1933, a position he held for 22 years. Under his aegis, the building thrived as an entertainment centre and the Rangers developed into a solid hockey team that won the Stanley Cup in 1940. He was associated with the team up until his death, serving later as chairman of the board and then honourary chairman.

Frank Selke

b. Berlin (Kitchener), Ontario, May 7, 1893
d. Ribale, Quebec, July 3, 1985

Small, wiry, and not the best hockey player, the 13-year-old Frank Selke formed a team and coached it in his hometown, thus beginning a career in hockey that endured some 60 years. He has been associated with numerous Memorial and Allan Cup–winning teams, but more famously he was with Toronto in the heyday of Leafs' success and in Montreal for the glory days of the 1950s. Selke was Conn Smythe's right-hand man at Maple Leaf Gardens almost from day one, and when Smythe went off to war, it was Selke who assumed all managerial responsibilities. He left the Leafs in 1946,

having won three Stanley Cups. His tenure in Montreal was marked by greater success, notably five Cups in a row from 1955 to 1960. Selke served for years on the Hockey Hall of Fame's Selection Committee. He was also salient to the building of the Hall's permanent home, which opened in 1961.

Frank Selke's long and distinguished association with the Hockey Hall of Fame culminated in 1979 when he received a scroll of thanks (pictured below) for his lifelong devotion to the game.

1961

August 26, 1961: The Hockey Hall of Fame Comes to Life

This was a crucial year in the history of hockey; the Hockey Hall of Fame finally had a building to call its own. On August 26, 1961, Prime Minister John Diefenbaker opened the doors of the $500,000 facility, which now enshrined some 89 members, including those elected at a meeting in Montreal on June 13, 1961. Complete financing for the building was provided evenly by the six National Hockey League teams.

Among the number of new inductees were eleven new Players, notably Maurice Richard who had retired only a year before. In order to "make sure that there were some players in the Hall with whom the youngsters of today would be familiar"—in the words of Selection Committee chairman Frank Selke—the Hall waived the mandatory five-year waiting period to induct Richard, the greatest right winger of his era. Additionally, there were three new Builders added and, for the first time, on-ice officials were also included. The new Hall also showcased memorabilia of hockey history, from rare 19th century artifacts to Richard's 500th goal puck. The Selection Committee consisted of the following men: Baz O'Meara, Cyclone Taylor, Al Pickard, James Dunn, Red Dutton, Milt Dunnell, Danny Gallivan, Frank Selke, Walter Brown, and Marcel Desjardins.

Curator Bobby Hewitson stands in front of the palatial new Hockey Hall of Fame at the Canadian National Exhibition grounds in Toronto.

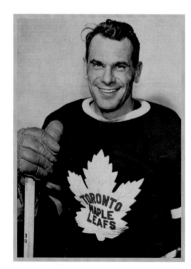

Syl Apps

b. Paris, Ontario, January 18, 1915
d. Kingston, Ontario, December 24, 1998

Apps was perhaps the finest man ever to play in the NHL, a consummate competitor but a gentleman from the day he entered the world. He was discovered at McMaster University by Conn Smythe, who watched Apps in a football game and signed him without ever having seen him skate. Apps returned the loyalty, playing his entire career with the Leafs and winning three Stanley Cups. As a rookie, in 1936–37, Apps led the league in assists and won the Calder Trophy. He won the Lady Byng Trophy in 1941–42, the year of his first Cup, and in 1943 he joined the army. Apps retired at age 33, in the prime of his career. He scored a hat trick in his final regular season game to pass the vaunted 200-goal mark. In the playoffs, his last moment on ice was as captain holding the Stanley Cup.

Few men led as dignified a life as Syl Apps. He finished sixth for Canada in the pole vault at the 1936 Olympics. He earned a degree in politics at McMaster. He was inducted into three sports halls of fame in Canada. He never drank or swore and was named Father of the Year in all of Canada. He was later named chairman of the Select Committee on Youth and then Minister of Correctional Services. When he died, hockey lost a legend, Canada lost an icon, and his family lost a model of virtue.

Syl Apps is seen during his days as captain, against Chicago in 1946–47.

Charlie Conacher

b. Toronto, Ontario, December 10, 1909

d. Toronto, Ontario, January 30, 1967

"The Big Bomber" was one of the first great superstars of the Toronto Maple Leafs. He played his best years on the Kid Line

with Joe Primeau and Harvey Jackson, the highest-scoring threesome in the league. Conacher scored 20 goals as a rookie in 1928–29 and then in five of the next six years led the NHL in goal scoring. In 1933–34 and 1934–35, Conacher also led the league in points during the days before the awarding of the Art Ross Trophy. He ended his career with Detroit and the New York Americans (he is seen here wearing number 6 for the Amerks) and then coached Chicago for two and a half years. Two of his brothers, Lionel and Roy, were later inducted into the Hall.

Charlie Conacher receives his Hockey Hall of Fame plaque from NHL president Clarence Campbell at the 1961 induction ceremonies.

Clarence "Happy" Day

b. Owen Sound, Ontario, June 1, 1901

d. St. Thomas, Ontario, February 17, 1990

Day came out of the Pharmacy program at the University of Toronto to turn pro with the St. Pats in 1924, and for the next 13 seasons he remained a fixture on the Toronto blue line. He captained the Leafs to their first Stanley Cup in 1931–32, and although he ended his career with a season with the Americans, he returned to Maple Leaf Gardens as coach in 1940 (seen here with two of his young players). For the next decade, he had an incomparable career. He led the team to five Stanley Cups, none more memorable than in 1942 when the team came back from 3-0 down to win

four in a row and capture an historic Cup, the first and only time that kind of comeback has been staged by a team in the finals. Day later became team general manager, and when he retired in 1957, he ended more than three decades' service to the franchise.

1961

George Hainsworth

b. Toronto, Ontario, June 26, 1895
d. Gravenhurst, Ontario, October 9, 1950

One of every five games Hainsworth played, he recorded a shutout; one of three victories was by shutout. In just 11 NHL seasons, Hainsworth recorded 94 blank sheets, a record bettered only by Terry Sawchuk who had 103 shutouts in more than double the games played. Hainsworth won the first Vézina Trophy, in 1926–27, and two years later, he won his third in a row by posting 22 shutouts in 44 games, a record that surely will never be broken. He spent all his years with Toronto and Montreal, winning two Cups with the Canadiens.

Joe Hall

b. Staffordshire, England, May 3, 1882
d. Seattle, Washington, April 5, 1919

He was called Mean Joe Hall or Bad Joe Hall all his playing days, for no one was more ferocious with his stick than the cover point cum defenceman who grew up in Manitoba. He began playing for Brandon and moved to Montreal in 1907 where he began his pro career in the Eastern Canada Amateur Hockey Association. Hall stayed in Quebec when the National Hockey Association formed and in 1910 joined the Quebec Bulldogs. He won two Cups with that team and became a member of the Canadiens in 1917 when the NHL replaced the National Hockey Association. Two years later, during the Cup finals against Seattle, he contracted a serious strain of influenza and died in hospital a few days later. For the first and only time, no winner of the Stanley Cup was decided.

Percy LeSueur

b. Quebec City, Quebec, November 21, 1881
d. Hamilton, Ontario, January 27, 1962

His entrance into the world of hockey was mythic. LeSueur played goal for Smiths Falls in the 1906 Cup challenge against Ottawa, and despite losing he played so well that the Senators hired him to guard the cage in game two of their next challenge against the Wanderers. His play nearly caused one of the greatest upsets of all time, and he had, in a matter of weeks, established himself as one of the finest goalies in all of Canada. LeSueur spent the next eight years in Ottawa, winning three Cups, before finishing his career in Toronto. He served in hockey for half a century, later as a referee, coach, and journalist.

Frank Rankin

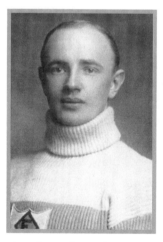

b. Stratford, Ontario, April 1, 1889
d. unknown

His was a short career, but Rankin made an impact in his native Stratford, starting in 1904 when he played junior hockey. A rover, he played on three Ontario Hockey Association champion teams (1906–09) before moving down to Toronto. He played for the Eaton Athletic Association and played in two seniors finals, losing the Allan Cup in 1912. Rankin also played at St. Mike's for two seasons, and he later coached the Toronto Granites, the team that represented Canada at the 1924 Olympic Winter Games.

Maurice Richard

b. Montreal, Quebec, August 4, 1921
d. Montreal, Quebec, May 27, 2000

By the summer of 1943, Maurice Richard was 22 years old and his reputation was suffering. In three successive seasons, the young man with bundles of talent had suffered serious injuries that cut short each season. Was he a glass hero or just slow to mature physically? In 1943–44, he scored 32 regular season goals and a league-leading 12 more in the playoffs en route to the Stanley Cup. The year after, he scored 50 goals in 50 games, a record that stood for four decades. Richard developed into what many fans and critics called the best player inside the blue line. He was a scorer, not a passer, and he drove to the net without much finesse (seen below with trademark determination and fire). He defended

himself and fought his own battles, and made as many friends in enemy rinks as admirers in his own. He assaulted a linesman in a game in Boston in 1955 and was suspended for the last three games of the regular season and all of the playoffs. On March 17, 1955, the Richard Riot was the fans' response to NHL president Clarence Campbell's suspension. By the time he retired in 1960, Richard had scored 544 goals, obliterating the previous record of 324 set by Nels Stewart. He had won eight Stanley Cups, and established himself as a hero, a French Canadian icon. He was the lower-class boy who became famous, and he had a competitive fire that could not be quenched. He played in the first 13 All-Star Games (1947–59) yet, amazingly, won only one individual trophy: the Hart in 1946–47.

The Hero Returns

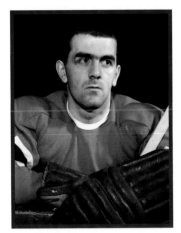

On April 8, 1952, Boston played in Montreal in game seven of the Bruins-Canadiens semifinals series. The score was 1-1 after the first period when Leo Labine nailed Richard with a check that knocked the Montreal star unconscious. He was helped off the ice and had six stitches sewn into his forehead above his left eye. He returned late in the second briefly, and then at 16:19 of the third, he scored the game-winning goal for the Habs. After the game, Bruins goalie "Sugar Jim" Henry gave the Rocket a reverential handshake.

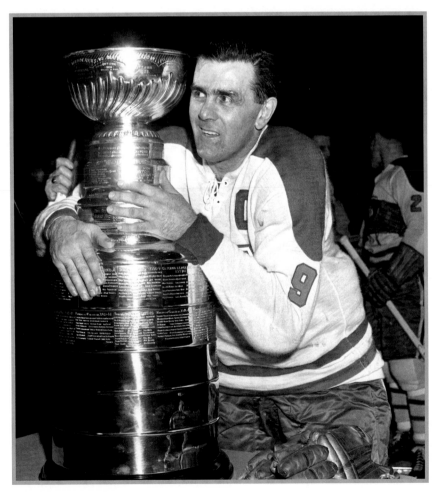

Maurice Richard held the Cup eight times during his 18-year career, including five in a row before retiring in 1960.

Milt Schmidt

b. Kitchener, Ontario, March 5, 1918

The Leafs weren't interested in him, and he took 18 games to score his first NHL goal after debuting in 1936. But make no mistake: Schmidt was one of the great centremen of all time, a man who was considered a playmaker extraordinnaire. Schmidt played on a line with Woody Dumart and Bobby Bauer—the

Bruins' Kraut Line was the top threesome in the game. Schmidt led the league in assists (30) and points (52) in 1939–40, the year all three placed 1-2-3 in league scoring, the first time that feat had been accomplished by linemates. He took off three and half years in the prime of his career to play his part in the Canadian army, and when he returned he spent the last part of his career on defence. One of the greatest nights in NHL history came on March 18, 1952, when Bauer came out of retirement to play on the line one more time. That night, Schmidt scored the 200th goal of his illustrious career. He won two Cups with the Bruins, and in 1950–51 won the Hart Trophy.

Oliver Seibert

b. Berlin (Kitchener), Ontario,
March 18, 1881
d. Kitchener, Ontario, May 15, 1944

A true pioneer, Seibert cut his first set of skate blades from solid steel, affixing them to a pair of shoes with screws. He skated on artificial ice in St. Louis around the turn of the 20th century and he became the first native Berliner to turn pro. Seibert came from a large family of hockey players, and under his leadership the Berlin Rangers won six successive Ontario Hockey

Association championships (1900–06). He could skate as fast backward as he could forward, and his son, Earl, later became a Hall of Fame NHLer in his own right.

Bruce Stuart

b. Ottawa, Ontario, 1882
d. Ottawa, Ontario,
October 28, 1961

His health in decline, Bruce Stuart attended the Hockey Hall of Fame induction ceremonies of 1961 in a wheelchair. He passed away just a short time later. Bruce and brother Hod played a number of years together, notably with Houghton and Pittsburgh in the first pro league in North America in 1902. Bruce became a fine rover and goal scorer with Portage and joined the Montreal Wanderers in 1907. The team won the Stanley Cup that year, but when Stuart had the chance to return home to Ottawa, he took it. He won two more Cups with the Senators, one in 1909 and the other in 1910 when he captained the team.

George Brown

b. Boston, Massachusetts,
October 21, 1880
d. Boston, Massachusetts,
October 17, 1937

In the early days of hockey in the United States, Brown was a champion of the sport in an executive capacity. In 1910, he organized the Boston Athletic Association team, which became a power in amateur play in the United States. Brown was integral to the building of the Boston Arena and later, when the Bruins moved into the

Garden, he helped establish the Can-Am league, forerunner to the American Hockey League. Brown later became general manager of both the Arena and Garden and ran the Boston Tigers as well.

Paul Loicq

b. Clermont, Belgium, August 11, 1888
d. March 26, 1953

When Loicq was inducted into the Hockey Hall of Fame, he was represented by Etienne Harford, Counsellor of the Belgian Embassy. Loicq played internationally for his native Belgium from 1908, the year the International Ice Hockey Federation was organized, until 1920, when he played at the Olympics. He later served as a referee, and in 1927 he was named president of the IIHF, a post he held for 20 years. It was under his guidance that hockey became an official sport at the Olympic Winter Games. Loicq was the first truly international inductee into the hall.

Fred Waghorn

b. Tunbridge Wells, England, 1866
d. 1956

Without Waghorn as a referee, who knows how different hockey might have turned out to be? He officiated more than 2,400 games over a career that spanned half a century. In one early contest, the puck split in two after a shot, half entering the net, half not. No goal, he ruled, because the puck was listed as one-inch thick in the rule book and the rubber that entered the net was only a half-inch thick. Thus was born the solid, one-piece puck. Waghorn also initiated the dropping of the puck to begin play—over the previous standard of placing of the puck between opponents. He discarded the traditional bell in favour of a whistle. And he started the Toronto Hockey League, the largest outdoor league in the world.

Chaucer Elliott

b. Kingston, Ontario, 1879
d. Kingston, Ontario, March 14, 1913

A fine athlete and executive in a number of sports, Elliot made his hockey contributions starting in 1903 when he became a referee. He distinguished himself for 10 years in the Ontario Hockey Association and later in the International league.

1961

Fred "Mickey" Ion

b. Paris, Ontario, February 25, 1886
d. Redmond, Washington, October 26, 1964

Ion ended his athletic career in 1912 to focus on becoming a referee. He started out west in the Pacific Coast Hockey League and later transferred to the NHL, where he became a respected whistle tooter. By the time he called his last game, in 1943, he was a legend for his impartiality and clarity of judgement. To him, this meant being tough and standing up to all hollers of objection and criticism from both benches. By the time Ion was inducted into the Hockey Hall of Fame (as shown here on the left), he had had both legs amputated by the onslaught of diabetes, though that affected neither his pleasure in attending the ceremonies nor the honour of being enshrined for his 30-year career.

Cooper Smeaton

b. Carleton Place, Ontario, July 22, 1890
d. Montreal, Quebec, October 3, 1978

Smeaton declined all offers to turn pro as a player, instead taking his love for hockey to the officials' room. He, like the players, began as an amateur, and in 1913 was named to the staff of the National Hockey Association. In 1917, with the formation of the NHL, Smeaton joined. He was manager of the Philadelphia Quakers for a single season (1930–31) but beyond that, he was a referee until 1937. He was referee-in-chief for six years and later became a trustee of the Stanley Cup.

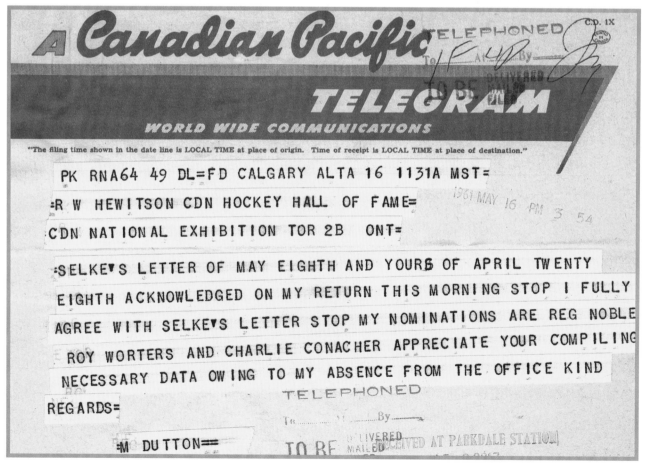

When members of the Selection Committee couldn't attend a meeting, they submitted their nominations by cable, as Red Dutton did this year.

1962

August 25, 1962: Remarkable Success

By the end of the 1962's Canadian National Exhibition, some 800,000 people had walked through the Hockey Hall of Fame, up from the 750,000 of the Hall's inaugural year. Curator Bobby Hewitson noted that the Stanley Cup was the one object everyone wanted to see. A special display of all 200-goal scorers also proved popular.

The Selection Committee inducted another large group of Players in 1962, and chairman Frank Selke promised that in 1963, the hall would catch up and induct as many of the oldtimers as it deemed necessary. For this year, his proposition was to include three Players up to the start of the NHL in 1917–18 (two of the three had to be alive), and three Players since that time.

"Punch" Broadbent

b. Ottawa, Ontario, July 13, 1892
d. Ottawa, Ontario, March 6, 1971

Right winger Broadbent got into the record books in 1921–22 by scoring a goal in each of 16 consecutive games. While playing for Ottawa that year, he led the league in both goals (32) and points (46). His tenure with the Senators began in 1912 in the National Hockey Association, but he left the team three years later to fight in the war (where he was awarded a Military Medal). He returned to hockey and Ottawa in 1918 and went on to win four Stanley Cups, three with the Senators and one, in 1925–26, with the Montreal Maroons. In all, he had 121 career goals in 303 NHL games.

Harry Hyland

b. Montreal, Quebec, January 2, 1889
d. Montreal, Quebec, August 8, 1969

Although he played in the NHL in his final year and that league's first, Hyland was a longtime star in the National Hockey Association with the Montreal Wanderers. He played the right wing, often in tandem with Gordie Roberts, and was a premier scorer of his day. Hyland won the Stanley Cup as a rookie in 1909–10. On January 27, 1913, at the height of his career, he scored eight goals in a 10-6 Wanderers win over Quebec. He started 1917–18 with the Redbands, but after the team's arena burned down, he transferred to Ottawa to finish his career.

Fred Maxwell

b. Winnipeg, Manitoba, May 19, 1890
d. Winnipeg, Manitoba, September 10, 1975

"Steamer" Maxwell was a speedy terror on the ice, a rover in seven-man hockey who was born to skate. He started with the Winnipeg Monarchs in 1909, and six years later, with the senior entry, won the Allan Cup. He refused all professional contract offers and soon moved into coaching, which career was marked by two notable accomplishments on the international stage: in 1920, he led the Winnipeg Falcons to the Allan Cup and then Olympic gold, and in 1935 he led the Canadians to gold at the World Championships.

Reg Noble

b. Collingwood, Ontario, June 23, 1895

d. Alliston, Ontario, January 19, 1962

The paths of Reg Noble and Jack Adams crossed twice. The first instance came in 1917-18 when both men played for Toronto, winning the Stanley Cup in the first year of the NHL. Noble spent more than seven years in Toronto, winning a second Cup in 1922 and a third, with the Maroons, in 1925–26. He then

played most of the rest of his career in Detroit under coach Adams. Noble played mostly left wing but he also spent a good deal of time as a defenceman. In all, he played 510 NHL games.

"Sweeney" Schriner

b. Saratov, Russia, November 30, 1911

d. Calgary, Alberta, July 4, 1990

In eleven NHL seasons, Schriner proved to be one of the league's top scorers and a tough but gentlemanly player. He was also a fine playmaker as a left winger with the New York Americans and the Maple Leafs, leading the league in points for two seasons (1935-37) while with the Amazing Amerks. Schriner won two Stanley Cups with the Leafs, one in the spring of 1942, the other three years later. He was named to the NHL's First All-Star Team twice, and by the time he retired in 1946 he had recorded 405 points in 484 games.

Alf Smith

b. Ottawa, Ontario, June 3, 1873

d. Ottawa, Ontario, August 21, 1953

The great right winger developed his skills at home in Ottawa and rewarded his hometown fans with great results. Smith played pro in Pittsburgh in 1902, but a year later he played for the local Silver Seven and captained that team to three successive Stanley Cups. He finished his career back in Pittsburgh, and—after dominating as one of the best scorers in the pro ranks—spent many years coaching.

1962

Franklin Ahearn

b. Ottawa, Ontario, May 10, 1886

d. Ottawa, Ontario,
    November 7, 1962

After an heroic tour of duty during World War I, Ahearn returned to Ottawa and decided to put hockey and the local Senators foremost on his list of priorities. He became a director of the team and then, in 1922, its owner. Under his guidance, the team won Stanley Cups in 1923 and 1927. Ahearn managed to hang onto the team after the Great Depression but was forced to sell some of his biggest stars and eventually had to give up ownership.

Walter Brown

b. Boston, Massachusetts, February 10, 1905

d. Hyannis, Massachusetts, September 7, 1964

An American who had a significant impact on the game at both an NHL and international level, Walter Brown had a long and distinguished hockey career. He was president of the Boston Bruins and Boston Garden but he also led many early American teams to the World Championships and the Olympics. His U.S. team won a silver medal at the 1931 Worlds, and he also took teams overseas in 1933, 1934, and 1937. Additionally, Brown was the man behind American entries in the 1936 and 1948 Olympics. He served as president of the International Ice Hockey Federation for three years (1954–57) and as vice president before and after (1948–54 and 1960–63). As a result, he was also later inducted into the International Ice Hockey Federation Hall of Fame as a Builder.

Walter Brown (left) receives his Hockey Hall of Fame plaque from Clarence Campbell.

Fred Hume

b. New Westminster, British Columbia, May 2, 1892
d. Vancouver, British Columbia, February 17, 1967

Politically, Hume was a mayor in both New Westminster and Vancouver. In sporting terms, his enthusiasm was for amateur and minor hockey. Hume introduced the New Westminster Royals as a hockey team and he was later vital to the formation of the Western Hockey League, one of the most important leagues in Canada.

James Norris

b. Montreal, Quebec, December 10, 1879
d. Chicago, Illinois, December 4, 1952

He may have earned his millions in the grain business, but his passion was hockey. Norris and his son, James D., bought the Detroit NHL franchise in 1933 and changed the team's name to Red Wings. They set the Stanley Cup as their target and hit a bull's eye in 1936, 1937, and 1943. Norris later had a controlling interest in the Chicago Stadium and Madison Square Garden (those on the outside began to call it the Norris Hockey League). Norris also championed the development of a farm system as a way to grow the NHL team.

Ambrose O'Brien

b. Renfrew, Ontario, May 27, 1885
d. Ottawa, Ontario, April 25, 1968

In 1909, the Eastern Canada Hockey Association rejected O'Brien's plea to allow his Renfrew Millionaires to join the league. Furious, O'Brien and his father established the National Hockey Association, a five-team league that included a Renfrew team stocked by O'Brien with the greatest stars: Cyclone Taylor, Fred Whitcroft, and Frank and Lester Patrick. Another team in the league was the Montreal Canadiens, thus starting the great success that was to become the bleu, blanc, et rouge of the Habitants. All thanks to the wrath and determination of O'Brien.

1962

Frank Smith

b. Orford Township, Ontario, June 1, 1894
d. Toronto, Ontario, June 11, 1964

Late in 1911, a group of men met in Toronto to discuss the formation of a new hockey league for children. Thus was born the Beaches Hockey League, which grew into the Toronto Hockey League and the Metropolitan Toronto Hockey League, the world's largest hockey body and the league that has sent more players on to the NHL than any other league in the world. Smith was named secretary and treasurer back in 1911, a position he held until retiring in 1962. Under his aegis, the league grew exponentially in importance and sophistication, giving tens of thousands of young boys the chance to play hockey in an organized set-up conducive to the development of skill and character.

Mike Rodden

b. Mattawa, Ontario, April 24, 1891
d. Kingston, Ontario, January 11, 1978

Rodden was the first man to be inducted into both the Hockey Hall of Fame and the Canadian Football Hall of Fame (for his many years as a successful coach). In hockey, he refereed some 2,864 games, 1,187 of which were in the NHL. He had been a player in his youth, and he also coached various teams in Toronto—but it was the tremendous respect players and coaches had for him that earned him special recognition in the Hall of greats.

MERVYN DUTTON
BOX 3900, POSTAL STATION A
CALGARY, ALBERTA
May 8th, 1962.

R.W. Hewitson, Secretary,
Hockey Hall of Fame,
Canadian National Exhibition,
TORONTO 2B, Ontario.

Dear Bobby:

Received your letter of April 30th and as per your request I am forwarding my selections for the Hockey Hall of Fame.

I have always felt that some consideration should be given to the election to the Hockey Hall of Fame, if possible, while a man is alive and after much consideration I am going to try and nominate two players living and one who has passed on.

My selection of Roy Worters which I have nominated several times is one that I feel should be recognized. Having played with him for many years and being a winner of the Heart Trophy and Vezina Trophy in the era of which he played gives him the qualifications to enter the Hockey Hall of Fame. Worters was possibly the smallest Goalkeeper that was ever in the National Hockey League and his intestinal fortitude was without question.

My second nomination is for Eddie Oatman whom I played hockey with in Calgary and who was a good example of an athlete keeping himself in shape the year around. His record of his many years of hockey is outstanding. He is now 72 years of age and I believe he qualifies to enter the Hockey Hall of Fame.

Dave Sweeney Schriner's record speaks for itself. He led the league in scoring two years with a club that did not have too much strength. He was among the top ten scorers in ten seasons, he was on two Stanley Cup teams and he was on two All Star teams. He was the Leagues leading Rooky in the season of 1933 & 34. After his retirement he established himself in business and has had much to do with fostering minor league hockey in Calgary.

At the meeting designated for June 4th I would like to find out from the selection committee what is the attitude towards minor officials such as Timekeepers, Penalty Timekeepers and so on, as some of these men gave a great deal of their time and effort and loyalty to our National game.

If there is any more information on the above mentioned players required, please contact me.

With kind personal regards, I am,

Yours sincerely,

M.A. Dutton.

MAD:mp

Red Dutton's articulate and thoughtful nominations for 1962 provide insight into the detail and seriousness with which Selection Committee members take their responsibilities.

1963

August 24, 1963: Forgotten Stars Enshrined en masse

The year 1963 was a time to catch up on inducting great players from the early days of hockey. In addition to the three Builders and one Official, the Selection Committee honoured some 23 Players, all but three of them old timers. The 1963 Committee included Frank Selke, Cyclone Taylor, James Dunn, Milt Dunnell, Walter Brown, Marcel Desjardins, Danny Gallivan, Red Dutton, and Al Pickard. The official announcements were made at the International and Athletic Day Luncheon at the Canadian National Exhibition.

1963

Harry Cameron

b. Pembroke, Ontario,
February 6, 1890
d. Vancouver, British Columbia,
October 20, 1953

By the time he left the NHL in 1923, Cameron was the highest-scoring defenceman in the league's young history, having scored 88 times in just 121 games. He had a unique shooting motion that produced a curved shot. Cameron won three Stanley Cups, one with the Toronto Blueshirts in the National Hockey Association in 1913–14 and two more with Toronto in the NHL. He also played extensively in the west and in the American Hockey Association before retiring.

"Rusty" Crawford

b. Cardinal, Ontario, November 7, 1885
d. Prince Albert, Saskatchewan, December 19, 1971

Crawford (pictured here on the left at the Hockey Hall of Fame ceremonies) played professional hockey for 20 years. The first half of his career was highlighted by his years with the Quebec Bulldogs in the National Hockey Association where he won a

Cup in 1912–13. He played for Toronto in the NHL's first year, winning a second Cup, and he passed the rest of his career in the west and then in the American Hockey Association with Minneapolis.

Jack Darragh

b. Ottawa, Ontario,
December 4, 1890
d. Ottawa, Ontario,
June 25, 1924

Brother Harold, a longtime NHLer in his own right, attended the Hall of Fame inductions to represent Jack, who had died many years earlier. Darragh, a left-hand shot who skated on the right side, was one of the first forwards to play "off wing." He had a great backhand shot and was known for his stickhandling. Darragh played his entire career—both amateur and pro—in his native Ottawa, winning four Stanley Cups in 1911, 1920, 1921, and 1923. In 121 NHL games he scored 66 goals.

Jimmy Gardner

b. Montreal, Quebec,
May 21, 1881
d. Montreal, Quebec,
November 6, 1940

By the time he retired in 1915, Gardner had won four Stanley Cups, all in Montreal. He won first with the Amateur Athletic Association in 1902 and 1903 before turning pro with Calumet, but he returned home in 1907 and spent the majority of his career with the Wanderers. A left winger, Gardner was one of the toughest men in hockey's early pro days.

Billy Gilmour

b. Ottawa, Ontario, March 21, 1885
d. Montreal, Quebec, March 13, 1959

He might have been christened Hamilton Livingstone, but everyone called him Billy. Gilmour was one of seven hockey-playing brothers, three of whom—Billy, Dave, and Suddie—starred for the Silver Seven. Billy played almost all of his career in Ottawa, winning the Cup in 1903, 1904, and 1905 with the greatest early team around.

Ebbie Goodfellow

b. Ottawa, Ontario, April 9, 1906
d. Sarasota, Florida, September 10, 1965

Ebenezer Goodfellow spent his entire 14-year, 557-game NHL career with Detroit. He won three Stanley Cups with the Red Wings and captained the team for four years. As a centreman, he was a hard-nosed player and when he shifted back to defence he had the hardest shot of all blueliners. Goodfellow won the Hart Trophy in 1939–40 and was twice a First Team All-Star.

"Shorty" Green

b. Sudbury, Ontario,
July 17, 1896
d. Sudbury, Ontario,
April 19, 1960

After completing his junior career, Green joined the Canadian army in World War I, returning in 1918 to help the Hamilton Tigers capture the Allan Cup the following spring. He returned to Sudbury to play for four years before joining the ill-fated Hamilton Tigers in 1923, the team that was suspended from the 1925 playoffs because the players went on strike for better pay. Green finished his career with the New York Americans in 1927 when a serious kidney injury ended his career.

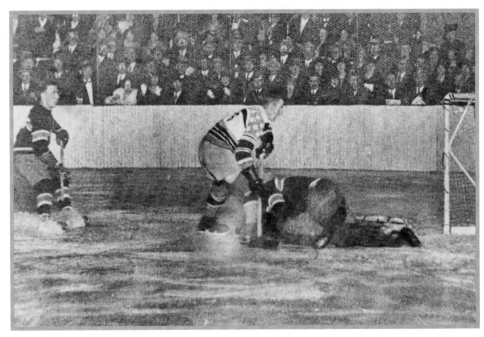

On December 15, 1925, Shorty Green scored the first goal in the history of Madison Square Garden, beating Montreal Canadiens goalie Herb Rheaume at 11:55 of the first period.

1963

"Riley" Hern

b. St. Marys, Ontario, December 5, 1880
d. Montreal, Quebec, June 24, 1929

He was a champion goalie for a number of years, making his most impressive mark with the Montreal Wanderers during the early years of the 1900s. Hern turned pro in Pittsburgh before moving to Portage in 1904 where for two years he was the best stopper in the International Hockey League. He joined Montreal in 1906 and won the Stanley Cup in four successive seasons (though there were a couple of losses by challenge along the way). Hern retired in 1911.

Tom Hooper

b. Rat Portage (Kenora), Ontario, November 24, 1883
d. Vancouver, British Columbia, March 23, 1960

An outstanding rover, Hooper made a name for himself in his hometown. Three times the Kenora Thistles played for the Stanley Cup. In 1903, they lost to Ottawa; in 1905, they lost again to the Silver Seven; and, finally, in 1907, they challenged the Montreal Wanderers and won. Kenora became the smallest town to win the Cup. A month later the Thistles lost a challenge to those same Redbands, setting a record for holding the Cup for the shortest time.

"Bouse" Hutton

b. Ottawa, Ontario, October 24, 1877
d. Ottawa, Ontario, October 27, 1962

Hutton was one of three members of the famed Ottawa Silver Seven to be inducted into the Hockey Hall of Fame in 1963, along with Harry Westwick and Billy Gilmour. Hutton guarded the goal for that great team, winning the Cup in 1903, 1904, 1905, and 1906.

Jack Laviolette

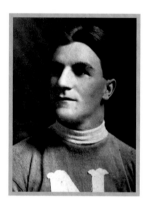

b. Belleville, Ontario, July 27, 1879
d. Montreal, Quebec, January 10, 1960

It was under the guidance and direction of Laviolette that the Montreal Canadiens franchise started in 1909. He organized the team, brought the players together, and captained it. He started as a defender but later moved up to play on a line with Didier Pitre and Newsy Lalonde. He played the last nine years of his career with the Habs, winning a Cup in 1915–16 and playing in the NHL in its first season and his last.

Billy McGimsie

b. Woodsville, Ontario, June 7, 1880
d. Calgary, Alberta, October 28, 1968

McGimsie played his entire, and brief, career in Rat Portage and Kenora, a time highlighted by the Thistles' win over Montreal for the Stanley Cup in 1907. He played centre and scored two goals in that two-game series, his last series in hockey.

Didier Pitre

b. Valleyfield, Quebec, September 1, 1883
d. Sault Ste. Marie, Ontario, July 29, 1934

Pitre was the first player signed to the Montreal Canadiens, in 1909, and he spent most of the next 14 seasons with the team, excepting one year on the west coast. In his prime, he weighed 200 pounds, thus earning the nickname Cannonball, but he also had great speed and a terrific shot. He started on the defence but soon moved up to form a forward combination with Jack Laviolette and Newsy Lalonde, and his scoring increased dramatically. In the National Hockey Association, he averaged better than a goal a game, and in 127 NHL games he had 64 goals. His one Cup victory came in 1915–16.

Joe Primeau

b. Lindsay, Ontario, January 29, 1906
d. Toronto, Ontario, May 14, 1989

Conn Smythe knew from the time Primeau was a teen that this was a player to watch. He signed the young Primeau to an option to join the Rangers, but when Smythe was fired by the Blueshirts, he managed to get Primeau into a Leafs uniform in 1928. Soon, Primeau was playing with Charlie Conacher and Harvey Jackson, and the Kid Line was born. Primeau was the centreman and playmaker, a superb passer who led the NHL in assists three out of four years from 1930 to 1934. He played his entire nine years with the Leafs, winning the Cup in 1931–32, the same year he won the Lady Byng Trophy. Primeau retired in 1936 when he was just 30 years old.

Joe Primeau was the only coach to win the Memorial Cup, Allan Cup, and Stanley Cup as a coach. After retiring, he coached the Marlies to the junior hockey championship in 1945 and 1947. In 1949–50, he guided the senior Marlies to the Allan Cup, and then as coach of the Leafs he won the NHL trophy in 1950–51 (which he hugs warmly here), courtesy of Bill Barilko's overtime heroics.

1963

Jack Ruttan

b. Winnipeg, Manitoba, April 5, 1889
d. Winnipeg, Manitoba, January 7, 1973

An amateur his whole life, Ruttan played most of his career in his native Manitoba, notably the 1912–13 season when the Winnipeg team won the Allan Cup. He later went on to coach and officiate in that city, where he remained a respected member of its hockey fraternity.

Earl Seibert

b. Berlin (Kitchener), Ontario, December 7, 1911
d. Agawam, Massachusetts, May 12, 1990

With Earl's induction, he and father Oliver became the first father-son combination to be elected into the Hall of Fame as Players. There was nothing sentimental about Seibert Jr.'s inclusion, either. He played in the NHL for 15 years and was a First or Second Team All-Star in 10 of those years. Seibert was a strapping defenceman, rough in his own end and skilled at moving the puck up ice. He started with the Rangers and won a Cup on Broadway in 1932–33. Five years later he was a champion again, this time with Chicago. He finished his career in Detroit, and in 645 games he recorded 89 goals and 276 total points.

Joe Simpson

b. Selkirk, Manitoba, August 13, 1893
d. Coral Gables, Florida, December 25, 1973

A speed demon on skates, Simpson certainly earned the moniker Bullet Joe. He was a defenceman who made fearless, headlong rushes, starting with the Winnipeg 61st Battalion team in 1915–16 that won the Allan Cup. After a three-year stint in the army, during which time he won the Military Medal, Simpson resumed his skating pursuits with Selkirk and then Edmonton. He joined the New York Americans in 1925 and spent the last six years of his career in the NHL with the Amerks. Simpson's style of play, as much as his accomplishments, earned him a place in the Hockey Hall of Fame.

Barney Stanley

b. Paisley, Ontario, June 1, 1893
d. Edmonton, Alberta, May 16, 1971

Stanley's name made the NHL ledgers because of a single game in 1927–28 when he filled in playing for a night (at the time, he was coach and manager). The meat of his career occurred out west, starting with Vancouver in 1915 when the Millionaires won the Stanley Cup. The right winger was an accomplished scorer wherever he went, and after retiring he coached for many years.

Marty Walsh

b. Kingston, Ontario, October 16, 1883
d. Gravenhurst, Ontario, March 27, 1915

His might not have been a long career, but it was spectacular nonetheless. Walsh was a centreman, a forward who scored almost at will. He attended Queen's University at the start of the 20th century and turned pro with the Canadian Soo in 1906. A year later, he joined Ottawa, the team for which he played the remaining five years of his career. Walsh won three Cups with the Senators and, in just 69 games with the team, he scored a remarkable 145 goals. In 1908–09, the year he won his first Cup, he scored 42 goals in just 12 league games.

Harry Watson

b. St. John's, Newfoundland, July 14, 1898
d. London, Ontario, September 11, 1957

Watson was the finest amateur player in the history of hockey. He played his entire career in Toronto, but he never gave in to the lure of the professional game and of playing for money. Watson starred with the Toronto Granites, winning the Allan Cup in 1922 and 1923 and then leading Canada to a gold medal at the 1924 Olympics. He scored 13 goals in one game and 37 goals in the five games of that tournament, records that will never be broken. But upon returning home, he refused the offers from Toronto and Montreal to play in the NHL. He retired an amateur, true to his beliefs.

Harry Westwick

b. Ottawa, Ontario, April 23, 1876
d. Ottawa, Ontario, April 3, 1957

He played his entire career in Ottawa with the exception of two unsuccessful games for the Cup in 1907. Westwick started with the Silver Seven in 1894 and endured some 15 seasons. The climax of his career came during 1903 to 1906 when the team won four successive Cups and withstood many challenges from all the top teams in the country. A rover, he was a leading scorer for the team.

Fred Whitcroft

b. Port Perry, Ontario, 1883
d. Vancouver, British Columbia, 1931

Whitcroft grew up in Peterborough where he developed into a successful junior player with local teams. He saw his first serious hockey action in 1907 with Kenora when the team was Cup champion, though he played only in the second challenge, the one the Thistles lost, and was not a member of the team that had won the Cup weeks earlier. In 1907 he moved out to Edmonton and captained the team for three years, taking it to another Cup challenge against the Montreal Wanderers in December 1908. He was a superb skater and stick-handler and often a leading scorer wherever he played.

"Phat" Wilson

b. Port Arthur (Thunder Bay), Ontario, December 29, 1895
d. Port Arthur (Thunder Bay), Ontario, July 26, 1970

The finest hockey player to come out of Port Arthur, Wilson never turned pro but enjoyed a 15-year career with local teams, competing at the highest level and winning three Allan Cups. From 1918 to 1933 he was a stalwart on defence, winning the Canadian amateur championship trophy in 1925, 1926, and 1929.

Leo Dandurand

b. Bourbonnais, Illinois, July 9, 1889
d. Montreal, Quebec, June 26, 1964

He wasn't a great player in his youth, but he loved hockey and spent his life in the game at an executive level. Dandurand was first part of the organizing committee in Ottawa for the

Canadian Amateur Hockey Association in 1914, but his life changed forever on November 3, 1921. On that date, he and partners Joe Cattarinich and Leo Letourneau purchased the Montreal Canadiens for the princely sum of $11,000. Dandurand remained owner until 1935, when he sold the team to the Montreal Arena Company. During his tenure, the team evolved into the famed Flying Frenchmen that featured some of the greatest players of all time, notably Howie Morenz, Newsy Lalonde, and Aurel Joliat.

Tommy Gorman

b. Ottawa, Ontario, June 9, 1886
d. Ottawa, Ontario, May 15, 1961

It was back in 1915 that Gorman first became associated with the Ottawa Senators, helping the team survive in the National Hockey Association during precarious times. In 1917, he became a founding member of the NHL with those Senators, and in the ensuing three decades he was part of seven Stanley Cups spread over four NHL teams. With Ottawa, he won in 1920, 1921, and 1923. He managed Chicago to a win in 1933–34 and a year later the Montreal Maroons. In the 1940s, Gorman transferred to the Canadiens and helped the team win the Cup in 1944 and in 1946. As a coach and manager, he was without compare.

Major Frederic McLaughlin

b. Chicago, Illinois, June 27, 1877

d. Chicago, Illinois,
December 17, 1944

McLaughlin was a champion of American-born hockey players at a time when it was both novel and perhaps unwise. He started in the game as owner of Portland in 1926 and soon after he purchased a controlling interest of the Chicago Blackhawks. His team won the Cup in 1933–34 with a patchwork lineup, and two years later he decided to stock his team with Americans. The experiment failed, but he drew attention to those native stars and helped promote the game in the United States. McLaughlin won his second and last Cup with the Hawks in 1938.

Bobby Hewitson

b. Toronto, Ontario,
January 23, 1892

d. Toronto, Ontario,
January 9, 1969

It was as an Official that Hewitson made his way into the pantheon of hockey greats at the Hall of Fame. His reputation as a referee had been established from 1924 to 1934 in the NHL. He was an athlete in his youth, and after his days as a zebra, Hewitson was active in

sports—in an executive capacity—for the rest of his life, notably as secretary of the Canadian Rugby Union. He later became curator of the Hockey Hall of Fame.

As part of his curatorial duties, Hewitson collected memorabilia whenever the opportunity arose. In March 1967 (pictured below), he acquired the goalie stick used by Terry Sawchuk to record a 100th career shutout and the stick of George Armstrong, used to fire Armstrong's 250th career NHL goal.

Connaught Park Jockey Club

R.R. NO. 2

AYLMER E., QUE.

MAY 2, 1963.

MR. HARRY I. PRICE,
CHAIRMAN,
HOCKEY HALL OF FAME,
CANADIAN NATIONAL EXHIBITION,
TORONTO 2B.

DEAR MR. PRICE:

THANK YOU VERY MUCH FOR YOUR LETTER ADVISING THE ELECTION OF MY LATE FATHER TO THE HALL OF FAME. NEEDLESS TO SAY WE ARE GRATIFIED AT THIS NEWS AND WILL MOST CERTAINLY BE REPRESENTED ON THE OCCASION OF THE OFFICIAL PRESENTATION.

PLEASE ACCEPT OUR THANKS FOR YOUR KIND INVITATION AND WE WOULD APPRECIATE BEING ADVISED OF ANY CHANGE IN DATE AS OUR RACING SEASON WILL BE OPEN AT THAT TIME.

SINCERELY YOURS,

FRANK GORMAN.

Tommy Gorman passed away before he was inducted into the Hockey Hall of Fame, but his son, Frank, attended the ceremonies on his father's behalf.

1964

August 29, 1964: NHLers Get Their Due

The Selection Committee added seven new names to its pantheon of greats, four Players, two Builders, and an Official. The only player from the pre-1939 era was Babe Siebert. The other three represented the 1939–45 era. The Committee also gave honourable mentions to a number of players who were close to being inducted, notably Harry Oliver, Marty Barry, Red Horner, Hugh Aird, Pit Lepine, and Alex Irvin. The Committee consisted of Frank Selke, Cyclone Taylor, Red Dutton, James Dunn, Milt Dunnell, Walter Brown, Marcel Desjardins, Danny Gallivan, and Baz O'Meara.

Doug Bentley

b. Delisle, Saskatchewan, September 3, 1916

d. Saskatoon, Saskatchewan, November 24, 1972

Bentley played 12 of his 13 years in Chicago, and although the team was never accomplished in the playoffs, he was one of the finest left wingers in the game. He led the league in goals twice, in assists three times, and in points in 1942–43, a year the Hawks didn't even make the playoffs. He played in five successive All-Star Games (1947–51) and when he retired in 1954, he was one of a select few to reach the 200-goal plateau, with 219 goals. (Pictured here, he plays for the Hawks against his brother, Max, who was with the Leafs at the time.)

Doug Bentley receives his Hockey Hall of Fame commemorative plaque from NHL president Clarence Campbell at the 1964 induction ceremonies.

Bill Durnan

b. Toronto, Ontario, January 22, 1916

d. Toronto, Ontario, October 31, 1972

Despite playing only seven seasons in the NHL, Durnan's goaltending legacy is a gigantic one. He won an Allan Cup with the Kirkland Lake Blue Devils in 1939–40 and then moved into the Montreal system. In 1943, he earned the starter's job, and in six of his seven seasons he won the Vézina Trophy. Durnan was ambidextrous and shifted his stick from one hand to the other, based on where the puck was (in this shot, he has the stick in his

right hand for playing to that side of his net). He missed only 17 games in his career and led the league in wins for four successive seasons (1943–47). He also won two Stanley Cups and was elected to six First All-Star Teams. During one stretch of the 1948–49 season, he had a shutout streak that lasted 309:21.

"Babe" Siebert

b. Plattsville, Ontario, January 14, 1904

d. St. Joseph, Ontario, August 25, 1939

Never known as a scorer, Siebert was instead noted for his intimidating rushes and his superb defensive play. He started in 1925–26 with the Maroons, winning a Stanley Cup as a rookie. In succeeding years, he played the left wing on the fabled S-Line with Hooley Smith and Nels Stewart. He was traded to the Rangers in 1932 and won a Cup that same season, but he ended his career back in Montreal with the Canadiens. Siebert retired in 1939 and was immediately appointed the Habs' coach for the coming season. Tragically, he drowned later that summer.

Jack Stewart

b. Pilot Mound, Manitoba, May 6, 1917
d. Troy, Michigan, May 25, 1983

One of the heaviest hitters of his era, Stewart permitted few enemy forwards past him during his 12 years in the NHL. He started with Detroit in 1939 and won his first Cup with the Wings in 1942–43, his last before going off to war. Two years later, he was back with the team and five years later he won his second championship. Stewart (pictured below fighting for the

Angus Campbell

b. Stayner, Ontario, March 19, 1884
d. Toronto, Ontario, 1976

puck against the Leafs) finished his career with Chicago during which time a back injury slowed him down. He played in four All-Star Games and was a three-time member of the First All-Star Team.

As a player, he was fair and determined, and off-ice he operated the same way. Campbell played in Cobalt from 1911 to 1914. In 1919, he became affiliated with the Northern Ontario Hockey Association and assisted in its amalgamation with the Ontario Hockey Association. He was appointed to the OHA executive that year and later elected to the executive committee. In 1949, he was presented with the OHA's gold stick for his outstanding service—of more than a decade—to amateur hockey.

1964

Frank Dilio

b. Montreal, Quebec, April 12, 1912
d. Montreal, Quebec, January 26, 1997

Dilio first started in hockey in 1931 when he was named secretary of the St. Anne's Juvenile Club in Montreal. He later joined the Junior Amateur Hockey Association and in 1939 became president of the JAHA for four years. In 1943, Dilio became registrar of the Quebec Amateur Hockey Association and in 1952 he added the duties of secretary to his portfolio (as pictured above). He retired in 1962, and a year later he was given the Meritorious Award by the Canadian Amateur Hockey Association for his outstanding service to amateur hockey in Canada.

Bill Chadwick

b. New York, New York, October 10, 1915

The officiating career of Bill Chadwick started first and foremost because his playing career was cut short by the loss of an eye in a hockey accident. Yet, for all the hundreds of NHL games he called, no one knew that he was—literally—half blind. Chadwick was known to be tough and fair, but his finest contribution was to give pro hockey hand signals to call penalties. For a holding infraction, he grabbed his wrist; for a tripping call he'd clip his knee, and so on. Thus was born the visual communication of penalties that has been used ever since.

1965

August 28, 1965: Foster Hewitt Takes Centre Stage

Although all new members to the Hockey Hall of Fame were inducted on the same afternoon in August, their selection to the Hall happened in two phases. The Builders—Foster Hewitt and Tommy Lockhart—were selected in January 1965, while the Players were selected in the summer. For the first time, Jim Norris, owner and president of the Hawks, and Gordon Juckes, secretary of the Canadian Amateur Hockey Association, participated in the selection process as members of the committee.

1965

Marty Barry

b. Quebec City, Quebec, December 8, 1905
d. Halifax, Nova Scotia, August 20, 1969

It was in 1927 that Newsy Lalonde signed Barry to play for the New York Americans for the coming season, but after just a few games Barry found himself in the minors for the better part of

two years. He joined Boston in 1929 and in six years averaged more than 21 goals as a centreman (here he lines up beside Happy Day of Toronto). His best years came with Detroit, though, where he played with Larry Aurie and Herbie Lewis. The trio led the Red Wings to Cups in 1936 and 1937, Barry winning the Lady Byng Trophy in the latter season. He retired in 1941 with 195 goals to his credit in 509 NHL games.

Clint Benedict

b. Ottawa, Ontario, September 25, 1892
d. Ottawa, Ontario, November 12, 1976

From the time he turned pro with Ottawa in the National Hockey Association in 1912 until the day he retired some 19 years later, there was no finer goalie than Clint Benedict. He played 13 of those years in the NHL, with the Senators and with the Montreal Maroons, during which time he proved to be the most resilient goalie in the circuit. Eight times he played the full schedule. He led the league in wins six times, in shutouts seven times, and in goals-against average seven times. He won 190 of the 362 games he played, and

he left the league with a stunning goals-against average of just 2.32. Most importantly, he won the Stanley Cup four times.

The First Mask

Midway through the 1929–30 season, Benedict was hit in the face by a Howie Morenz shot that shattered the goalie's nose. On the night of February 20, 1930, he made history by playing a game wearing a face mask. Here was what the *Toronto Star* said

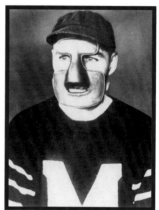

of the novelty: "Clint Benedict, veteran goaler of the Montreal Maroons, has set a new fashion for netminders by wearing a face mask. Benedict was still suffering from the broken nose he sustained when one of Howie Morenz's shots crushed in his face, and fearing that even a slight jolt might cause further injury, he secured a heavy leather nose and mouthguard. He wore it throughout the game, setting a precedent for the major leagues, and setting what also may become a fashion among the much-battered goalers of the league. The mask is much like the noseguards worn by football players, but is strapped on firmly over the top of the head and under the chin. Benedict claimed it did not interfere with his vision, which is the important factor and the main argument that has been advanced against the use of wire masks such as those employed by baseball catchers."

Art Farrell

b. Montreal, Quebec, February 8, 1877
d. Ste-Agathe-des-Monts, Quebec, February 7, 1909

Farrell played all of four years of hockey with the Montreal Shamrocks, starting in 1897. He won two Stanley Cups with the team, playing wing on a line with Harry Trihey and Fred Scanlan. This threesome revolutionized the game in that they stressed passing and teamwork over individual rushing and singular play. Farrell scored four goals in one playoff game and five in another, career highlights. In 1899, he wrote the earliest extant hockey book, and before he died at 31 of tuberculosis he wrote two other books on the sport.

"Red" Horner

b. Lynden, Ontario, May 28, 1909

In his letter to the Hockey Hall of Fame Selection Committee in support of the nomination of Red Horner, Conn Smythe wrote: "Red Horner was captain of our club for six or seven years in the days when we had great players and his team was never out of the playoffs. Red Horner played in the time when defencemen were of the calibre of Shore, Johnston, Abel, Seibert, Red Dutton and a host of other great players. At no time in any game did he suffer in comparison with any of these other players with respect to his ability." Indeed, Horner won one Cup with the team and went to the finals on six other occasions. He led the NHL in penalty minutes for eight successive seasons, but as Smythe went on to report: "I would venture to state that his penalties never hurt us at any time… Of all the great body checkers there have been in the National Hockey League, no one hit a man fairer or harder than Red Horner."

Red Horner receives his honourary plaque from NHL president Clarence Campbell at the 1965 induction ceremonies.

Syd Howe

b. Ottawa, Ontario, September 28, 1911
d. Ottawa, Ontario, May 20, 1976

In his first six seasons in the NHL (1929–35), Howe played for four teams, but from February 1935 until his retirement in 1946, he played exclusively for Detroit. He won three Stanley Cups with the Wings and, unusually, played in both the shortest and longest overtime games in league history to that time. The longest, a six-overtime affair on March 24–25, 1936, remains the longest. He also scored the winner just 25 seconds into the game against the Americans. Howe also scored six goals in a game on February 3, 1944, a feat that went unmatched for 24 years. In all, he scored 237 goals in 698 NHL games.

Jack Marshall

b. St. Valier, Quebec, March 14, 1876
d. Montreal, Quebec, August 7, 1965

Wherever Marshall played, victory followed. During his 17-year career, he won some six Stanley Cups with four different teams, starting with the Winnipeg Victorias in 1900–01. He later transferred to Montreal and won with the Amateur Athletic Association in 1902 and 1903, and four years later he was back at it with the Wanderers. Marshall also won with the Toronto Blueshirts in 1913–14 as a playing coach, and he retired in 1917 just before the formation of the NHL. He played every position but goal during his career and was considered a pioneer in the east for adopting the tube skate long before most of his contemporaries.

Bill Mosienko

b. Winnipeg, Manitoba, November 2, 1921
d. Winnipeg, Manitoba, July 9, 1994

On March 23, 1952, Mosienko set a record that has survived half a century and may survive many years longer. He scored three goals in just 21 seconds against Lorne Anderson of the Rangers on the final day of a dismal season for Chicago (pictured below). Over and above that remarkable feat, Mosienko was the fastest skater in the league. Small and quick, he played with the Bentley brothers, Max and Doug, to form the Pony Line. In his first full season, 1943-44, Mosienko scored 32 goals, his career best. He won the Lady Byng Trophy in 1944–45 by going the entire 50-game season without incurring even one minor penalty. He played all his 711 NHL games with the Hawks, scoring 258 goals and 540 points.

Blair Russel

b. Montreal, Quebec, September 17, 1880
d. Montreal, Quebec, December 7, 1961

Russel played his entire career with the Montreal Victorias until 1908 when the Eastern Canada Amateur Hockey Association became a professional league. He retired an amateur, and when he hung up his skates he was considered the best left winger hockey had ever seen. He was renowned for his speed and combination work with Russell Bowie, and Russel was among the most gentlemanly players of his era as well. He had a seven-goal and six-goal game to his credit and averaged more than a goal a game throughout his playing days.

Ernie Russell

b. Montreal, Quebec,
October 21, 1883
d. Montreal, Quebec,
February 23, 1963

Despite playing his entire career with the Montreal Wanderers, Russell's membership with the Montreal Amateur Athletic Association caused him to be suspended by the Redbands for the 1908–09 season. Not coincidentally, that was the only year the team did not win the Stanley Cup during the years 1906–1910. Russell was one of the premier scorers in the country up to his retirement in 1914. In 1906–07 he recorded a hat trick or better in five successive games, and he finished the year with 43 goals in just nine games.

Fred Scanlan

b. unknown   d. unknown

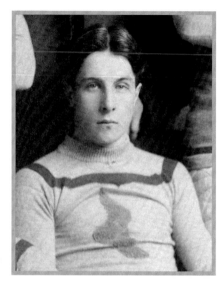

A member of the great Montreal Shamrocks team of the late 1800s, Scanlan played forward with Harry Trihey and Art Farrell, forming a threesome that moved the puck quickly and skillfully as a group. The team won the Cup in 1899 and 1900, and after another year Scanlan moved out west to join the Winnipeg Victorias for the last two years of his career. He was also known for his stamina and great shot.

Foster Hewitt

b. Toronto, Ontario, 1903
d. Toronto, Ontario, April 21, 1985

No amount of praise or flood of words can overstate the importance of Foster Hewitt to hockey. He broadcast his first game on March 23, 1923 at the Mutual Street Arena, an Ontario Hockey Association intermediate game, and for more than half a century he was the voice of hockey. When Maple Leaf Gardens opened in 1931, he served as the master of ceremonies and then walked up to his famous gondola to call the game. Hewitt gave the world the greatest expression in the game—"He shoots! He scores!"—and broadcast to the nation every home game from the Gardens. Through him, the Leafs became Canada's team, and because of him, fans could follow and cheer on their bladed heroes. In addition to his NHL work, Hewitt also covered important games from the Olympics and World Championships. He established his own radio station in Toronto, CKFH, the last two letters being his own initials. He carried on the broadcasting tradition to his son, Bill, and toward the end of his distinguished career he

made sure to leave the gondola with an expression that became as famous as the one he introduced many years ago. On September 28, 1972, his voice boomed out the now immortal words, "Henderson has scored for Canada!" as he described the conclusion of the greatest showdown in hockey history, the 1972 Canada–Soviet Union Summit Series.

August 28, 1965: Foster Hewitt Takes Centre Stage

Tom Lockhart

b. New York, New York, March 21, 1892

d. New York, New York, May 18, 1979

Lockhart devoted his life to hockey in New York, starting in 1933 when he organized the Eastern Amateur Hockey League. Two years later, he was named league president and in 1937 he increased his scope to cover all of the United States. He started the Amateur Hockey Association of the United States and was immediately elected its president. He was also closely linked to the New York Rovers for nearly two decades and also served as the business manager of the Rangers. Later still, Lockhart was a member of the United States Olympic Committee and with the International Ice Hockey Federation Council.

CLUB DE HOCKEY CANADIEN INC.

2313 ST. CATHERINE ST. WEST · TEL. WELlington 2-6131 · MONTREAL 25, P.Q.

June 7, 1965

To all Members of the
Hockey Hall of Fame Committee and
Hockey Hall of Fame Selection Committee

Gentlemen:

Meeting – Monday, June 7, 1965

The following names have been submitted to the Hall of Fame Committee and to the Members of the Selection Committee and from these the members of the Selection Committee can make as many nominations as the rules permit at the time of the meeting.

For your convenience we shall list them. Old-timers who, by recommendation of the Hall of Fame Committee, should receive serious consideration today:

BLAIR RUSSELL   FARRELL AND SCANLON
JACK MARSHALL   of the 1899/1900 Cup-winning
ERNIE RUSSELL   Shamrocks

Then we have:

SYD HOWE   RED HORNER
FRANKIE BRIMSEK   MARTY BARRY
HARRY OLIVER

from the mid-twenties and thirties....and from a somewhat later era

BILLY MOSIENKO   HECTOR "TOE" BLAKE

and two names of which there should be special mention – CLINT BENEDICT, who was suggested as an afterthought by Baz O'Meara, and NICK BAWLF of Kingston who perhaps should be named to the Sports Hall of Fame rather than the Hockey Hall of Fame.

In any case you have this letter and all the data to which you can refer. Hope your selections will meet with universal approval. It goes without saying that there will be criticism regardless of what we decide.

My thanks to all of you for attending today's meeting and carrying on the work of the Hockey Hall of Fame.

Sincerely yours,

Frank J. Selke.

FJS:D

This letter from Selection Committee chairman Frank Selke in 1965 reveals part of the process for inductions.

1966

August 27, 1966: Clarence Campbell Leads the Way

Ten new names were added to the Hockey Hall of Fame honour roll this year, and the NHL led the inductees. Head of the class was Clarence Campbell in the Builders category, league president since 1946 and still another decade away from retirement. Ted Lindsay, fiery as ever, did not attend the stag affair. "If my family can't share in this, I won't go," he said. And he didn't go. The next year, the induction ceremonies were open to wives, girlfriends, and children, and have become the most important social function of the hockey season.

Max Bentley

b. Delisle, Saskatchewan, March 1, 1920
d. Saskatoon, Saskatchewan, January 19, 1984

By the time he retired in 1954, only Maurice Richard had more active-player goals than Bentley's 245. He was called the "Dipsy Doodle Dandy from Delisle" because of his creativity with the puck, as a passer and stickhandler both. He turned pro in 1940 with Chicago, joining his brother, Doug, and forming a potent combination. Max led the league in scoring in 1945–46 and 1946–47, the latter year beating Maurice Richard 72 points to 71 on the final day of the season. He also won the Hart Trophy in 1945–46 and the Lady Byng in 1942–43. But the team was weak, and early in the 1947–48 season, he was sent to Toronto in a five-for-two deal, such was his value, according to Leafs' general manager Conn Smythe. The trade worked wonders for Toronto, as the team won the Stanley Cup in three of the next four years.

Toe Blake

b. Victoria Mines, Ontario, August 21, 1912
d. Montreal, Quebec, May 17, 1995

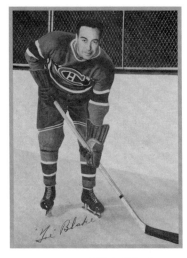

Few men have had spectacular effects on hockey in two ways, but Blake's successes as a player were matched if not exceeded by his longtime tenure as coach of the Montreal Canadiens, the team with which he was affiliated virtually all his life. He played a few games for the Montreal Maroons in 1934–35, the year the team won the Stanley Cup, but in the summer he was traded to the crosstown Habitants. For the next 13 seasons, he was their fixture on the left wing, most notably when he played with Maurice Richard and Elmer Lach on the famous Punch Line. In 1938–39, Blake led the league in scoring with 47 points and was named winner of the Hart Trophy. He became known as Old Lamplighter for his goal scoring exploits, six times recording more than 20 in a season. In his early days he was known for his temper, and it was one of the great events when, in 1945–46, he won the Lady Byng Trophy after accruing just one minor penalty all year! He won two Cups with the team, but his career was cut short in the 1947–48 season when he broke his leg badly.

Coach Toe

In 1955, the Canadiens were looking for a coach to replace Dick Irvin and they called upon Toe Blake, the man the team felt was best capable to handle Maurice Richard, a former linemate but a temperamental character. In his 13 years behind the bench, Blake established records that have never been bettered. He led the team to eight first-place finishes and eight Stanley Cups, starting in his rookie season

(here he celebrates victory in 1957). The team won an unprecedented five in a row (1956–60) and three more in the 1960s before he retired in 1968.

Butch Bouchard

b. Montreal, Quebec, September 11, 1920

At 6'2" and 205 pounds, he was a giant in the NHL, during the height of the Original Six. Bouchard made the team in 1941, an excitable, skilled, but raw talent in need of grooming and ice time. He developed into the most reliable defenceman on the Canadiens, physically intimidating but never violent. Bouchard played 15 years with the Habs, winning four Stanley Cups and playing the role of quiet superstar, the blueliner who plays his best when he's not noticed. He didn't score many goals or make fancy plays; he just kept the puck out of his own net. In all, Bouchard played in six All-Star Games and was a First Team All-Star three times.

Frank Brimsek

b. Eveleth, Minnesota, September 26, 1915
d. Virginia, Minnesota, November 11, 1998

They called him Mister Zero for good reason. He entered the league in 1938 and in his rookie season Brimsek won more games than any other goalie (33), recorded more shutouts (10), had the lowest goals-against average (1.56), led his team, the Bruins, to a Stanley Cup, and won the Calder Trophy. The rest of his 10 years wasn't bad, either. Despite missing a year and a half to army duty, he won 252 of 514 games played and recorded 40 shutouts. He won a second Vézina Trophy in 1941–42 and was a First Team All-Star twice. A stand-up goalie, he was happy to use his stick on encroaching forwards, and he played with a cockiness that flummoxed many players.

1966

1966

Ted Kennedy

b. Humberstone, Ontario, December 12, 1925

At first, Conn Smythe was furious that Frank Selke had acquired a 17-year-old named Ted Kennedy from Montreal for the rights to Frank Eddolls—a player Smythe liked. But once "Teeter" put on the blue and white Maple Leafs sweater for the first time in 1943, Smythe's anger was quelled and his fears allayed. Kennedy was not the smoothest or swiftest skater, but he might have been the most competitive man ever to play for the Leafs (pictured here driving to the Chicago net against goalie Al Rollins). He

played all his 14 seasons with Toronto and won five Stanley Cups, averaging nearly 20 goals a season. He was also the master of the faceoff and the undisputed leader of the Leafs. He played in six All-Star Games and won the Hart Trophy in 1954–55, his last full season in the league.

Elmer Lach

b. Nokomis, Saskatchewan, January 22, 1918

Despite the injuries, Lach was a consistent scorer his whole career. From the time he joined the Canadiens in 1940 until the time he retired 14 years later, he was one of the team's catalysts, too. No finer example can be cited than the 1944–45 season. That was the year his linemate, Maurice Richard, scored 50 goals

in 50 games, but it was Lach who won the league's scoring title that year with 80 points. He was given the Hart Trophy for that season, and the centreman led the NHL in points again in 1947–48. He was equally skilled as a scorer or passer, and valued as both a defensive player and offensive star. Lach was a First Team All-Star three times, and ended his career with 623 points in 664 career regular season games. He also won three Cups with the Habs.

Ted Lindsay

b. Renfrew, Ontario, July 29, 1925

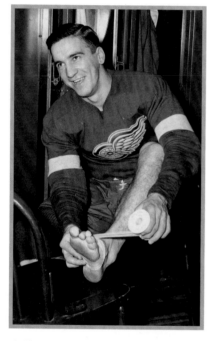

On ice or off, few players can claim to have made the impact on hockey that Terrible Ted Lindsay made. When he started with Detroit in 1944, he was a wild gun out of St. Mike's in Toronto, a left winger with remarkable skill and a temper frightening in its scope. Soon, he was playing alongside his best friend, Gordie Howe, and the old man of the line, Sid Abel. The Production Line was the highest-scoring threesome in the league, and in 1947–48 Lindsay led the league with 33 goals. In 1949–50, the year of the team's first post-war Stanley Cup, he won the Art Ross Trophy by recording 78 points. He led the team to four Cups in the early 1950s and fought for every square inch of ice he ever skated on. In the middle of the decade, though, he tried to establish a players' association to help offset the dictatorship that was the NHL. No sooner had he got a player rep from each team onside, though, than he was traded to Chicago, the worst team in the league, and the momentum was quashed by the owners. Nonetheless, it was these efforts that later led to the formation of the National Hockey League Players' Association in 1967. Lindsay retired from Chicago and the game in 1960, but four years later he decided to return to the Wings for one year (seen here in action against the Leafs, Lindsay played in eleven consecutive All-Star Games (1947–57) and was a First Team All-Star eight times.

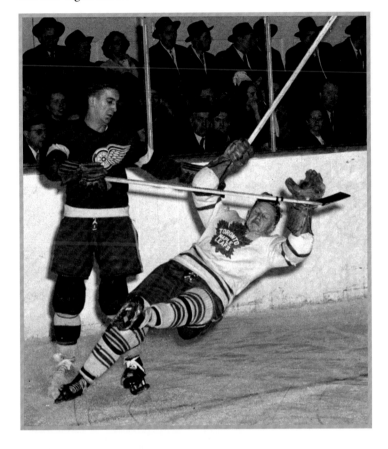

"Babe" Pratt

b. Stony Mountain, Manitoba,
January 7, 1916
d. Vancouver, British Columbia,
December 16, 1988

Cyclone Taylor himself endorsed the nomination of Babe Pratt into the Hockey Hall of Fame. Wrote Taylor: "Perhaps more than any other defenceman in the history of the game, he [Pratt] demonstrated the theory that often a good offence is the best defence." That is, Pratt, at 6'3" and 215 pounds, was the biggest defenceman in the game and a great puck carrier. In his first 140 games with the Leafs he scored 47 goals, a staggering number for a blueliner of the day. He started with the Rangers in 1935, and after winning a Cup on

Broadway in 1940, he wound up at Maple Leaf Gardens early in the 1942–43 season. He won the Hart Trophy with Toronto the next year and scored the Cup-winning goal in game seven for the Leafs in the 1945 finals.

Ken Reardon

b. Winnipeg, Manitoba,
April 1, 1921

It is a tribute to his reputation and skills that he made it into the Hockey Hall of Fame despite playing only 341 NHL games in seven seasons. Reardon was a fearless defenceman who moved around his own end with reckless abandon. He started with the Canadiens in 1940, but after just two seasons he left the team to join Canada's war efforts. During this time, he played for the Ottawa Commandos and won the Allan Cup in 1943 with one of the finest amateur teams ever assembled. Upon returning in 1945, he led the team to a Stanley Cup. He retired in 1950 with 122 points to his credit, but it was his style of play, not his statistics, that fans and critics remembered most vividly.

Clarence Campbell

b. Fleming, Saskatchewan, July 9, 1905
d. Montreal, Quebec, June 24, 1984

Before he became president of the NHL in 1946, Campbell had led a full life. In 1924, he graduated from the University of Alberta, at 18 the youngest ever to leave the school with a degree. Two years later, he was named a Rhodes scholar. He practised law and worked as a referee in his spare time, and in 1940 he joined the Canadian army.

August 27, 1966: Clarence Campbell Leads the Way

In 1945 he was named assistant to Red Dutton, and when Dutton resigned a year later, Campbell took control of the NHL. He served for more than 30 years and guided the league through enormous change. Under his iron hand, he established the non-fraternization rule, which forbade players on opposing teams from conversing in public. He inaugurated the All-Star Game and established the players' pension fund. He increased the schedule and expanded the league from six to 12 to 14 teams and beyond.

The Richard Riot

In March 1955, Clarence Campbell suspended Maurice Richard for the rest of the regular season (three games) and all of the playoffs, after the Rocket went berserk during a game in Boston and struck linesman Clifford Thompson. The suspension caused social outrage in Montreal. Not only did it cause Richard to lose what was almost certainly going to be his only scoring title, it weakened the Habs enough that they lost to Detroit in seven games in the Cup finals. It also pitted what was seen as an English dictator against a French-Canadian hero and victim. On March 17, Campbell attended the Montreal-Detroit game at the Forum to show his conviction behind the decision. The first period was calm and the Wings held a commanding 4-1 lead, but, during the intermission, someone tossed a smoke bomb in the direction of Campbell and from there all hell broke loose. Garbage, tomatoes, and bottles were thrown in his direction, but he endured the assault with stubborn pride. The mayhem spilled to the streets and lasted days, and Richard himself made public appeals to quell the violence. It was perhaps the lowest point in NHL history, but Campbell's resolute handling of the crisis earned him praise from all corners of the sporting world.

NHL president Clarence Campbell takes a seat during a quiet time at the Forum, unlike the night of March 17th, 1955, the night of the infamous Richard Riots.

1967

September 2, 1967: Turkey Face Acknowledged

In an effort to scale back on the number of inductees, the Selection Committee for the Hockey Hall of Fame elected only three new Players and one Official to its roster of greats. The move was hailed as a sign of maturity for the Hall, which had dedicated much of its efforts in the last few years to catching up on its old timers inductions. Once again the induction ceremonies occurred on Sports and Citizens Day at the Canadian National Exhibition in Toronto.

September 2, 1967: Turkey Face Acknowledged

Walter "Turk" Broda

b. Brandon, Manitoba, May 15, 1914
d. Toronto, Ontario, October 17, 1972

One of the biggest steals Conn Smythe ever made during his decades at the helm of the Leafs was to buy goalie Broda from Jack Adams in Detroit (for the paltry sum of $8,000) in 1936. Broda went on to play his entire 14-year career with Toronto, back-

stopping the team to five Stanley Cups, despite missing two full seasons during the war. The "Fabulous Fat Man," as the media dubbed him, rarely missed a game and was considered the best playoff goalie of all time when he retired in 1952. He won the Vézina Trophy twice (in 1940–41 and 1947–48), but more important he was toughest to beat when a game was on the line. In 101 career playoff games, Broda won 60 of those games and had a goals-against average of just 1.98.

Neil Colville

b. Edmonton, Alberta, August 4, 1914
d. Richmond, British Columbia, December 26, 1987

Cyclone Taylor nominated Colville to the Hall of Fame, concluding his letter of support with the simple declaration, "I regard Neil Colville as a worthy candidate for enshrinement in the Hockey Hall of Fame." Indeed. Colville played his whole career with the Rangers, joining the team as the top centre for the 1935–36 season. He played on a line with brother Mac on the right wing and Alex Shibicky portside, and the three formed the team's most important offensive unit. Colville led the Blueshirts to a Stanley Cup in 1940 and he spent most of three years in the army during the war. During that time, he captained the Ottawa Commandos to the Allan Cup. Early in the 1948–49 season he was forced to retire after suffering a serious groin injury, though he went on to coach the team for a while. In 464 games with the Rangers, Colville had 99 goals and 265 points. He later served on the Hall's Selection Committee.

Harry Oliver

b. Selkirk, Manitoba, October 26, 1898
d. Selkirk, Manitoba, June 16, 1985

In an era when the game was being formed, Oliver played like a gentleman on the ice and behaved like one off it as well. He neither smoked nor drank, and spent only cursory time in the penalty box. He weighed just 155 pounds, but he skated like the wind and moved with balletic grace. Oliver cut his teeth with Calgary in the early 1920s and joined Boston in 1926. He played the right wing and was a pure goal scorer, helping the Bruins win the Cup in 1928–29. In 351 career games with the team, Oliver had 109 goals. He played the last two and a half years of his career with the New York Americans before retiring late in 1936, his career marked by an effortless on-ice grace.

"Red" Storey

b. Barrie, Ontario, 1918

Although he was a superb athlete in his own right and officiated some 2,000 hockey games, Storey rates his most exciting playoff as: "the '50–'51 series when the Rocket scored those two overtime goals in Detroit." Storey won two Grey Cups with the Toronto Argonauts (of the Canadian Football League) in 1937 and 1938 and then refereed in the NHL from 1950 until 1959, when he resigned after a falling out with Clarence Campbell (who allegedly criticized him in public for "freezing" during a Montreal-Chicago playoff game). Nonetheless, Storey was well respected by the NHL fraternity and many tried to coax him back to the ice. As Conn Smythe said at a surprise party for Storey, the night before the induction, "The NHL was forced to fire bad referees, but Storey was not one of them. He, in effect, fired us, and that was good." Storey remained in hockey for many years after, living in Montreal and appearing in various roles to support the game at all levels in Canada. His induction for his career as NHL referee was well deserved.

1968

June 11, 1968: The All-Time Leading Scorer in 1942

In the case of the 1968 Hockey Hall of Fame induction, smaller did not mean poorer. One Player was inducted and he was exceptional. The Selection Committee also inducted two outstanding Officials to join him.

1968

Bill Cowley

b. Bristol, Quebec, June 12, 1912
d. Ottawa, Ontario, December 31, 1993

Perhaps there has never been as sporting a gesture in hockey as on February 17, 1943 when Bill Cowley wrote the NHL and requested the removal of one assist from his scoring record: "On January 16, during a game played here [Boston] against the Rangers, Art Jackson was awarded a goal when Warwick threw his stick to prevent a score. The official scorer has credited me with an assist for having made the play which put Jackson in a scoring position. I feel that this assist was not justified owing to the fact that Jackson did not actually score the goal, it being awarded as a result of the foul called on the Ranger player. Therefore, may I ask that you eliminate this assist from your official scoring records." And it was. Cowley finished that year with 45 assists, tying—not breaking—his own NHL record for helpers in a season. He was regarded as the best playmaker of all time, playing 12 of his 13 seasons in the league with Boston.

Cowley took the team to the Cup in 1939 and 1941 and won the Hart Trophy in 1940–41 and 1942–43. In February 1942, he recorded his 573rd point to become the all-time scoring leader in the league, surpassing Syd Howe. In 1943–44, he had 71 points in just 36 games, an average of 1.97 points a game. This record endured until 1980–81 when Wayne Gretzky broke it.

Jimmy Dunn

b. Winnipeg, Manitoba,
March 24, 1898
d. Winnipeg, Manitoba,
January 7, 1979

After suffering injuries in World War I that prevented him from pursuing a hockey career as a player, Jimmy Dunn moved into an executive capacity in Manitoba. He started as secretary of the Manitoba Amateur Hockey Association until 1941 when he became vice president. After three more years, he became president for six years, and in 1950 he became vice president of the Canadian Amateur Hockey Association. Five years later, he was named president of the CAHA, and in 1961 he became a member of the Selection Committee of the Hockey Hall of Fame. Over the course of his lifetime, Dunn also served in a variety of capacities for other sports.

Jim Hendy

b. Barbados, British West Indies,
May 6, 1905
d. Cleveland, Ohio, January 14, 1961

His was likely the most atypical start to a life in hockey. Hendy emigrated to Vancouver at age six and, over the next few unhappy years, ran away several times, travelled the world, and held a variety of unsatisfying jobs. He ended up in New York, and then, more specifically, at Madison Square Garden. Hendy had a deep interest in the game's statistics, a topic that no one had previously taken a fancy to. In 1933, Hendy published his first annual Hockey Guide, a "facts 'n' stats" book that he published himself every year for a quarter-century. In 1951, he handed all his work over to the NHL, which used his information as the basis of today's mammoth NHL Official Guide & Record Book. He later worked for the Rangers in their publicity department and became the president of the United States Hockey League and general manager of the Cleveland Barons in the American league.

1969

August 21, 1969: Detroit Alumni Have Their Night

The Induction Ceremonies were a gala affair for 1969 as six new men, four of them Players, were enshrined in the Hockey Hall of Fame. Master of ceremonies was none other than Conn Smythe, and past inductees in attendance included Toe Blake, Turk Broda, Ted Kennedy, Angus Campbell, Jimmy Dunn, Foster Hewitt, Frank Fredrickson, Cyclone Taylor, Milt Schmidt, Sylvio Mantha, and Joe Primeau. A singular moment came when Gordie Howe made the introductions for Sid Abel, who had been a teammate with Howe in the 1940s and was now his coach!

Bruce Norris (left) and Sid Abel celebrate their induction into the Hockey Hall of Fame.

Sid Abel

b. Melville, Saskatchewan, February 22, 1918
d. Detroit, Michigan, February 7, 2000

At 24, Abel (pictured, foreground left) was named captain of the Red Wings, the team with which he spent most of his career, starting in 1938–39. He played on two of Detroit's greatest lines, first with the Liniment Line with Don Grosso and Eddie Wares and later on the great Production Line with Gordie Howe and Ted Lindsay. In the former, he was a young star, and in the latter he was the experienced centre, playing alongside two of the great youngsters of the game. Abel won three Stanley Cups with the Wings, one before he went off to war, and the other two after combat. He led the NHL in goals in 1948–49 with 28, the year he won the Hart Trophy, though he had a career high of 34 the following season. After finishing his career in Chicago, Abel returned to the Motor City where he became a coach and general manager, living the rest of his life in the area that had been so good to him as a player.

Bryan Hextall

b. Grenfell, Saskatchewan, July 31, 1913
d. Portage la Prairie, Manitoba, July 25, 1984

In 449 NHL games, all with the Rangers, Hextall recorded 187 goals and 362 points. He took the team to a Stanley Cup in 1940, the year he led the league in goals with 24. The next year he was again top sniper with 26, and in 1941–42 he was the league's scoring leader with 56 total points. A right winger, Hextall was named to the NHL's First All-Star Team three times and Second All-Star Team once—clear evidence of his skill.

Leonard "Red" Kelly

b. Simcoe, Ontario, July 9, 1927

There was very good reason why the Selection Committee waived the three-year waiting period to induct Kelly into the Hockey Hall of Fame: he had not one great career, but two. The first came with Detroit and lasted the better part of 13 seasons. Kelly played mostly defence, though he was occasionally shifted up to the left wing, and with the Wings he evolved into one of the best blueliners in the game. He was a First Team All-Star with the Wings six times in a seven-year span (1950–57) and he won four Lady Byng Trophies, even though the Lady Byng is rarely given to defencemen. In 1953–54, Kelly was awarded the James Norris Trophy, and he represented the team for nine successive years at the All-Star Game. He also won four Stanley Cups with the greatest Wings team of all time. Had he retired in 1960, he would still have been inducted into the Hall. A trade, however, gave him new life. He was sent to Toronto, and it was there that coach Punch Imlach moved him permanently to centre and revived his career. Kelly won four more Cups with the great Leafs teams of the 1960s, and such was his reputation by this point that often when captain George Armstrong missed a game, it was the redhead Kelly who played as captain designate (pictured below). By the time Kelly retired in 1967, on the eve of expansion, he had played 1,316 regular season games and 164 more in the playoffs (in the days when the post season was never more than two rounds of play).

August 21, 1969: Detroit Alumni Have Their Night

Red Kelly (#4 in white, above) started his career as a defenceman with the Red Wings before moving to centre with the Leafs (below).

Roy Worters

b. Toronto, Ontario, October 19, 1900

d. Toronto, Ontario, November 7, 1957

Worters' grandson attended the induction and accepted the plaque on Worters' behalf in 1969. Red Dutton presented, which was only fitting, since he had recommended this tiny goalie to the Selection Committee: "With what he lacked in

stature he made up for in determination and intestinal fortitude," wrote Dutton in his letter to the Committee. Dutton then related Worters' methods in the days before the blocker was part of the goalie's paraphernalia. "He was the first goalkeeper I had ever seen to use the back of his hands to divert pucks to the corner, and you very seldom scored on a rebound on Roy. His hands took terrible punishment and I marvel at the little guy and the way he had splints put on his fingers before a game." Indeed, Shrimp, as he was known, played in the NHL from 1925 to 1937, mostly with the ill-fated New York Americans. He won the Hart Trophy in 1928–29 and the Vézina two years later, and despite playing on a bad team (he made only 11 playoff appearances) he retired with 67 shutouts to his credit and a remarkable goals-against average of 2.27.

Al Leader

b. Barnsley, Manitoba, December 4, 1903

d. Rancho Mirage, California, May 8, 1982

As a player, Leader went as far as junior and senior hockey, but his true calling was in a suit, not in a uniform. He journeyed to the United States as a player, but in 1933 he was named secretary of the Seattle City League. He became manager, and later coach,

in that league, and in 1940 he formed the Defense Hockey League. In 1944, Leader was named secretary of the Pacific Coast Hockey League and four years later, when it became a pro league, he was appointed president, a position he held for more than a quarter-century. He also acted in an administrative capacity in amateur hockey throughout the United States, notably with the American Hockey Association.

Bruce Norris

b. Chicago, Illinois, February 19, 1924

d. Florida, January 1, 1986

His father, James, bought the Detroit Red Wings in 1933, and Bruce moved up the ranks from vice president of the team to president in 1955, succeeding his sister, Marguerite, at the ripe old age of just 31. He played college hockey until a serious knee injury ended any serious aspirations, but he always enjoyed skating whenever he got the chance (in the photo above he makes the moves on goalie Hank Bassen). He remained day-to-day boss of the team until 1982 when he sold the Wings, and during his tenure he guided the team to steady performances throughout the 1950s and 1960s. He also saw to major renovations of the Olympia and to the construction of the Joe Louis Arena in 1979.

1970

Conn Smythe again emceed the Hall of Fame induction dinner of 1970, and the tone was one of merry celebration. This year, the Selection Committee added three Players and one Builder.

August 27, 1970: Dye and Gadsby Join the Elite

1970

Bill Gadsby (left) receives his Hockey Hall of Fame plaque from Ebbie Goodfellow, an Honoured Member in his own right.

Cecil "Babe" Dye

b. Hamilton, Ontario, May 13, 1898
d. Chicago, Illinois, January 2, 1962

Clarence Campbell had this to say about Dye at the induction dinner: "He was a minuscule man by modern standards, only 5' 8" and 150 pounds flat out, but in one span of 170 games with Toronto St. Pats, Dye scored 174 goals. That's the highest scoring average per game in NHL history and will never be broken." Indeed, despite his small stature, Dye was known for his tremendous shot. While playing with Toronto in the early days of the NHL, he led the league in goal scoring three times and in points twice. His only Stanley Cup came with the St. Pats in 1921–22, when he set a record that still stands by scoring nine goals in the five-game finals series against Vancouver. In 271 career NHL games, Dye had an incredible 201 goals.

Bill Gadsby

b. Calgary, Alberta, August 8, 1927

Even in the 21st century, the list of players who stayed in the NHL for 20 years is a short one. But make no mistake, Gadsby's name is on it. He started with Chicago in 1946 and by 1966 (when he retired), his face had seen hundreds of stitches from

his 1,248 games on defence. He played in eight All-Star Games and was a First Team All-Star three times, but he never won the Stanley cup or an individual award. He divided his career fairly evenly between the Rangers, Chicago, and Detroit, making it to the Cup finals with the Wings three times in the 1960s, coming up second-best each time.

Tom Johnson

b. Baldur, Manitoba, February 18, 1928

He was the "hidden" superstar on Montreal in the 1950s, as one newspaper put it. He was the defenceman who was never appreciated enough because he played on a team with Doug Harvey, the unquestioned king of the blue line. Nonetheless, Johnson played in eight All-Star Games, won six Stanley Cups, and was awarded the Norris Trophy for 1958–59. He never played the power play—that was Harvey's bailiwick—but he was a great penalty killer. He had great speed and was ever-reliable defensively. His disciplined play also earned him the trust of every coach for whom he played.

Although an unheralded Canadiens defenceman during their ages of glory, Tom Johnson won six Stanley Cups with Montreal.

Bob LeBel

b. Quebec City, Quebec,
September 21, 1905
d. Longueuil, Quebec
September 20, 1999

There was nothing in hockey Bob LeBel focused on that he didn't accomplish. He played up to senior level before realizing he could do more as an administrator than a player, and in 1944 he founded the Interprovincial Senior League, acting as president for the first three years. By 1955 he had become president of the Quebec amateur league, and in 1960 he attained the highest post possible: president of the International Ice Hockey Federation, which he held for two years. In 1964, LeBel was named a lifetime member of the Canadian Amateur Hockey Association and of the Quebec Amateur Hockey Association. From 1961, he sat on the Hall's Governing Committee.

> June 16, 1970
>
> Mr. Robert LeBel
> 26 Peter St.
> Chambly, P.Q.
>
> Dear Mr. LeBel:
>
> On behalf of the Governing Committee and the Selection Committee of the Hockey Hall of Fame, may I extend to you sincere congratulations upon being elected a member of the Hall. And may I add my own personal congratulations.
>
> As both secretary and curator of the Hall, one of my functions is to assemble background material to be used in our annual publication Hockey's Heritage. I am enclosing the information sheet we have about you, but wonder if you might wish to add anything of interest, so that our account may be correct and complete. An early response would be appreciated as we shall soon be going to press on the current edition.
>
> Hockey Hall of Fame induction ceremonies, as I believe you know, are scheduled for Thursday, August 27, at approximately 7 p.m. An official invitation confirming this will be forthcoming at a later date, so please keep it in mind.
>
> Again, sincere congratulations.
>
> Yours sincerely,
>
> HOCKEY HALL OF FAME
>
> M.H. (Lefty) Reid
> Curator and Secretary

A copy of the letter sent to Bob LeBel to announce his induction into the Hockey Hall of Fame.

1971

August 26, 1971: Harvey Jackson Stirs Debate

It was, perhaps, the most awkward moment in the history of the Hockey Hall of Fame. On June 9, 1971, Frank Selke, Sr., chairman of the Selection Committee, announced three names of Players who had been inducted into the Hall. Then, he cleared his throat and explained the final nominee accepted: "The next selection is going to be a controversial one... Just as I said Sawchuk was the best goalie I ever saw... It's like I've said before... Harvey Jackson was the classiest player I ever saw. I mean for style and poise and all that... Unfortunately, he was his own worst enemy." Indeed, Conn Smythe, chairman of the Hall's board, resigned after learning of Jackson's inclusion, such was the vehemence of his anger. "If the standards are going to be lowered," he challenged, "I'll get out as chairman of the board." He was venting not against Jackson's irrefutable skill and grace on the ice, but rather his post-career, off-ice lifestyle, which eventually led to premature death (in 1966), caused by liver failure. Since then, the great member of the Kid Line had been nominated twice for hall of fame induction, and Smythe's iron will had won the day so far; no player who drank and led the high life was going to be enshrined. The Selection Committee of 1970, though, begged to differ, arguing that Jackson was being inducted because he was a great player—no more, no less. That Committee included Selke, Red Dutton, Cyclone Taylor, Marcel Desjardins, Baz O'Meara, Gordon Juckes, Milt Dunnell, Jimmy Dunn, Danny Gallivan, and Ebbie Goodfellow. Their opinion carried the day, and all these years later no fan could argue that Jackson's career didn't merit inclusion in the Hall.

Harvey Jackson

b. Toronto, Ontario, January 19, 1911
d. Toronto, Ontario, June 25, 1966

Toronto trainer Tim Daly dropped the young Jackson's ego down a peg when he said he was "nuthin' but a busher" at Jackson's first training camp, and although the epithet stuck for the rest of his life, Jackson quickly developed into the best left winger in the NHL. He joined the Leafs in 1929 and for 10 seasons patrolled the left side for Conn Smythe's men. Jackson was primarily a scorer, and 1931–32 was the best season of his career. He led the league with 53 points and led the team to the Stanley Cup. He was named to the First All-Star Team for the first of four such honours. In all, Jackson played 633 games and scored 241 goals.

Gordon Roberts

b. Ottawa, Ontario, September 5, 1891
d. Oakland, California, September 2, 1966

In his first days as a hockey player, Roberts suited up for the Ottawa Senators, Cup champions in 1909, but two years later he moved to Montreal in order to study medicine at McGill University. He joined the local Wanderers and played in the National Hockey Association, which enabled him to pay for his education. A left winger, Roberts was an outstanding scorer with the team, but he didn't veer from his path of being a doctor. In 1916 he moved out to Vancouver to start his practice, and in 1916–17 he set a new

Pacific Coast Hockey Association record by scoring 43 goals in 23 games. Soon he was down in Seattle, and in 1920 he continued south to Oakland, where he could run a successful obstetrics practice but where there was no high-level hockey. Roberts retired as an enigma to the hockey world, and a great athlete in the world of medicine.

Terry Sawchuk

b. Winnipeg, Manitoba, December 28, 1929
d. Long Beach, New York, May 31, 1970

Brilliant on-ice or off, Sawchuk was as magnificent in the nets as he was unhappy. Nobody endured more physical pain during so long a career, and no goalie had more success. He died at age 40 during a summer accident, and the Hockey Hall of Fame waived the waiting period a year later to ensure he got his place in hockey greatness as soon as possible. Sawchuk played so well in an emergency situation in the 1949–50 season that after just seven games general manager Jack Adams knew this was his goalie for the future. He traded Harry Lumley in the summer of 1950, even though Lumley had just led the Wings to the Stanley Cup. But Adams did not make a mistake. In his first five seasons, Sawchuk led the league in victories every year, led in shutouts three times and went on to win three Vézina Trophies. He had 56 total shutouts in that short time, and won three Cups as well. Sawchuk was clearly the best. He was brave beyond words and suffered untold injuries, both to his body and to his psyche. He was a poor sleeper and was uncommunicative off-ice, but in the crease he was a competitor of the first order. He went on to play for Boston,

Detroit's Terry Sawchuk set records for a goalie that endured more than 30 years, and his 103 career shutouts is one that might never be broken.

though he retired briefly because of stress, and returned to the Wings two years later. He later shared goaler's duties with Johnny Bower in 1966–67, winning a fourth Cup at age 38, and he didn't retire until 1969, by which time he was with the Rangers. Sawchuk set records for games played (972) and wins (446) that lasted three decades, and his 103 career shutouts (plus another 12 in the playoffs) is one of hockey's most elusive records. He won

rookie of the year in three consecutive years in three different leagues (United States Hockey League, American Hockey League, NHL) and played in a record 11 All-Star Games.

Sawchuk played in goal for the Leafs during the historic 1966-67 season when the Leafs became the oldest team to win the Stanley Cup.

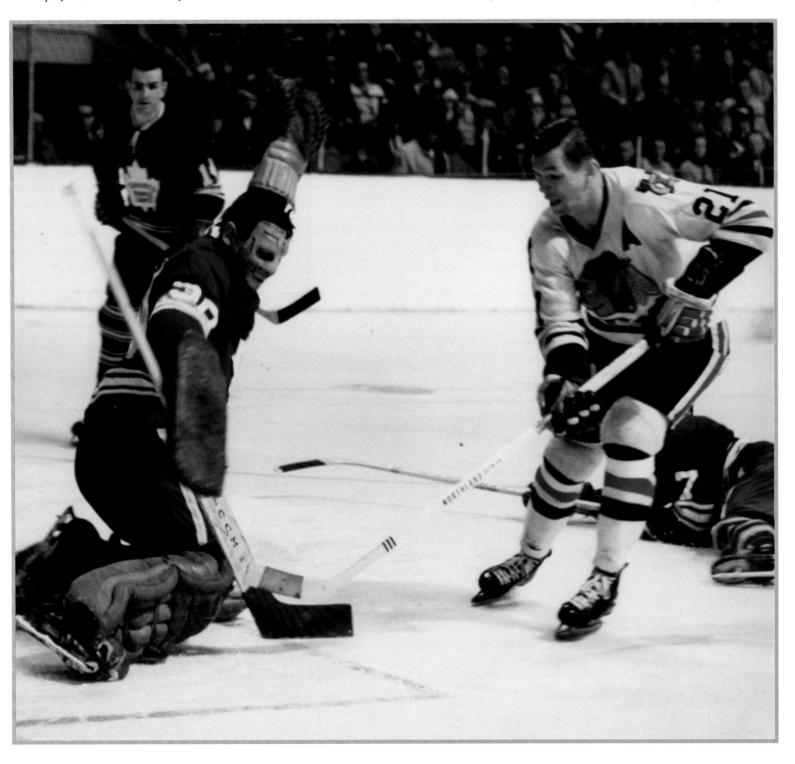

1971

Ralph "Cooney" Weiland

b. Egmondville, Ontario, November 5,1904
d. New England, July 3, 1985

After helping the Owen Sound Greys win the Memorial Cup in 1924–25, Weiland took his hockey act to Minneapolis in the American Hockey Association, where his teammate was goalie

Tiny Thompson. In 1928, the pair was acquired by Boston, and so began two illustrious Hall of Fame careers. Weiland won the Cup as a rookie in 1928–29, and although he had just 11 regular-season goals, he was the hero in the playoffs. Boston beat Montreal in the semifinals in two games, both going to a 1-0 score, and Weiland scored the two Boston goals. The year after he led the league with 43 goals in just 44 games and was at the top of the points parade with 73. It was his finest season. "Besides being an offensive threat," Frank Selke, Sr. wrote in his recommendation to the Hockey Hall of Fame Selection Committee, "he was a great exponent of the poke check, which made him effective defensively, especially killing penalties." In 509 career games, Weiland had 333 points. He went on to coach Harvard for more than 20 years and became a member of the rare 300-win club in the National Collegiate Athletic Association.

Arthur Wirtz

b. Chicago, Illinois, January 23, 1901
d. Chicago, Illinois, July 21, 1983

Wirtz's association with hockey began back in 1931 when he and James Norris combined forces to buy the Detroit Red Wings. Two years later, they and James D. Norris saved the Chicago Black Hawks, and in the ensuing years they also bought

controlling interest in Madison Square Garden in New York, the St. Louis Arena, and other arenas with which they helped develop farm teams for their NHL clubs. Wirtz and James D. Norris bought the Hawks outright in 1954 and spent all their energies building that team into a winner, a project that culminated in 1961 with the Stanley Cup. In 1966, Wirtz was instrumental in bringing hockey to St. Louis. He sold his interest to the Salomon family in order to ensure ethical development of the team, and Wirtz later became chairman and president of the Hawks, while his son, William, took control of the day-to-day operations of the hockey team. Arthur Wirtz sold his interests in the team in 1979.

1972

August 24, 1972: Taking Their Rightful Place

It was an historic night at the Canadian National Exhibition in Toronto this year as two players—Gordie Howe and Jean Béliveau—were inducted into the Hockey Hall of Fame without having to wait the usual three years before qualifying for enshrinement. When speaking of Howe, Joe Primeau said it best: "We now have hockey's equivalent to baseball's Babe Ruth in our Hall of Fame." Indeed, Howe was the all-time leader in games played, goals, assists, and total points. Primeau went on to say, "He's not only the greatest right winger of all time, he's the greatest hockey player of all time. No one gave rival coaches more nightmares, and I speak from experience." Béliveau was in Munich at the Summer Olympics and was not in attendance, but the dinner was full of hockey luminaries, from Bobby Orr and Phil Esposito, to Frank Selke, Sr. and Clarence Campbell.

1972

Jean Béliveau

b. Trois Rivieres, Quebec, August 31, 1931

At first, the Montreal Canadiens were happy to see Béliveau go to Quebec City to develop after junior hockey. But when he got there, he became the highest-paid player in hockey. He was revered, happy, and a superstar. He had no desire to go anywhere else. In 1950–51 and 1952–53, he was called up briefly by the

Habs, scoring six goals in five games. It was clear he was going to be a star in the NHL—if the team could convince him to sign. He balked, and the Habs were forced to buy the entire Quebec senior league and make it a professional league, thus forcing Béliveau to honour his contract, which stated that when he turned pro he would play only for the Canadiens. He signed the day of the 1953 All-Star Game (the Games used to take place at the start of the year), and thus began his full-time, lifelong association with le Club de Hockey Canadiens. In 20 years with the

Montreal captain Jean Béliveau, seen here in a game against the Leafs, was a combination of gentleman and indomitable spirit on ice.

team, he won 10 Stanley Cups, a record broken only by teammate Henri Richard. Béliveau achieved every possible milestone a player can hope to: he played 1,125 games, scored 507 goals and 1,219 points. He won the Hart Trophy in 1955–56, the same year he won the Art Ross Trophy, and he won a second Hart Trophy in 1963–64. He played in 13 All-Star Games and in 1965 was

the initial recipient of the NHL's newest trophy, the Conn Smythe, to honour the best player of the playoffs. Béliveau captained the Habs with honour and distinction for the last 10 years of his career, a gentleman on the ice and a loyal Montrealer off it.

Bernie Geoffrion

b. Montreal, Quebec, February 16, 1931

It was on March 16, 1961 that Boom Boom Geoffrion got his name into the record books when he scored his 50th goal of the season to tie his idol Maurice Richard for most goals in a year. Geoffrion accomplished the feat in 62 games (the Rocket had done it in 50), and it was Geoffrion's only 50-goal season of his distin-

guished 16-year career, 14 of which were spent with the Canadiens. He had won the Calder Trophy in 1951–52, his first full season, scoring 30 times and establishing himself as a premier scorer. In 1954–55, he led the league with 38 goals and 75 points to win the Art Ross Trophy. For his fine season, he was also awarded the Hart Trophy. Although he played in 11 All-Star Games, Geoffrion made only one First All-Star Team, a circumstance explained by the fact that guys named Howe and Richard were fixtures on that roster for the duration of their careers.

Geoffrion averaged nearly a point a game (822 in 883 games) and he was legendary for his ability to play through extraordinary pain. He earned his nickname for his use of the slapshot, and although he wasn't the first man to use that hard shot, he was certainly the first to perfect it and use it regularly to intimidate goalies and score.

Harry "Hap" Holmes

b. Aurora, Ontario, February 21, 1892
d. Fort Lauderdale, Florida, June 28, 1941

In 16 seasons of professional hockey, Holmes was, with Georges Vézina, the finest goalie in the game. He started with the Toronto Blueshirts in the National Hockey Association in 1912, and won his first of four Stanley Cups two years later. He and teammates Frank Foyston and Jack Walker then moved out west to play in the Pacific Coast Hockey Association where Holmes played the majority of his career. He won a Cup with Seattle in 1917, returned east to help Toronto win in 1918, the first year of the NHL, and then settled in to an eight-year stint with Seattle and Victoria. Holmes led the Cougars to a Cup in 1925, but a year later the Western Hockey League folded and he returned to the NHL with Detroit. In his final season, 1927–28, the 36-year-old recorded 11 shutouts and posted a goals-against average of 1.73 before retiring. In 1961, the American Hockey League named its best goalie award after him.

1972

The greatest goal scorer of all time, until Wayne Gretzky arrived, Gordie Howe shovelled 801 goals into opponents' nets.

Gordie Howe

b. Floral, Saskatchewan, March 31, 1928

When Gordie Howe retired in the spring of 1971, he was considered by one and all to be the best player ever to skate in the NHL or in any other league. He had played 25 years in the league and was the all-time leader in every offensive category. Flash back to the start of his career, though, and nothing seemed that certain. He first attended New York Rangers training camp but was so homesick he fled the camp to return to the farm. Detroit's general manager convinced him to attend Red Wings camp in 1945, and the rest, as they say, is history. Howe played a year in Omaha and in 1946 joined the NHL. He soon formed a long friendship with Ted Lindsay, and the two played on a line with Sid Abel called the

Production Line, because of its prolific scoring. Howe's career and life almost ended early in the 1950 playoffs when he landed headfirst into the boards after missing a check on Toronto's Ted Kennedy, but after a summer of recuperation, he came back with a vengeance, leading the league in goals, assists, and points in 1950–51. It was the first of six scoring championships he won and the first of four in a row. In his final 22 seasons, he never

Howe battles with Allan Stanley around the goal (photo far left), a job he was quite comfortable with on a regular basis (above).

failed to score at least 23 goals, a record that won't likely be broken. Howe also won six Hart Trophies and was also respected as the toughest player of his era. He retired because of arthritis in his wrists, but soon after his induction he was lured to the fledgling World Hockey Association because of the prospect of playing with his sons, Marty and Mark. The incredible and improbable story continued through the 1979–80 season when Hartford joined the NHL from the other league and the Howe

family played one last season together. At the age of 52, Howe still scored 15 goals and had a plus-minus rating of +9, playing in every game and doing nothing but adding to his legend as the greatest player. That final season climaxed at the 1980 All-Star Game when he was named to the team for the 23rd time, another record. The ovation given him at the new Joe Louis Arena in his old town is still regarded as the most memorable in All-Star Game history.

Gordie Howe admires his Hockey Hall of Fame ring with his sons—Marty and Murray—and daughter Cathy and wife Colleen.

1972

"Hooley" Smith

b. Toronto, Ontario, January 7, 1903
d. Montreal, Quebec, August 24, 1963

Smith grew up in Toronto and played his best amateur hockey with the Toronto Granites, the team that easily captured gold for Canada at the 1924 Olympics in Chamonix, France. Upon his return, he was overwhelmed with offers to turn pro, and he accepted the Ottawa bid. Smith starred on a line with Frank

Nighbor and Cy Denneny, winning a Cup in his third season, 1926–27. He was then traded to Montreal, and it was with the Maroons that he had his best years. He played on the right wing with Nels Stewart and Babe Siebert, the threesome being dubbed the 3-S Line or, simply, the S-Line. They were big, strong, ferocious, and offensively intimidating, leading the M's to a Cup in 1935. Smith ended his career with the Bruins and New York Americans. He played in 715 career games and scored exactly 200 goals, among the first players to reach that magical plateau of the NHL's early days.

Weston Adams

b. August 9, 1904
d. Boston, Massachusetts, March 19, 1973

His father, Charles, was the first owner and president of the Boston Bruins in 1924 when the team entered the NHL. In 1931, Weston was named president of the newly acquired Boston Cubs of the Can-Am league, and four years later he succeeded his father as head man of the Bruins. Under his guidance the team won the Stanley Cup in 1939 and 1941, at which point Weston joined the war efforts. He resigned as Bruins president in 1950, a position to which he returned in 1964 and where he sought with single-mindedness to strengthen the farm system and scouting staff. He retired for good in 1969 and a year later enjoyed the fruits of his labour as the Bruins won the Cup.

1973

August 23, 1973: Doug Harvey Gets in a Year Too Late

The good and the bad collided head-on at this year's induction. Doug Harvey, considered the greatest defenceman of all time (not counting the ongoing career of Bobby Orr), was inducted by unanimous decision. But in Harvey's estimation, the induction came a year too late. He was upset that he hadn't been named the previous year, with Gordie Howe and Jean Béliveau, two other greats who had the customary waiting period waived. No such honour was accorded Harvey, and as a result he refused to attend 1973's banquet and celebration. Cyclone Taylor, a member of the Selection Committee, was diplomatic in his explanation: "Doug would have gone in last year had he been out of hockey three years, but he kept unretiring. He was the finest defenceman I ever saw play. There is no doubt about his right to be in the Hall of Fame." Implications were that—like Harvey Jackson—Harvey had been kept out a bit longer because of his drinking problems, a suggestion Taylor dismissed. "That has nothing to do with it. We enshrine them for their hockey… He was spectacular, colourful, excellent."

August 23, 1973: Doug Harvey Gets in a Year Too Late

Doug Harvey

b. Montreal, Quebec, December 19, 1924
d. Montreal, Quebec, December 26, 1989

The honours, the respect, the reputation were without compare during his playing days. Harvey joined Montreal in 1947 and for 14 years was the backbone of the Canadiens' defence. In many ways, he was also its offence. He presaged Bobby Orr, not in terms of scoring points but in creativity with the puck. He never scored more than nine goals in a given season, but he was a perfect passer and moved the puck like no other defenceman in the game. Harvey won six Cups with Montreal, including the great stretch of five in a row from 1956 to 1960. He left the team in 1961 to coach and play for the New York Rangers, later accomplishing something unique—winning a trophy while coaching the team. Harvey won the Norris Trophy that first season with the Blueshirts, his seventh. He had won the previous year with the Habs, and so became the only defenceman to win in consecutive years with different teams. He was a First Team All-Star 10 times and played in 13 All-Star Games. In 1,113 games Harvey registered 540 points, but it was his style of play— his ability to control a game and determine its outcome almost single-handedly—that earned him accolades.

Harvey (#2 white) was as spectacular with the puck heading up ice as he was in his own end preventing goals.

1973

Charlie Rayner

b. Sutherland, Saskatchewan, August 11, 1920
d. Langley, British Columbia, October 6, 2002

Long before Ron Hextall or Martin Brodeur handled the puck like a defenceman or skated like a forward there was Charlie Rayner, a goalie who almost scored on a solo rush and who even played the power play point four or five times during his years with the Rangers. He entered the NHL with the Americans in 1940 and played a year and a half before joining Canada's war efforts. In 1945, upon resuming his career, he joined the Rangers and established himself as a great goalie playing on not-so-great teams. Only twice did he make the playoffs, coming closest to a Cup in 1950 when the team lost to Detroit in overtime of game seven. It was that season he was named winner of the Hart Trophy. Rayner never had a winning season, but he had 138 wins in 424 appearances and was respected for his brilliant performances in a losing cause. In 1946–47, for instance, he led the NHL in shutouts with five, even though the team missed the playoffs. He also played in three All-Star Games.

Goalie Charlie Rayner stops a penalty shot by Toronto's Tod Sloan during the '50-'51 season.

Tommy Smith

b. Ottawa, Ontario, September 27, 1885
d. Ottawa, Ontario, August 1, 1966

His NHL ledger looks pale, 10 games in his final season of pro, with Quebec in 1919–20. The truth, though, was that Tommy Smith was among the greatest goal getters of the pre-NHL era. He started with Ottawa in 1905 and moved down to Pittsburgh to play in the first fully pro league a year later. From there, he moved around, though he missed most of 1909–10 because of typhoid fever. Smith landed with Quebec in the new National Hockey Association in 1912 and it was there he won his only Stanley Cup. He retired in 1917 after a season with the Canadiens, and two years later he made a brief comeback with the Bulldogs. His brother Alf was inducted into the Hockey Hall of Fame in 1962.

Hon. Hartland de Montarville Molson

b. Montreal, Quebec,
May 29, 1907
d. Montreal, Quebec,
September 28, 2002

His father was one of the founders of the Canadian Arena Company, the backbone of professional hockey in Montreal. Hartland was a fine amateur player who made it to the Memorial Cup finals in 1926 with Royal Military College after which he pursued a business career.

August 23, 1973: Doug Harvey Gets in a Year Too Late

In 1938, he became assistant secretary-treasurer of Molson Brewery Limited, though his tenure was interrupted by a colourful career in the military. Molson went on to became president and chairman of the Canadian Arena Company and the Canadiens club from 1957 to 1968, when Molson's owned the team. He was a member of the NHL's finance committee that helped build the Hockey Hall of Fame in 1961 and he also worked to improve the NHL's pension fund.

Frank Udvari

b. Yugoslavia, January 2, 1924

Fate played a large role in the life of Udvari, who grew up in Kitchener, his adopted home from the age of seven. He was coaching a local team when, one night, the referee didn't show and he volunteered to be arbiter. Three years later, he was in the NHL, and after a few games fate would again have a hand in his becoming, almost overnight, a full-time NHL referee. In 1952, long-time zebra Georges Gravel became ill early in the season and missed most of a year. Despite his inexperience, Udvari was thrust into the spotlight. He handled every difficult situation well and quickly became respected as the best in the business. During his 15 years, he never missed a game because of injury, and he retired on August 1, 1966—only so that he could become the league's referee-in-chief.

During a break in action, referee Frank Udvari confers with the penalty timekeeper.

1974

August 22, 1974: Catching Up with the Golden Oldies

Toronto was the theme to this year's inductees; three of the seven men—Billy Burch, Carl Voss, and Tommy Ivan—grew up in that city, while two others—Dickie Moore and Charles Hay—had connections to Hogtown during their careers. For Ivan in particular, the induction was sweet reward for a career in coaching, a career that evolved out of an injury preventing Ivan from playing. "This is like winning the Stanley Cup," he said, upon learning of the announcement to enshrine him. "I just hope I'm worthy of the honour, something I had sort of hoped for but never really expected."

1974

Billy Burch

b. Yonkers, New York,
   November 20, 1900
d. Toronto, Ontario,
   November 30, 1950

Burch first saw the light of day in New York, but he grew up in Toronto and played junior locally with Aura Lee. He turned pro with the Hamilton Tigers in 1922–23 and two years later he won the Hart Trophy. The team went on strike before the playoffs and was disqualified, costing Burch his best chance at a Stanley Cup. He went with the team to New York the next year, where it played as the Americans, and he was the team's first captain. In 1926–27 he won the Lady Byng Trophy. The 1932–33 season was his last—a season split between Boston and Chicago and cut short because of a broken leg that forced him to retire.

Art Coulter

b. Winnipeg, Manitoba, May 31, 1909

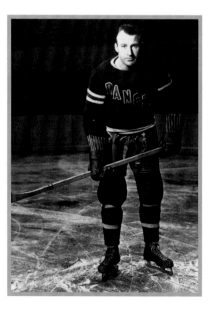

His strength and endurance were the stuff of legend, and Coulter made his reputation as a defensive defenceman rather than a rusher. He broke into the NHL with Chicago toward the end of the 1931–32 season and for three and a half years was a rock on the Hawks blue line, notably in 1933–34 when the team won its first Stanley Cup. He was later made captain of the team and, soon after, traded one-for-one to the Rangers for Earl Seibert. It was on Broadway that Coulter spent the last six and a half seasons. He won a second Cup in 1940 and was named to four Second All-Star Teams in an era when Hall of Fame defencemen were numerous.

Tommy Dunderdale

b. Benella, Australia, May 6, 1887
d. Winnipeg, Manitoba, December 15, 1960

The all-time leading scorer in Pacific Coast Hockey Association history, Dunderdale spent most of his career out west. His family moved from Australia to Ottawa in 1904, and a few years later continued west to Winnipeg. Along the way, Dunderdale played hockey. A small and fleet centre, he moved east in 1909 to play for the Montreal Shamrocks and Quebec Bulldogs, but in 1911 he moved west to Victoria. For fully the first half of his career he averaged better than a goal a game, and in 12 seasons, his total stood first among all men. He was a First Team All-Star six times, though he never won a Stanley Cup.

Dickie Moore

b. Montreal, Quebec, January 6, 1931

It was his amazing ability to play with pain and to recover from injury after injury that got Moore from the streets of Montreal to the Hockey Hall of Fame. In 1949 and 1950, he won consecutive Memorial Cups with the Royals and Jr. Canadiens, respectively, and in 1951 he joined the Canadiens for half a season. He spent 12 seasons in all with the Habs, a time noteworthy for both personal and team accomplishments. Moore helped the club win six Stanley Cups, one in 1953, the others consecutively from 1956 to 1960. In 1957–58 he led the league with 36 goals and 84 points, and the next year he set a single-season scoring record with 96 points, besting Gordie Howe's record by one. Moore also played in six All-Star Games and was named to two First All-Star teams. Yet through it all, he was plagued by injuries. His bad knees troubled him his whole life. He had at least three shoulder separations, a broken hand and wrist, the last of which was particularly troublesome. He spent the last three months of the 1957–58 season in a cast, yet still managed to lead the league in points. Toward the end of his career he came out of retirement twice, once to play for Toronto, the other time to join the fledgling St. Louis Blues. In 719 total games, Moore had 261 goals and 608 points.

Dickie Moore (with puck) played nearly 20 years in the NHL, finishing his career with the expansion Blues in St. Louis.

Charles Hay

b. Kingston, Ontario, 1902
d. Toronto, Ontario,
October 24, 1973

The father of Bill Hay (current chairman of the Hockey Hall of Fame) Charles Hay was a businessman out west for most of his life. Everything changed when he retired, though. On December 10, 1968, he attended a meeting in Ottawa set up by the Task Force on Sport, ostensibly to bring people together who could

help centralize and give structure to hockey in the country. The result was Hockey Canada, the prime focus of which was to promote international competition. Hay became president just a few months after its inception, and under his guidance and leadership, Canada was able to organize the Summit Series, the most important tournament ever played. Later, Hay used his many business connections for fundraising and financing various programs and projects for Hockey Canada. His legacy has lived on in the many roles that the Canadian Hockey Association now fills in hockey at all levels—national, amateur, and international.

Tommy Ivan

b. Toronto, Ontario, January 31, 1911
d. Chicago, Illinois, June 24, 1999

A fractured cheekbone prevented Ivan from realizing his dream to play hockey for a living, but he subsequently became a referee and then coach. He was hired by Detroit to coach the farm team in Omaha. His first year behind the bench coincided with the first pro year for a 17-year-old named Gordie Howe, and soon after they were both in Detroit. Ivan was the only NHL coach of the day who never played pro, but that didn't stop him from winning six consecutive division titles and three Stanley Cups. He left Motor City in 1954 to assume general manager duties in Chicago, and it was under his leadership that the Hawks established a superior farm system. Ivan also coached six All-Star Games and can boast a perfect 6-0 record, something no one before or since can claim.

Anatoli Tarasov

b. December 18, 1918
d. Moscow, Russia, June 23, 1995

It was under the brilliant leadership of Tarasov that Soviet hockey established itself as a world power and maintained that high reputation for decades. He had been an above-average player in the late 1940s when hockey was in its earliest development in the Soviet Union, but his true calling came as a coach, first with

Central Army in the 1950s and then the national team starting in 1963. Tarasov's methods were influenced by the Canadian style, but he went beyond merely mimicking what he saw. He interpreted and, in many ways, improved on those methods. He was no player's best friend, but he got every ounce of energy and skill from every player who ever skated under him. Tarasov accumulated ten gold medals in World Championship play in the 1960s and into the early '70s—as well as three Olympic golds in 1964, '68, and '72. By the time he retired he was known as the godfather of Soviet hockey, such was the reverence and respect he was accorded by everyone in the Soviet hockey system for his astounding international success.

Carl Voss

b. Chelsea, Massachusetts, January 6, 1907
d. Lake Park, Florida, September 13, 1994

In 1950, Voss was lured away from his post as president of the United States Hockey League to become the NHL's first referee-in-chief. For the next 15 years, he devoted his life to officiating the game and brought the quality of play interpretation to higher standards. Voss conducted clinics, trained officials, and scouted and critiqued their every performance—doing everything possible to improve the officials' ability to call a fair game. He started as the only employee in that branch of the NHL, and by the time he left, there were 23 in the department. Thanks to his efforts, the number and quality of officials increased exponentially and gave the league a solid base from which to choose the finest men. Voss had been a nine-year NHLer as a player and holds the distinction of being the only man to win the rookie of the year award (pre–Calder Trophy days) during a season in which he was traded.

1975

August 28, 1975: Leafs Take Centre Stage

In 1975, the Hockey Hall of Fame induction dinner moved away from the Canadian National Exhibition for the first time when it was held at the Royal York Hotel in Toronto, the most popular spot in the city for visiting players and executives.

1975

George Armstrong

b. Skead, Ontario, July 6, 1930

The longest-serving captain in Maple Leafs history, George Armstrong was a paradigm of leadership and skill. From 1957 to 1969 he wore the hallowed "C" for the team, and he still holds records for most seasons (21) and most games played (1,187) with Toronto. Armstrong was never a phenomenal offensive star in the way modern captains are. He had just four 20-goal seasons, but he led by example and was a reliable two-way player. Under him, the team won four Stanley Cups and he appeared in seven All-Star Games. He has remained with the team ever since retiring in 1971, as scout, coach, and alumnus, a representative of Toronto's great and glorious years.

"Ace" Bailey

b. Bracebridge,
* Ontario, July 3, 1903*
d. Toronto, Ontario,
* April 7, 1992*

He played just seven and a half seasons and 313 NHL games—all with Toronto—but Bailey was one of the top right wingers of his era. He had seasons of 22, 22, and 23 goals from 1928–31, and in the first of those years he also led the NHL with 32 total points. Bailey was a fleet forward with a quick shot, though his career ended prematurely because of a vicious Eddie Shore check in Boston the night of December 12, 1933.

Leafs captain George Armstrong fights with Serge Savard for the puck.

Ace Bailey receives his ring during induction ceremonies at the Royal York Hotel.

The Birth of the All-Star Game

Eddie Shore ended Ace Bailey's career out of a misunderstanding. Shore had been checked off the puck hard in the Toronto end, and as he came back, he thought Bailey was the one who had hit him. Shore upended the Toronto forward from behind, and

Bailey's head cracked the ice with near tragic results. Doctors had to perform three emergency brain operations in the coming days to save the player's life, and although he lived, his career was assuredly over. The NHL turned a negative into a positive, though. On February 14, 1934, the league held a special game in Toronto, the Leafs facing an all-star team of players from the rest of the league. During the pre-game ceremonies, Shore was introduced to the crowd and Bailey shook his hand at centre ice as the Gardens erupted in applause. All was forgiven, and the All-Star Game was born, becoming an annual affair, starting in 1947.

Gord Drillon

b. Moncton, New Brunswick, October 23, 1913

d. Saint John, New Brunswick, September 23, 1985

The career of Gord Drillon began in 1936 when the Leafs brought him into the lineup as a temporary replacement for the injured Charlie Conacher. He proved to have such a scoring knack around the net that coach Dick Irvin couldn't send him back to Syracuse, and for the next seven seasons Drillon was one of the highest and most consistent scorers in the league. In his second season, 1937–38, he led the NHL with 26 goals and 52 points. He won the Lady Byng Trophy and was named to the First All-Star Team. In 1941–42, his last year with Toronto, Drillon played on a line with Bob Davidson and Syl Apps, a threesome that led the team to the Stanley Cup. He was sold to Montreal in the summer and finished his career playing a year with the Canadiens. Drillon played just 311 NHL games, but scored 155 times, an average of better than 22 goals a year in an era when 20 was something to brag about.

Glenn Hall

b. Humboldt, Saskatchewan, October 3, 1931

It's true, in a sense, that records are meant to be broken, but there is at least one in hockey that will never, ever be broken. Over a period of seven years and 502 games, goalie Glenn Hall played every minute of every game for Detroit and Chicago. He appeared briefly for the Wings in 1952–53 and 1954–55, and he played so well that general manager Jack Adams knew he could trade Terry Sawchuk and rely on Hall. No greater compliment can be given a puckstopper. Hall started the 1955–56 season with Detroit and it wasn't until November 7, 1962 (when he wrenched his back during a game) that he had to leave the crease. Hall won the Calder Trophy in 1955–56, a season in which he recorded a league high of 12 shutouts. He led the league in wins three times and shutouts six times, and was named to the First All-Star Team seven times. He was traded to Chicago in the summer of 1957 with Ted Lindsay and four years later won his only Cup, with the Hawks. In 1967 he was claimed by St. Louis in the expansion draft and shared the

goaltending duties with Jacques Plante. Amazingly, the pair won the Vézina Trophy in 1968–69, when Hall was 38 and Plante 40. Hall had won a Vézina on his own in 1962–63 and shared one with Denis DeJordy in 1966–67. By the time he retired in 1971 he had played 906 games and 53,484 minutes—both second only to Sawchuk—and his 84 shutouts placed him third all-time.

Goalie Glenn Hall played in 502 consecutive games, a record for the netminding brethren that will never be broken.

Pierre Pilote

b. Kenogami, Quebec, December 11, 1931

To Pilote, induction into the pantheon of greats struck the right chord. "It's the last chapter at the end of the book," he said years later. "You play for so many years, and then one day they say, 'Hey, you're one of the best.' It makes you feel good." One of the best, indeed. He started with Chicago in 1955 as a young rookie and sixth defenceman on a weak team, but by the fall of 1961, he was wearing the "C" on his sweater after holding the Stanley Cup in his hand the previous spring. He led the league in assists and points that playoff season and assured his place in NHL history. Pilote was a First Team All-Star from 1962–67, a run of five years that has few comparisons. En route, he won three successive Norris Trophies (1962–65) and played in eight straight All-Star Games. The only season he didn't play for the Hawks was his last, 1968–69, when he dressed for Toronto.

Everyone called Pierre Pilote "Pete," but he was also known as one of the top defencemen in the game during the 1960s when the Hawks were at the height of their powers.

1975

Frank Buckland

b. Gravenhurst, Ontario, 1901
d. Peterborough, Ontario, June 23, 1991

In nominating Frank Buckland for the Hockey Hall of Fame, Ontario Hockey Association president Cliffe Phillips wrote: "Longevity itself does not deserve the distinction of election, but Mr. Buckland has made amateur hockey a life work and, to this day, his thoughts dwell not on the past victories, but instead on fresh new approaches to today's hockey problems." A fitting tribute, to be sure, for Buckland, who started in hockey in 1927 and represented the game the rest of his life. He began as a coach in Toronto, and in 1932 coached in Peterborough for eight years. He became a member of the Ontario Hockey Association executive and in 1955 was named its president, serving a two-year term. In 1961, he was made treasurer of the OHA and brought it into a financially stable position. Four years later he was honoured with the Canadian Amateur Hockey Association's Meritorious Award and later made a life member of the OHA.

William Jennings

b. New York, New York, December 14, 1920
d. New York, New York, August 17, 1981

Jennings graduated from Princeton and Yale universities to start a career in law, but in 1962 that career dovetailed with the New York Rangers when he became that team's president and governor. He swiftly made an impression on the NHL and was vital to the league's expansion efforts, which doubled the teams from six to 12. He continued to fight for further expansion to 18 teams, including a second franchise in the New York area, which he saw as a key city in the NHL's future. To that end, he also helped establish a New York office for the league, and he provided great support for the development of amateur hockey, notably through the Metropolitan (New York) Junior Hockey Association.

1976

August 26, 1976: The China Wall Joins the Enshrinees

It was on June 8, 1976, that the Hockey Hall of Fame announced its newest Honoured Members. This year there were just two worthy Players added, along with three Builders.

1976

Johnny Bower

b. Prince Albert, Saskatchewan, November 8, 1924

They called him the China Wall because, as the joke had it, he was just as old. True enough, the legendary goalie didn't retire until age 45, by which time he was the all-time winningest goalie in pro hockey (American Hockey League and NHL combined). Bower started in the AHL in 1945 and seemed destined for a long and happy career in the minors. After eight years, he played every game for the Rangers in 1953–54 and was the only goalie to play every minute of every game for his team. The year after, though, he was replaced by the younger Gump Worsley and was back in the minors for the better part of four more seasons. Then the Leafs claimed him, and quickly he established himself as a top-six stopper. For the next dozen years he guarded the Leafs' cage with unflinching loyalty, leading the team to four Stanley Cups. He had been a three-time MVP in the American Hockey League, and in the NHL he won two Vézina Trophies and played in four All-Star Games. He led the league in goals-against average four times, and when he retired he had 250 wins in 552 appearances.

The great Johnny Bower played 25 seasons of pro hockey in the AHL and NHL, playing in his last game, with the Leafs, at age 45.

Bill Quackenbush

b. Toronto, Ontario, March 2, 1922
d. Newton, Pennsylvania, September 12, 1999

The fast fact that stands out in the playing career of Bill Quackenbush is that after 14 years in the NHL, he accrued just 95 penalty minutes. In fact, in 1948–49, he went the entire season without a single minor and, as just reward, became the first defenceman to win the Lady Byng Trophy. He retired in 1956 with 222 assists to his credit; only Red Kelly had more in the history of the game. Quackenbush (seen above with the puck) was a fine rusher and passer, but he was also a solid, though not vicious, hitter in his own end. He played only with Detroit and Boston and never won a Stanley Cup, though in testament to his reputation he appeared in eight All-Star Games.

1976

Jack Gibson

b. Berlin (Kitchener), Ontario, September 10, 1880
d. Calgary, Alberta, October 7, 1955

Elmer Ferguson of the *Montreal Herald* wrote of Gibson: "He played the game with excellence... He helped promote it, improve it, and make it the spectacle which so many people the world over enjoy today." Indeed, he began as a player with Berlin in junior hockey in 1895 and later played with Portage, but during this time he realized that the game was moving from the amateur to pro ranks. Gibson became part of the history of that change. He established the world's first pro league in 1902, the International League, with teams in Michigan, Pittsburgh, and the Canadian Soo. He set up a dental practice in Michigan and played until 1907, at which time he retired to Calgary to practice dentistry full-time.

Phillip Dansken Ross

b. Montreal, Quebec, January 1, 1858
d. Ottawa, Ontario, July 7, 1949

It was a career in journalism that took Ross into the hockey world and unwittingly on to the Hockey Hall of Fame many years after his death. He was a reporter for a number of newspapers, primarily in Montreal and Toronto, until 1886 when he bought half of the *Ottawa Journal*. He bought the other half five years later, and during his time in Ottawa he became acquainted with Lord Stanley of Preston, Canada's governor-general. When Lord Stanley donated a special trophy to the hockey world shortly before his departure to England, he appointed two men to act as custodians—trustees—of the Cup,

Ross and Sheriff John Sweetland. Ross remained a trustee until the day he died, more than half a century later, during which time he dealt with many challenges, adjudicated many an argument, and finally oversaw the trophy's transition from amateur award to pro award.

William Wirtz

b. October 5, 1929

His father owned the Detroit Red Wings and later Chicago Black Hawks in 1952, at which time young William joined the executive. A graduate of Brown University two years earlier, William Wirtz became vice president of the team and in 1966 also became a governor on the NHL's board. The year 1966 was also the same year that Wirtz stepped up to be president of the Hawks. In the 1970s he was elected to five consecutive two-year terms as chairman of the NHL Board of Governors, helping to oversee the first collective bargaining agreement in pro sports and seeing the league through continued expansion and the development of international competition.

1977

August 25, 1977: Long-Serving Players Make it into the Hall

For the second year in a row, only two Players were inducted into the Hockey Hall of Fame, and this year they were two of the longest-serving men in league history. Alex Delvecchio still holds the record for his 24 years and 1,549 games of continuous service to one club (Detroit), and Tim Horton played more games than any other defenceman in league history (1,446)—until Larry Murphy bettered that mark in the 21st century.

Alex Delvecchio

b. Fort William, Ontario, December 4, 1932

Few players enjoyed the career that Alex Delvecchio did, and only a handful stayed on the ice as long as the man they called Fats. He made his Wings debut toward the end of the 1950–51 season and stayed with the team as a player until early in the 1973–74 season, when he retired to become the team's head coach. In between, his achievements were extraordinary. He won the Cup three times in his first four full seasons and played in 13 All-Star Games. He won three Lady Byng Trophies (1958–59, 1965–66, and 1968–69) and had 13 years of scoring 20 or more goals. In addition to his 1,549 games played—all with the Red Wings—he scored 456 goals and a total of 1,281 points.

Tim Horton

b. Cochrane, Ontario, January 12, 1930
d. St. Catharines, Ontario, February 21, 1974

He was the strongest player in the league, though he used that tremendous strength as a pacifier. Still, no one on the blue line had a more formidable reputation than Tim Horton. Between 1949 and 1952 he had two brief call-ups with the Leafs, and at training camp in 1952 he made the team full time. In all, he played 20 years with Toronto, anchoring a defence that was critical to the four Stanley Cups the Leafs brought home in the 1960s. Horton was a powerful skater and could rush the puck well, though he scored only a few goals during his years. He later played for the Rangers, Pittsburgh, and Buffalo, where he was reunited with coach Punch Imlach. Horton's career and life ended one night driving home to Buffalo from a game at Maple Leaf Gardens when he was involved in a fatal single-car highway crash. Horton played in seven All-Star Games and was a First or Second Team All-Star six times.

Alex Delvecchio (foreground) played 24 years in the league, each and every one of them with Detroit, a record.

Miles "Tim" Horton (left) set a record for defencemen by playing in 1,446 regular season games during his lengthy NHL career.

"Bunny" Ahearne

b. County Wexford, Ireland, 1901
d. Gloucestershire, England,
    April 11, 1985

Bunny Ahearne became the secretary of the British Ice Hockey Association in 1933 and remained so for some 40 years. As such, he was the manager of the 1936 Olympic team that defeated Canada 2-1 and won the gold medal, a singular achievement in British hockey history. After World War II, Ahearne became an executive member of the International Ice Hockey Federation. He was named vice president in 1954 and president three years later, positions he held alternately until his retirement in 1975.

Harold Ballard

b. Toronto, Ontario, July 30, 1903
d. Toronto, Ontario, April 11, 1990

Harold Ballard's involvement in hockey began in Toronto when he took the Sea Fleas to the World Championships in 1933 and won a silver medal from a 2-1 loss to the United States in the deciding game. He later became involved with the Toronto Marlies, and in the early 1960s he, Stafford Smythe, and John Bassett bought the Maple Leafs from Conn Smythe. A decade later, Ballard became sole owner of the team and ruled the most popular and powerful team in the league for close to two decades. His was a significant voice with the NHL's Board of Governors, and thanks to his influence the Gardens played host to Team Canada's training camp in 1972 and the Canada Cup finals four years later. (He is pictured below on the left celebrating a Cup win with Red Kelly.)

1977

Joe Cattarinich

b. Levis, Quebec, November 13, 1881
d. New Orleans, Louisiana, December 7, 1938

"As someone who has followed the activities of the National Hockey League since the mid-1920s," began Marcel Desjardins in his nomination for Builder induction, "I look at the list of Hockey Hall of Fame members and note that a name is missing—the name of Joseph Cattarinich." Cattarinich played goal as a junior and one day was so impressed by an opponent that he beseeched his club to sign the other goalie as his replacement! That goalie turned out to be Georges Vézina—proving that even at that point Cattarinich was a shrewd observer of talent. Later in life, on November 3, 1921, he and two partners—Leo Dandurand and Louis Letourneau— bought the Montreal Canadiens. Cattarinich remained owner until 1935, and during these years he built a team of speed and skill unmatched in previous years. The Flying Frenchmen, as the team was called, featured immortals such as Howie Morenz, Newsy Lalonde, and Aurel Joliat, and won three Stanley Cups under the watchful eye of Cattarinich.

1978

September 13, 1978: The Masked Man Leads the Way

While players can be inducted only after having been retired for three years or more, Builders inductees don't face the same restrictions. Thus, as soon as Sam Pollock announced his retirement in the spring of 1978, he was given consideration for induction. Builders were announced on April 11, 1978, while Players were informed in June, two separate votes deciding the honour roll for the year.

1978

Andy Bathgate

b. Winnipeg, Manitoba, August 28, 1932

Perhaps no more appropriate, or ironic, combination of inductees occurred than this year when Bathgate and Jacques Plante entered the Hockey Hall of Fame together. For it was Bathgate who, on November 1, 1959, drilled Plante in the forehead with a hard shot that changed the course of hockey.

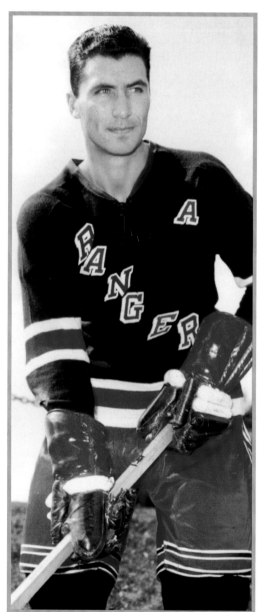

Plante went to the dressing room for stitches, came back out onto the ice wearing a face mask, and goaltending hasn't been the same since. Bathgate was renowned for his shot. When he played for the Guelph Biltmores in junior, his reputation for withstanding great pain was almost as mighty as that shot. He got to the NHL with the Rangers in 1952 and quickly established himself as the best player on the team. He scored 20 goals in his first full season and by 1958–59 had doubled that, recording his first and only 40-goal year, the year he won the Hart Trophy. His personal high-water mark came three years later when he won the scoring title and led the league in assists and, of course, points. In 1963–64, Bathgate was traded to Toronto during the season, and this turned out to be the only Stanley Cup year of his career. He later played for Detroit and Pittsburgh to close out his 17 seasons in the NHL. During that time, Bathgate played 1,069 games and scored 349 goals and 973 points. He played in eight consecutive All-Star Games, from 1957 to 1964.

Jacques Plante

b. Shawinigan Falls, Quebec, January 17, 1929
d. Geneva, Switzerland, February 26, 1986

There were two distinct parts to Jacques Plante's career, the first consisting of his Stanley Cup years with Montreal, the second his many and final years of pro when he continued to prove himself among the best the game has seen. He played a few games for the Habs in 1952–53 and a few more the year after, but it was at training camp in 1954 that he established himself as the team's current and future star. He won his first Cup in 1955–56, the first of five in a row, and he also won the Vézina Trophy that year, the first of a record five in a row as well. He won a sixth Vézina in 1961–62. Montreal said goodbye to him in 1963, but Plante played another decade still, with lesser teams that didn't win the Cup, most notably St. Louis where he and Glenn Hall shared an improbable Vézina in 1968–69. He was a First Team All-Star three times and played in eight All-Star Games. By the time he left the NHL in 1973 Plante had appeared in 837 games and recorded 82 shutouts.

Goalie Jacques Plante displays his trademark acrobatics. He was pioneering for his use of the mask as well as communicating with his defencemen.

1979

September 12, 1979: Number Four the Youngest Ever

The second that Bobby Orr announced his retirement, the Selection Committee snapped into action and made sure the great defenceman would be honoured as soon as possible. Ironically, he was sharing the spotlight with Harry Howell, the man who won the Norris Trophy in 1966–67, the last year before Orr took possession of it for the next eight.

Harry Howell

b. Hamilton, Ontario, December 28, 1932

Despite playing 1,411 regular season games over 21 years in the NHL, Howell never even made it to the Stanley Cup finals. It was the only regret the defenceman had, and the only success he did not enjoy during an otherwise spectacular career. He started

with the Rangers in 1952 playing on a bad team that rarely made it to the playoffs at all. Yet he was always singled out as the team's best defenceman, the premier shot blocker in the league, and a superior talent moving the puck up ice. He played 17 years with the Blueshirts and was the first man to have a special night at Madison Square Garden. In 1966–67, he won the Norris Trophy, and was the last man to do so before Bobby Orr took control of it. In an era of great blue-liners on great teams, Howell nonetheless played in seven All-Star Games and was a respected player every day he was in the league.

Bobby Orr

b. Parry Sound, Ontario,
March 20, 1948

Nobody played the game the way Bobby Orr did. A strong and powerful skater, he was a defenceman who not only handled the puck better than anyone, he rushed with it and barreled in on goal. He was the master of the give-and-go, the king of the end-to-end rush, the measure of future great defenceman to this day. He was playing junior hockey in Oshawa at age 14, and he was a star

and saviour for Boston in 1966 at age 18. Orr achieved what no defenceman before or since did: he won the scoring championship twice, in 1969–70 and 1974–75. He set season records for goals (46 in 1974–75), and assists (102 in 1970–71) as well, became the first and still only defenceman to have five 30-goal seasons. He led Boston to two Stanley Cups, in 1970 and 1972, the city's first since 1941. In both years, he was the man who scored the winning goal. Orr revolutionized the game, to be sure. His abilities on offence forced coaches to try to check him. He was called a fourth forward. He won the Norris Trophy eight successive seasons and was named to the First All-Star Team eight times in a row. He won two Conn Smythe Trophies and the Hart Trophy three times. Yet through it all, he was pained and slowed by serious knee injuries. He missed the Summit Series in 1972 because of a summer operation. He missed most of the rest of his career with knee injuries from 1975 on, but on one knee he led Canada to victory in the 1976 Canada Cup. In just nine full seasons and 657 games in 11 years total, Orr amassed 915 points. He was, in short, the greatest defenceman the world has ever seen. At 31, he was the youngest player ever inducted into the Hockey Hall of Fame.

The Goal

On Mother's Day 1970, May 10, Boston hosted St. Louis for game four of the Stanley Cup finals. Up 3-0, Boston could earn the trophy with a win, but after three periods the score was tied 3-3. Early in the overtime, Boston got the puck into the Blues' end, and Orr kept the puck in at the blue line and moved down the boards. He fed the puck to Derek Sanderson, headed for the net, and took the return pass. Quickly, he chipped the puck between goalie Glenn Hall's legs and raised his arms in celebration. At that very moment, St. Louis defenceman Noel Picard hooked his stick around Orr's ankle and helped propel Number Four high into the Garden air, making this the most photogenic Cup goal ever recorded. There he is, the greatest of the great, flying through the air after wining the 1970 Cup for the Boston Bruins!

1979

Montreal's Henri Richard won an incredible eleven Stanley Cups during his 20 years in the NHL, more than any other player, including his more famous brother, Maurice.

Henri Richard

b. Montreal, Quebec, February 29, 1936

He didn't have the same spirit as his more famous brother, and certainly not the same temper and tenacity, but Henri Richard won more Stanley Cups—11—than any hockey player. In 20 seasons, he drank from the Cup more than half those years, an astonishing record even by Montreal standards. He also played in 10 All-Star Games and won the Bill Masterton Trophy in 1973–74, but Richard also ended his career with 1,046 points, almost 100 more than Maurice. He led the league in assists twice and had his number 16 retired at the end of his career, his induction into the Hockey Hall of Fame a fitting tribute to his unparalleled on-ice success.

Gordon Juckes

b. Watrous, Saskatchewan, June 20, 1914
d. Melville, Saskatchewan, October 4, 1994

He was a player in his native Saskatchewan during the 1930s, but the war changed his life. Once peace prevailed, Juckes rose  through the executive ranks of the sport. He became president of his provincial amateur hockey association in 1953 and his climb peaked in 1959 when he assumed a similar post for the Canadian Amateur Hockey Association For the next 18 years he served the organization as executive director after his term as president expired, and in 1967 the International Ice Hockey Federation bestowed upon him its diploma of honour for his contributions to the game. He later served on the boards of the Canadian Olympic Association and Hockey Canada, and his incomparable hockey stamp collection is an integral part of the Hockey Hall of Fame's holdings.

1980

September 8, 1980: The Year of the Goalie

For the first time since moving away from the Canadian National Exhibition, the induction dinner was held at the Hotel Toronto (though the following year it was back at the Royal York). This was the year of the goalie, as two of the three honoured Players were members of the net set. The Builders were announced on May 1, 1980, and the Players on June 10. The Selection Committee underwent changes at this time, as the death of Lynn Patrick and the retirement of 87-year-old Frank Selke left two positions vacant. These were ably filled by Tommy Ivan and Bill Hay. The dinner itself was a raucous affair hosted by Dave Hodge of *Hockey Night in Canada*. Lou Nanne introduced Gump Worsley and Bob Hesketh said a few words about Lumley.

1980

Harry Lumley

b. Owen Sound, Ontario, November 11, 1926

d. London, Ontario, September 13, 1998

The career of goalie Harry Lumley is laced with success of the first order. When he made his debut with Detroit toward the end of the 1943–44 season, he was, at 17, the youngest goalie ever to play in the NHL. A year later, he assumed duties as the number-one man, and a year after that he played every minute of every game. He played the full schedule five times in his career and led the NHL in wins twice, 1948–49 and 1949–50, the second of those coming during his Stanley Cup year. In all, Lumley played for five of the six Original Six teams (it was only Montreal that he didn't play for). His best personal season was 1953–54 with Toronto when he set a modern-day record with 13 shutouts. He won the Vézina Trophy that year with a goals-against average of just 1.86. By the time he retired in 1960, Lumley had earned 71 shutouts in 803 career games.

Lynn Patrick

b. Victoria, British Columbia, February 3, 1912

d. St. Louis, Missouri, January 26, 1980

This was a most unlikely success story, a career that began out west where Patrick played no hockey at all. When he moved east to Montreal in his teens, he made up for lost time and the hockey genes of hockey's most famous family kicked in. Lester Patrick, Lynn's father, signed his son to the Rangers, a move that was greeted with skepticism if not anger by those who saw the move as nepotistic. Lynn joined the Blueshirts in 1934 and started slowly, but he soon adjusted to the fast pace of pro hockey and developed into a fine forward for the team. He helped bring the Cup to Broadway in 1940, and in 1941–42 he proved his father irrefutably correct when he led the NHL in goals with 32. Lynn's career more or less ended in 1943 when he went off to war, though he came back for one final season in 1945–46. He later served as coach and general manager for much of the rest of his life.

Goalie Harry Lumley sits for a portrait with his best hockey friend, the Vézina Trophy.

Lorne "Gump" Worsley

b. Montreal, Quebec, May 14, 1929

In 1952, the young and agile Gump Worsley made the Rangers out of training camp and for the next 10 years he was the starting goalie almost every night (except for '53–'54). He won the Calder Trophy by posting a record of 13-29-8 and a goals-against average of 3.06 on a weak team. This exemplified the way his career went in New York: great goalie, weak team. When he was traded to Montreal in the summer of 1963, his career took off. Playing in a hockey environment, Worsley won four Cups in five years with the Habs and shared in two Vézina Trophies, the first in 1965–66 with Charlie Hodge, the second two years later with a young Rogie Vachon. Worsley played the last four and a half years with Minnesota, and it wasn't until the 1973–74 season, his 21st and final one in the NHL, that he finally relented and wore a face mask. In 861 career games, the Gumper won 335 games and recorded 43 shutouts.

Goalie Gump Worsley exhibits Original Six bravery, coming out to block a shot while lunging at the skates of St. Louis's Red Berenson.

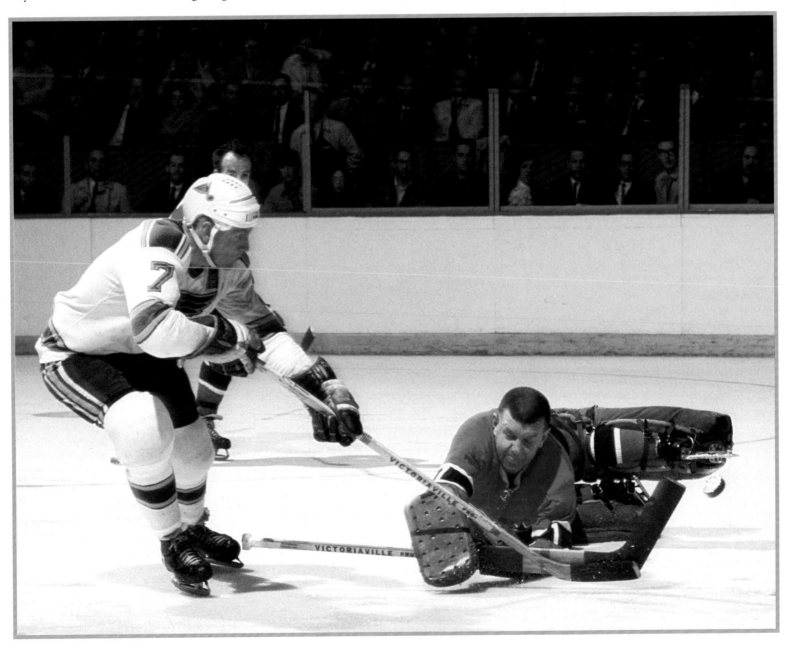

September 8, 1980: The Year of the Goalie

Jack Butterfield

b. Regina, Saskatchewan, August 1, 1919

After breaking his back during World War II, Butterfield started working for his uncle, Eddie Shore, as public relations man in Springfield in 1945. He learned the ropes of every facet of team and arena management over the years until 1957 when Shore thought enough of him to name him as an alternate governor at American Hockey League meetings. In 1966, Butterfield became president and treasurer of the league and helped the AHL deal with the severity of 1967 NHL expansion, which doubled teams in that league and crippled the supply of players to his own. He rewrote the constitution and amended players' contracts to deal with the World Hockey Association, and he helped bring the AHL back from the brink to a healthy, 10-team league. He later worked with the NHL's Rules Committee and wrote the schedule himself for the AHL for some 14 years. His name is synonymous with the success of what remains today the prime feeder and development league for the NHL, a grade below the National league in quality, but a vital ingredient in the structure of professional hockey in North America.

1981

September 15, 1981: The Timmins Induction

The annual induction this year was presided over by master of ceremonies Tim Ryan, and—as was the case for most years—each new Honoured Member was introduced by a distinguished guest or friend. Frank Mahovlich was paid tribute by Red Kelly; Johnny Bucyk by Bob Wilson; Allan Stanley by Harry Howell; and Official John Ashley by Carl Voss. The Selection Committee now included chairman Tom Fitzgerald and voters Milt Dunnell, Danny Gallivan, Gord Juckes, Ebbie Goodfellow, Neil Colville, Charles Coleman, Tim Moriarty, John Mariucci, Tommy Ivan, Bill Hay, and Jean Béliveau.

1981

Johnny Bucyk

b. Edmonton, Alberta, May 12, 1935

From his junior days with the Memorial Cup–winning Edmonton Flyers in the 1950s to the day he retired in 1978, Bucyk was a credit to the game. Tough, gritty, and a hard but clean hitter, he was also a skilled left winger who played some 23 seasons and 1,540 NHL games. Only Gordie Howe, Phil Esposito, and Stan Mikita had more career points than Bucyk's total of 1,369. Bucyk began with Detroit in 1955 but after a year and a half was traded to Boston for Terry Sawchuk. While Sawchuk wound up returning to the Red Wings, Bucyk has been a member of the Bruins organization ever since. He had 15 20-goal seasons in his career, peaking in 1970–71 when, as a 35-year-old, he scored 51 goals and 116 points in the year. He won two Cups in Boston, in 1970 and 1972, and captained the team the last four years of his career. He never led the league in any offensive category, but he was among the most consistent and longest-serving players in league history. He won two Lady Byng Trophies (in 1970–71 and 1973–74) and played in seven All-Star Games.

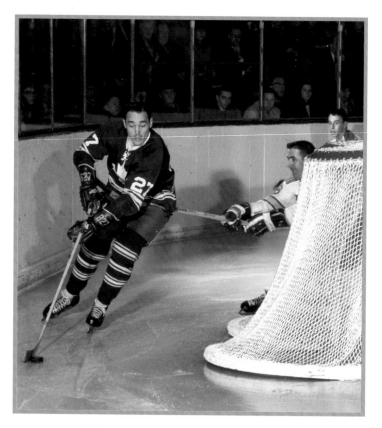

Frank Mahovlich

b. Timmins, Ontario, January 10, 1938

He never had a 50-goal or 100-point season, but the Big M finished with 533 goals and 1,103 points, surpassing the commonly used benchmarks for greatness (500 goals, 1,000 points) used to distinguish a Hall of Famer from the rest of the pack. Mahovlich spent the first ten and a half seasons in Toronto, winning four Stanley Cups, and, in 1960–61, coming tantalizingly close to the 50-goal mark, finishing with 48. He won the Calder Trophy as a rookie in 1957–58, oddly his only individual award during his 18 years in the NHL. He was often beloved by the fans and considered the finest left winger in team history, but when he was traded to Detroit and on to Montreal, his career came to life a second time. He won Cups with Montreal in 1971 and 1973 after recording 49 goals with Detroit in 1968–69. Mahovlich was a First All-Star three times and Second All-Star six more times, and he played in an amazing 15 consecutive All-Star Games.

Allan Stanley (#26, middle) was never the fastest skater, but he was among the smartest defencemen the NHL has ever seen.

Allan Stanley

b. Timmins, Ontario, March 1, 1926

He was called Snowshoes by his teammates because he was a slow-moving defenceman, but he made up for this deficiency by reading the play better than anyone. By consequence, he got to where the puck was well in advance, a superb defensive defenceman who always seemed to be in an opponent's way. Stanley played the first six and a half years with the Rangers and moved quickly on to Chicago and Boston, but in his first nine seasons he was in the playoffs only once. Nonetheless, he had a fine reputation, and when the Leafs acquired him at the start of the 1958–59 season, his career took off. Stanley played for the four Cup victories for the Leafs in the 1960s using his traditional and impeccable style of reliable, unspectacular defence. He ended his career with the Flyers, by which time he had been in the NHL for 21 years and 1,244 games.

1981

John Ashley

b. Galt, Ontario, March 5, 1930

Like many a Canadian boy, Ashley grew up playing hockey, moving up from junior to the American Hockey League to senior hockey in Stratford. When the league went bankrupt, he turned to officiating, signing his first contract with the NHL in 1959 and spending most of that rookie season in the minors. Ashley worked 17 games as a linesman in the NHL and then turned to refereeing, the occupation that would consume the rest of his skating days. He had the whistle for a total of 605 regular-season games and another 59 in the playoffs, including three game sevens in the 1971 quarter-finals, semifinals, and finals, the first ref to be assigned the toughest game three times in a row.

1982

September 8, 1982:
The Legacy of Montreal Captains Continues

With the induction this year of Yvan Cournoyer, Montreal boasted a string of team captains who went on to the Hockey Hall of Fame's honour roll. In fact, the last Montreal captain not inducted was Walt Buswell who was team leader in 1939–40.

Yvan Cournoyer

b. Drummondville, Quebec, November 22, 1943

He was as fast on skates as he was gentlemanly, but his competitive juices overcame his size (5'7" and 178 pounds) and earned him a remarkable 10 Stanley Cups in a 15-year career with Montreal. Yvan Cournoyer started with the team at the end of the 1963–64 season and was used sparingly at first, mostly on the power play. But by 1966 he had established himself as a brilliant right winger who went on to record 12 consecutive seasons of 25 goals or more. Cournoyer played in the 1972 Summit Series and used that tournament as a springboard to his best year. In the 1973 playoffs, he set an NHL record with 15 goals, led the Habs to another Cup, and won the Conn Smythe Trophy. The Roadrunner was never a First Team All-Star but he played in six All-Star Games. His career ended prematurely because of a recurring back injury.

Yvan Cournoyer, the Roadrunner, was one of many Montreal captains to have a Hall of Fame career before retiring.

Rod Gilbert had 13 seasons of 24 goals or more for the Rangers, and his 406 career goals is still a team record.

Rod Gilbert

b. Montreal, Quebec, July 1, 1941

After breaking his back in junior and nearly losing his leg from subsequent operations to correct the back, Gilbert went on to play 18 seasons with the Rangers, setting some 20 team records. He never won a Stanley Cup, but his 1,021 points at his retirement in 1978 was second in league history for right wingers—behind a fellow named Howe. The peak of his career came in 1971–72 when he played on a powerful line with Jean Ratelle and Vic Hadfield. Gilbert scored 43 goals and finished

with 97 points. It was the one and only year he was also named to the First All-Star Team. In 1975–76 he was awarded the Bill Masterton Trophy to acknowledge his remarkable career after overcoming near-debilitating injury. In all, Gilbert played in 1,065 games and scored 406 goals, and in 1991 he was given the Lester Patrick Trophy for his contribution to hockey in the United States.

1982

Norm Ullman

b. Provost, Alberta, December 26, 1935

There were three strikes against Ullman during his career. One, he played centre during an era when most of the finest centres in league history were at their peak. Two, he was just about the most quiet and unassuming player on and off the ice and was almost incapable of standing in the spotlight. Three, his timing caused him to arrive in the NHL with Detroit in 1955 at the end of the Red Wings' Cup dynasty and be traded to Toronto in 1968 right after the Leafs' 1960s dynasty ended. On the plus side, he was one of the greatest players of all time, a man who ranked seventh on the all-time scoring list when he left the NHL in 1975. Ullman played 1,410 regular-season games and in 16 of his 20 years he scored at least 20 goals. He led the league in scoring in 1964–65 when he had 42 goals, but because of the league depth at centre he was named to only one First and one Second All-Star Team. Nevertheless, he played in eleven All-Star Games. Ullman was hard-nosed but a sportsman, a superb passer and strong positional player. He finished with 490 goals, 739 assists, and 1,229 total points (below, he challenges Leafs goalie Bruce Gamble).

Emile Francis

b. North Battleford, Saskatchewan, September 13, 1926

"I firmly believe that Mr. Francis is a worthy candidate for admission to the Hockey Hall of Fame and I request respectfully that the Governing Committee give due consideration to this application." So wrote Brian O'Neill at the end of his nomination of Emile Francis as a Builder. Francis played goal for some 17 years in the NHL and the minor pros. He retired because of injuries to both shoulders and was immediately offered a coaching job in the Rangers' system. He used the opportunity to work his way up to Broadway during the 1965–66 season, and for the next decade he was coach or general manager (and sometimes both) for the team, making the playoffs the last nine years in a row. He left in 1976 to become president and general manager in St. Louis, and it was for his years of success and dedication to those teams and to the overall welfare of the league that O'Neill's nomination was successful.

1983

September 22, 1983: Chicago Takes Centre Stage

Of course, every induction features hockey's greatest players, but this year's honourees were a particularly spectacular foursome: Bobby Hull and Stan Mikita of Chicago, superstars from the 1960s, Harry Sinden, Builder and leader in Boston and for Team Canada, and Ken Dryden, who led Montreal to six Stanley Cups in the 1970s. The Selection Committee included Tom Fitzgerald, Milt Dunnell, Danny Gallivan, John Mariucci, Ebbie Goodfellow, Gordon Juckes, Neil Colville, Charles Coleman, Tim Moriarty, Tommy Ivan, Bill Hay, and Jean Béliveau. Larry Mann emceed the induction dinner and, as was the tradition, each player was introduced by someone special: Ken Dryden was introduced by brother, Dave; Bobby Hull by brother, Dennis; Stan Mikita by Scott Mikita; and, Harry Sinden by long-time Boston associate, Tom Johnson.

1983

Ken Dryden

b. Hamilton, Ontario, August 8, 1947

Few players in NHL history made as dramatic or successful an entrance into the league as did Dryden in the spring of 1971. Called up for the final few games of the 1970–71 season, he had a 6-0-0 record in the regular season and was named the starter for Montreal in the playoffs. He stoned Bobby Orr and the Cup-champion Bruins en route to a remarkable run to the Cup, won the Conn Smythe Trophy for his outstanding play, and then, a year later, won the Calder Trophy as rookie of the year. In that first full season, Dryden had a record of 39-8-15. His style was unlike anything shooters had seen before, his stretchy, 6'4" body covering the net quickly, getting in front of every

shot. There were no open-net goals on Dryden, no softies from centre ice. He played only seven and a half seasons and appeared in only 397 regular-season games, but he won six Stanley Cups and only twice—in 1972 and 1975—had to shake hands after a playoff series loss.

His record of 258-57-74 was outstripped only by his playoff numbers: 112 games played, 80 wins, and just 32 losses. He won or shared the Vézina Trophy five times, and at 36 years of age he was one of the youngest men to be inducted into the Hockey Hall of Fame.

Bobby Hull

b. Pointe Anne, Ontario, January 3, 1939

Almost from the instant Bobby Hull broke into the NHL with Chicago in 1957, he was feared and respected for his tremendous strength and his booming shot. In his third season he led the league in goals (39) and points (81), winning his first of three Art Ross Trophies. The next year, he led the Hawks to their first Stanley Cup since 1938, and although the team never won another championship, it was as strong as any throughout the 1960s. Hull hit the 50-goal mark for the first time in 1961–62, and four years later he set an NHL record with 54 goals. Key to his success was his terrific slapshot, which he didn't invent but certainly perfected. That year, 1965–66, he also won the Hart Trophy and his second Art Ross. In 1968–69, he improved his own record by scoring 58 times, and in his 15 seasons with Chicago he scored a total of 604 goals, second only to Gordie Howe on the all-time list. After leaving to play in the WHA for seven seasons, Hull returned for a final NHL year with Winnipeg and Hartford, where he played with Howe and Dave Keon. Hull played in 12 consecutive All-Star Games and retired as the premier left winger the game has ever known.

Bobby Hull had it all: speed, strength, and a phenomenal shot. In a career that lasted four decades, no one played the left wing with the same excitement as the "Golden Jet."

1983

The World Hockey Association Is Born

The bravest thing Hull ever did during his career was to leave the NHL and accept a million-dollar contract offer from the Winnipeg Jets in the summer of 1972. The deal gave the World Hockey Association credibility, gave Hull a great deal of money, and paved the way for dozens of others to follow to the pirate league. For Hull, the move was also symbolic, for he was proving there was more money available to the players than the NHL owners let on. Thanks to Hull, the World Hockey Association not only set down its roots, it also ensured better contracts for all players in pro hockey, regardless of league or reputation.

Stan Mikita

b. Sokolce, Czechoslovakia, May 20, 1940

Mikita (below, left) played all of his 22 seasons and 1,394 games with Chicago, and in 1966–67 he made history by winning three individual trophies—the Hart, the Art Ross, and the Lady Byng. It was his first of two in a row for the Hart, and his third of four for the Art Ross, but it was the Lady Byng that was a remarkable

achievement. Early in his career, Mikita was a brash and volatile forward out to prove himself in the NHL and fight for his survival. He turned his game around, though, and discovered the more he stayed out of the penalty box, the more he played and scored and contributed. Mikita was on the Cup-winning Hawks team of 1960–61. He was a First Team All-Star six times and played in nine All-Star Games—and at one time had a stretch of 14 seasons scoring at least 24 goals. He ended his career in November 1979 after continued back problems, but by that time he had scored 541 goals and amassed 1,467 points. He was also a member of Team Canada 1972.

Harry Sinden

b. Collins Bay, Ontario, September 14, 1932

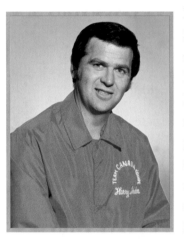

It was as a Builder that Harry Sinden took his place among the greats at the Hockey Hall of Fame, and it was great teams in Boston and with Team Canada that he built. Sinden was a player in his youth, but he was never quite good enough to make the NHL. He turned to coaching, and when the Bruins hired him in 1966, he was, at 33, the youngest coach in league history. He joined the Bruins at the same time an 18-year-old named Bobby Orr started out, and the two, it might be said, made each other's career. Orr became the best player ever, and Sinden guided the Bruins to a Cup in 1970. He left the team and was soon hired to coach Team Canada for the Summit Series in 1972. It was in large part to his brilliant adjustments and deployment of players that Canada won that series. Sinden returned to the Bruins fold and became general manager, a position he held for 28 years, during which time the Bruins missed the playoffs exactly twice.

1984

September 25, 1984:
The Most Famous Speech of All is Honoured

The three Player inductees this year all had their finest moments in the 1970s. In a decade crammed with great moments and accomplishments, Phil Esposito, Bernie Parent, and Jacques Lemaire contributed much to the game. They all won Stanley Cups in the 1970s and all retired around the same time. They also all played against each other in some of hockey's most competitive battles.

1984

Phil Esposito

b. Sault Ste. Marie, Ontario, February 20, 1942

A good four years in Chicago at the start of Phil Esposito's career turned into a record-shattering eight and a half years with Boston. Esposito retired in 1981 as the second all-time leading scorer behind only Gordie Howe. Esposito came to Boston in a multi-player deal on May 15, 1967, and, ironically, he led the league in assists his first year in Beantown. Nonetheless, he also scored 35 goals and increased that to 49 the year after, when he again led the league in helpers with 77. His 126 total points marked the highest total ever for one season, and he won the Art Ross and Hart Trophies for his efforts. But he wasn't finished. In 1969–70, Esposito led the league in goals for the first time, with 43, and the year after he set the standard by recording 76 goals

and 76 assists, 152 points, a mark that stood until Wayne Gretzky came along a generation later. It marked the first of five straight years he scored at least 55 goals, another incredible feat, and it was his first of four scoring championships in a row as well. Esposito was traded to the Rangers where he still had five 30-goal seasons left in him, but he is most remembered for his play in the 1972 Summit Series. His leadership on ice and his inspiring

speech after game four in Vancouver remain to this day great examples of skill and determination. Esposito retired having played 1,282 games and scoring 717 goals and 1,590 points, remarkable numbers all, and clear reason to ensure his place in the Hockey Hall of Fame.

Jacques Lemaire

b. LaSalle, Quebec, September 7, 1945

One of the slickest two-way centres to play for the Montreal Canadiens, Jacques Lemaire was a testament to hard work and perseverance. He developed in the Montreal system with the Junior Canadiens and made the NHL team in 1967. During his 12 years, he never won a major individual award and never made an All-Star Team—he only went out and won eight Stanley Cups. Lemaire never failed to score at least 20 goals in a season, but he was also a fine checker. Three times he had more than 90 points in a season and only once did he not make the playoffs (1970). He had 835 points in 853 career games, averaging nearly a point a game while being a plus player in the +/- statistics every year he was in the league.

Montreal's Jacques Lemaire (middle) was equally adept at scoring and playing solid defence, abilities which helped his team win eight Stanley Cups during his career.

Bernie Parent

b. Montreal, Quebec, April 3, 1945

Bernie Parent was a fine goalie for 13 years in the NHL, but for two of those he was the best goalie on the planet, the major reason why the Philadelphia Flyers won the Stanley Cup in 1973–74 and 1974–75. In those two seasons he won the Vézina Trophy both years (albeit shared with Tony Esposito in the first season). He led the league both years with 47 and 44 wins, respectively. He led the league in shutouts each season with 12. His goals-against average was the lowest, and in the playoffs he was so undisputedly fantastic that he became the first and only goalie to win consecutive Conn Smythe Trophies. Like his idol, Jacques Plante, Parent was a stand-up goalie who played the angles and was rock solid positionally. He waited for the shooter to make the first move, and he had tremendous reflexes. His years with Boston and Toronto were fine ones, but—before an eye injury ended his career too early—his best years in the business were with the Flyers.

Philadelphia goalie Bernie Parent styled his own play after Jacques Plante, wearing the same kind of mask and playing the angles with a like patience.

1984

George "Punch" Imlach

b. Toronto, Ontario, March 15, 1918
d. Toronto, Ontario, December 1, 1987

When general manager Punch Imlach fired coach Billy Reay and took over the reins of the Toronto Maple Leafs early in the 1958–59 season, he promised the city a playoff spot. With five games left in the season and trailing five points behind the Rangers, he continued to promise, and when the Leafs squeaked in on the final day of the season, Punch was hailed as a genius. The Leafs lost to Montreal in each of the next two finals, but Imlach proved his genius in the 1960s, leading the team to four Stanley Cups. Most notable was the 1967 victory in which he relied on the oldest team in league history to win. He was tough on his players and made as many enemies as friends in the dressing room—but four Cups is enough to make admirers and believers out of even the most adamant adversaries.

Jake Milford

b. Charlottetown, Prince Edward Island, July 29, 1914

Before World War II, he was a player. After the war, he made enough money to settle down on a farm—until the mayor of Brandon asked Milford to help organize a junior team to be called the Wheat Kings. The rest is history. Milford joined the Rangers' system in 1959, going first to Omaha and then St. Paul, where he won four championships in eight years. The Canadian Hockey League's coach of the year trophy was named after him, and in 1973 he joined the Los Angeles Kings as general manager. Four years later, he joined the Vancouver Canucks. Milford's acumen was often perfect. He acquired great players like Richard Brodeur and Thomas Gradin for next to nothing, and by 1982 the Canucks were playing for the Stanley Cup.

1985

September 12, 1985: Celebrating the Birth of the Hall

"The 25th Annual Hockey Hall of Fame Dinner," as this year's induction was billed, featured a little bit of everything: an Original Six left winger (Bert Olmstead), a Stanley Cup goalie (Gerry Cheevers), and one of the classiest centres to play the game (Jean Ratelle). Olmstead had been retired many a year, while Cheevers and Ratelle were only recently out of the game. All, though, were worthy additions to the Hall's honour roll.

1985

Gerry Cheevers

b. St. Catharines, Ontario, December 7, 1940

The Leafs let Cheevers out of their system because they felt they had plenty of talent in goal, so at the 1965 Intra-League Draft, the Boston Bruins claimed Cheesey and turned him into a Stanley Cup winner. He spent two seasons working his way into the Boston goal, but by 1967 he was the number-one man. Over the next five years, he won two Cups and established himself as the best money goalie in the business, a goalie who never had the best goals-against average, but one who would never give up a goal at a critical time. He never won an individual award and never recorded any spectacular statistic, but he was a winner. In 1972, Cheevers left for the World Hockey Association, returning to the NHL in 1976 and spending his final four years back in the Bruins' goal. He was renowned for his famous, "stitched" mask, which featured black slashes to indicate where he was hit on the face by the puck and how many times the mask saved him from serious cuts or certain death. In 418 NHL games, Cheevers won 230 times. In the playoffs, he had a tremendous record of 53-34 in 88 games.

Bert Olmstead

b. Sceptre, Saskatchewan, September 4, 1926

Left winger Bert Olmstead (above, right) broke into the NHL with Chicago in 1948 but just two and a half years later he was traded to Detroit and on to Montreal, where he played the core of his career. Olmstead had his best years on a line with Jean Béliveau and Bernie Geoffrion, and although he was the most unheralded and least spectacular of the three, he was the straw that stirred the drink, as it were. He helped the Habs win four Stanley Cups in the 1950s, reaching his peak in 1954–55 and 1955–56 when he led the NHL in assists with 48 and 56, respectively. That second total was a league record. Olmstead finished his career with the Leafs, playing four years in Toronto before retiring in 1962 as a Cup champ again. "Olmstead couldn't skate," Jacques Plante once said. "He wasn't stylish, either. All he could do was win."

Jean Ratelle

b. Lac Ste. Jean, Quebec, October 3, 1940

It's impossible to comprehend why or how Jean Ratelle never won a Stanley Cup. In 21 NHL seasons, he played 1,281 games and produced nearly a point a game from start to finish (491 goals, 1,267 points). He turned pro with the Rangers toward the end of the 1960–61 season and for 15 and a half seasons represented the Blueshirts with skill and class. He never had more than 28 penalty minutes in a season, and the centreman led the team to the Cup finals in 1972, only to lose to the Bruins. That 1971–72 season was his finest. He scored 46 goals and 109 points (both career highs) and won both the Lester Pearson Award and the Lady Byng Trophy. He was in the playoffs each of the final 15 years of his career, and his prospects for a Cup looked bright in 1975 when he was traded to the Bruins. Yet, the team never won, and Ratelle retired in 1981 as one of the greatest players in the game. He had 13 consecutive seasons of 25 goals or more and he played in five All-Star Games. When he left the ice for the last time, everyone around the league tipped his hat and said, there goes a player.

1985

John Mariucci

b. Eveleth, Minnesota, May 9, 1916

d. Minneapolis, Minnesota, March 23, 1987

In the years during and immediately after World War II, Mariucci was an average defenceman with Chicago, playing parts of five seasons with the Hawks. But it wasn't until after he retired that he earned himself a place in American hockey history and

the epithet "Godfather of Minnesota hockey." In 1952, Mariucci started recruiting players for the University of Minnesota and promoting high school hockey in his home state. When he began his efforts, high school hockey was close to non-existent. By 1980, there were more than 150 programs producing NHL-calibre players on a regular basis. Mariucci was also closely involved with international teams. He coached the United States to a silver medal at the Cortina Olympics in 1956 and in 1967 became assistant general manager to the new Minnesota North Stars franchise in the NHL. "John Mariucci, through his philosophies about the American boy, has done more for hockey in the United States than any person that I can relate to," wrote Walter Bush in his nominating of Mariucci for the Hockey Hall of Fame. "He did it all for the love of the game and his beliefs."

Rudy Pilous

b. Winnipeg, Manitoba, August 11, 1914

d. St. Catharines, Ontario, December 4, 1994

While playing hockey in the Rangers' system, Pilous was told by Frank Boucher in no uncertain terms that he didn't have the skating skills needed to make the NHL. Pilous went to St. Catharines where he played senior hockey briefly and then

established a junior team called the Falcons, thus beginning a 42-year career in a variety of administrative positions. In 1946 he moved to Buffalo as a scout, and a year later he turned a weak Houston franchise around to win the United States Hockey League championship during his first year there. Ditto for San Diego in the Pacific Coast Hockey League a year later, and from there he moved to Louisville and then back to St. Catharines to run the TeePees, the team with which he won the Memorial Cup in 1954. Pilous coached Chicago to the Stanley Cup in 1960–61 and he later coached in Denver for a number of years. He coached Bobby Hull and the Winnipeg Jets in the World Hockey Association and won three Avco Cups with the Jets before returning to the minors in St. Catharines in the Leafs system.

1986

September 10, 1986: Vancouver Plays Host to the Induction

For the first time, the Hockey Hall of Fame chose to hold its induction dinner outside Toronto, choosing the Hotel Vancouver, in Vancouver, British Columbia. The event was sold out and proved a fine success, with Steve Armitage hosting the evening and Bob Robertson providing comic relief. Leo Boivin was introduced by Emile Francis; Dave Keon by Jim Keon; and Serge Savard by fellow teammate John Ferguson. The Selection Committee this year included Danny Gallivan, Jean Béliveau, Alex Delvecchio, Milt Dunnell, Red Fisher, Bill Hay, Tommy Ivan, Gordon Juckes, John Mariucci, Tim Moriarty, Bud Poile, and Fran Rosa. On June 20, 1986, the NHL made another important decision regarding the Hall, which first opened in 1961 and was quickly outgrowing its home. It decided to put in motion redevelopment plans to bring the Hall up-to-date with new entertainment, updated exhibitry, expanded space, and exciting ways to draw more fans to the game. It would be seven years still before these plans reached maturity and the Hall moved to its present location in the heart of downtown Toronto.

1986

Leo Boivin

b. Prescott, Ontario, August 2, 1932

Leo Boivin's induction into the Hockey Hall of Fame was refreshing because it proved that numbers are not everything. A defenceman, he scored a scant 72 goals in 1,150 NHL games, and he never won a trophy of any sort. But, he was heads and shoulders the best hitter in the game, a rock on the blue line who could not be passed. Lynn Patrick compared him to Eddie Shore. Tim Horton called him the toughest defenceman to play against. His hip check was patented and his reputation admired throughout the league. He went to the Cup finals three times, twice with Boston with which he spent most of his career, and once with Detroit in 1966. He was Bruins captain for three years (1963–66) and played in three All-Star Games.

Dave Keon

b. Noranda, Quebec, March 22, 1940

At the age of 20, in 1960, Dave Keon (below, right) left St. Mike's College to play for the Toronto Maple Leafs. Twenty-two years later, he retired as one of the greatest players the game has known, a man tenacious and driven, gentlemanly and successful. He won the Calder Trophy for 1960–61 on the strength of his 20 goals and perfect two-way play. He played 15 years with the Leafs, winning two Lady Byng Trophies while averaging better than 20 goals a year. Keon rarely took a penalty and had only one fighting major in his career. He won four Cups with the Leafs and was named Conn Smythe winner in the 1967 playoffs, the last year the Leafs won. He succeeded George Armstrong as team captain, but in 1975 he left the team to sign with Minnesota in the World Hockey Association. He returned to the NHL four years later, closing out his career with Hartford. Keon played in eight All-Star Games and incurred just 117 penalty minutes in 1,296 regular-

season games. He retired in 1982 with 396 goals and 986 career points, one of the classiest, hardest working players in the game.

Serge Savard

b. Montreal, Quebec, January 22, 1946

In a career full of highlights and accomplishments, perhaps Savard's greatest boast is that he was the only player not to play in a loss during the 1972 Summit Series. That series took place at the height of his powers (though he had been slowed by two serious leg breaks in previous years). Savard broke in with the Habs in 1966–67 and went on to win eight Stanley Cups with the Habs in his 15 years on their blue line. He won the Conn Smythe Trophy in the 1969 playoffs for his outstanding performance, and he captained the team toward the end of his career. He was part of the so-called Big Three defence of Montreal, also featuring Larry Robinson and Guy Lapointe. After retiring in 1981, he was lured back to the ice by the Winnipeg Jets, where he played for a year and a half. Only once did his team not qualify for the playoffs in his career. Savard earned 439 points in 1,040 career games and won the Bill Masterton Trophy in 1978–79 for his dedication to the game.

Serge Savard of the Canadiens (left) was one of the Big Three on the Montreal defence, along with Larry Robinson and Guy Lapointe, all known for offensive abilities and great strength inside their own blueline.

1986

Bill Hanley

b. Balleyeast, Northern Ireland, February 28, 1915
d. Toronto, Ontario, September 16, 1990

In 1946, more or less out of the blue, Hanley was offered a job by Spiff Evans of Maple Leaf Gardens to act as a timekeeper for junior games. He accepted, and soon after he was doing the same for the Leafs. The Ontario Hockey Association then asked him to work on statistics for the league, and when he accepted this full-time position, the die was cast and hockey was to become his life's work and passion. His responsibilities grew, his acumen became more respected and demanded, and soon Hanley was made secretary-manager of the league, overseeing its daily operations for decades. He turned the league into the foremost developmental system for NHL players, and through the implementation of the draft in 1969 most pros came from the OHA. Hanley was responsible for changing officiating from a two-referee game to a one-referee, two-linesmen format.

1987

June 15, 1987: The Roadshow Moves to the Motor City

For the second year in a row, the Hockey Hall of Fame induction dinner travelled outside Toronto—and for the first time it went to the United States. Appropriately, Detroit's Westin Hotel was the host venue, for Builder and NHL president John Ziegler was a native of that city. George Michael was the master of ceremonies for the night, and the usual introductions were made by people close to the newest Honoured Members: Bobby Clarke was introduced by Ed Snider; Ed Giacomin by Hugh Delano; Jacques Laperriere by Ron Caron; and Matt Pavelich by Scotty Morrison. John Ziegler was introduced by his son, John Ziegler III.

Bobby Clarke

b. Flin Flon, Manitoba, August 13, 1949

Love him or hate him, no one who played with or against Bobby Clarke can deny he was one of the most competitive players of the modern era. He played his entire career with Philadelphia, starting in 1969 when the diabetic rookie went to training camp in the hopes of proving that a 5'10" fireplug with a serious disease could play a full schedule effectively. Irony of ironies, he missed only a handful of games in his 15 years in the league, and no one spoke about diabetes except to pay him compliment after compliment for his perseverance and performance. Clarke increased his goal scoring in each of his first four years, peaking at 37 in 1972–73. Playing on a line with Bill Barber and Reg Leach, the three terrorized the league for a number of productive years. Clarke recorded more than 100 points three times, and each time he did he also won the Hart Trophy (1972–73, 1974–75, 1975–76). He was the consummate leader, the youngest captain in league history, the man who inspired his teammates by his words and deeds on the ice and off. He took

the team to two Stanley Cups (in 1974 and 1975), and in 1982–83 won the Selke Trophy for his superb two-way play. Tenacious and determined, Clarke finished his career in 1984 and averaged better than a point a game: in 1,144 games, he had 1,210 points.

Ed Giacomin

b. Sudbury, Ontario, June 6, 1939

The rise of Giacomin's career coincided with the rise of the Rangers to a Cup-contending position in the late 1960s and early 1970s. Not a tall man, he was a quick goalie who played well positionally and inspired his teammates. Giacomin joined the Rangers in 1965 and from 1966 to 1970 played in all but 28 of his team's games. He led the league in wins three years in a row (1966–69) and kept his goals-against average under 3.00 for most of his career. In 1970–71, he and Gilles Villemure shared the Vézina Trophy, and the year after Giacomin took the Blueshirts to the finals where they lost to Bobby Orr and the Bruins. He finished his career in Detroit and played in six All-Star Games. After retiring in 1978, Giacomin ended with 610 games played and 289 victories.

Jacques Laperriere

b. Rouyn, Quebec, November 22, 1941

In nominating Laperriere to the Hockey Hall of Fame, Red Fisher wrote simply that, "His contribution to hockey makes him worthy of our strongest consideration for admittance." Fisher based his summary on obvious and salient facts of the defenceman's career. Laperriere played his first full season for Montreal in 1963–64 and won the Calder Trophy. In all, he played 12 seasons with the Canadiens, winning six Stanley Cups, the first coming in 1965. He won the Norris Trophy in 1965–66,

the year he won his second Cup, and he became the team's best blueliner for size and mobility. He was a First Team All-Star twice and played in five All-Star Games, though his career ended early because of a serious knee injury in January 1974. In all, he played 691 games and had 282 points. In 1972–73, he led the league with a plus-minus rating of +78.

Montreal's Jacques Laperriere (far right) never had the flashy style of Doug Harvey or the fan worship of Jean Béliveau, but he quietly won six Stanley Cups with the Canadiens nonetheless.

1987

John Ziegler

b. Grosse Pointe, Michigan, February 9, 1934

A graduate of the University of Michigan Law School, Ziegler came to the NHL via his studies rather than his slapshot. In the late 1950s and into the 1960s, he worked for the Olympia, the Red Wings, and Bruce Norris, and these ties helped him join the NHL's Board of Governors in 1966. A decade later, he was elected its chairman, and in September 1977 he was named president of the NHL, succeeding Clarence Campbell. Under Ziegler, the NHL took in four World Hockey Association franchises in 1979 and developed a strong base as a 21-year league. Ziegler worked closely to establish player-owner relations that were second to none in any sport, promoting the National Hockey League Players' Association while being fiscally responsible to the owners. In 1984, he was given the Lester Patrick Trophy for outstanding service to hockey in the United States.

Matt Pavelich

b. Park Hill Gold Mines, Ontario, March 12, 1934

As soon as the Hockey Hall of Fame Board of Directors changed eligibility from Referees to Officials, Frank Udvari nominated Pavelich as a potential inductee. Thus, Pavelich became the first linesman to enter the Hall. He started officiating at age 14 and went on to become the referee-in-chief for the Northern Michigan Intermediate League. He moved up as an official in the American Hockey League (where Carl Voss was impressed) and made his first NHL appearance on October 11, 1956. By the time he retired in 1979, Pavelich had worked an incredible 1,727 regular-season games, 245 more in the playoffs, and 11 All-Star Games. "He has been a role model for many of today's younger officials, and it is most fitting that he be honoured as the first linesman in the category of on-ice Officials," Brian O'Neill, the Hall's chairman of the board, declared.

1988

September 7, 1988: A Deluxe Potpourri of Talent

Goalies, forwards, and defenders were all represented at this year's induction, as were three Original Six teams: Montreal, Boston, and New York. For the first time, an important member of a 1967 expansion team was inducted: Philadelphia owner Ed Snider. The dinner was back home in Toronto, where it has remained ever since with one exception (1991).

1988

Tony Esposito

b. Sault Ste. Marie, Ontario, April 23, 1943

Certainly it can't hurt to have a future Hall of Famer shooting on you as a kid if you want to grow up to be an NHL goalie. Tony Esposito had just that advantage in his brother, Phil. "Tony O" started in Montreal, and although he played 873 games with Chicago after, it was his 13 games with the Habs in 1968–69 that gave him his only Stanley Cup. The Habs let him go in the Intra-League Draft of 1969 and the Hawks claimed him. Esposito immediately became one of the league's top goalies and had one of the finest rookie seasons ever for a puckstopper. In 1969–70, he led the league in wins with 38 and he set a modern-day record with 15 shutouts, a mark that still stands. His goals-against average was 2.17 and he won the Vézina Trophy and was named a First Team All-Star—all in his first year! Esposito perfected the butterfly style of goaltending and was one of the busiest goalies of his day. He played half the games of the Summit Series in 1972 and retired with 423 wins to his credit, a figure that is still fifth most on the all-time list. He also shared a second Vézina Trophy with Gary Smith in 1971–72 and tied for a third with Bernie Parent in 1973–74.

Guy Lafleur

b. Thurso, Quebec, September 20, 1951

Drafted first overall by Montreal in 1971, Lafleur lived up to his advanced billing by becoming one of the team's greatest right wingers. His stride was powerful and fluid, his shot hard and accurate, his play gentlemanly but determined. He was a credit to the game for all his 1,126 games in the league. He scored 29 goals as a rookie after a junior career in which he averaged nearly two goals a game, and by 1974–75 Lafleur had reached 50 goals and 100 points for the first of many times. He finished that year with 53 and 119, respectively, and the year after he won his first Art Ross Trophy with 125 points. It was his first of three successive scoring titles and first of five seasons in a row scoring at least 52 goals. Lafleur also won five Stanley Cups, and earned the Conn Smythe Trophy in 1977. He won three Lester B. Pearson Awards too, and three years after retiring in 1985 he was inducted into the Hockey Hall of Fame. However, just a few weeks after the induction dinner, Lafleur came out of retirement to play for the Rangers, and a year later he joined the Nordiques in Quebec for two final seasons. He retired finally in 1991 after scoring 560 goals and 1,353 points in just 1,126 games. He also averaged better than a point a game in the playoffs (134 in 128 games). Lafleur became only the second Hall of Famer after Gordie Howe to play in the NHL after being inducted.

1988

"Buddy" O'Connor

b. Montreal, Quebec,
June 21, 1916
d. Montreal, Quebec,
August 24, 1977

At 5'7" and 145 pounds, O'Connor was hardly a big man, but try to get the puck away from him and his skills were fully evident. More a passer than a scorer, he played senior hockey for the Montreal Royals, centering the Razzle Dazzle Line with wingers Pete Morin and Gerry Heffernan. The trio moved up to the Canadiens in 1941 and fit right in to the NHL. O'Connor helped the team to two Stanley Cups, in 1944 and 1946, but in the summer of 1947 he was traded to the Rangers. He proved the Habs wrong by having his finest season. O'Connor scored 24 goals and won both the Hart and Lady Byng Trophies to solidify his place as one of the best centres in the game. When he retired in 1951, he had scored 140 goals and had 397 points in 509 games. More incredibly, he incurred only 34 penalty minutes during his career.

Brad Park

b. Toronto, Ontario, July 6, 1948

In 17 years of NHL play, Brad Park never missed the playoffs. Never. He started with the Rangers in 1968, a young defenceman cut from the same cloth as his prime adversary, Bobby Orr. In 1971–72, he scored 24 goals and took the Blueshirts to the finals against Orr and the Bruins, and came up just short. Park hit the 20-goal mark three times during his career and reached 50 points in a season 10 times. When he was traded to the Bruins in 1975, he and Orr formed the best blue line tandem in league history, albeit for just a few games before a serious knee injury sidelined Orr again. Park had a similar powerful stride and a keen offensive ability to pass and move up ice. He acted as a fourth forward and scored 213 goals in his career, but like Orr he was weakened over the years by knee

injuries. Park finished his career with Detroit, retiring in 1985 with 1,113 games under his belt and 896 points to his credit. He won the Bill Masterton Trophy in 1983–84 for his perseverance, despite the injured knees, and he played in nine straight All-Star Games at one stretch (1970–78).

Cut from the same cloth as Bobby Orr, Brad Park had phenomenal puck-rushing skills and worked as a fourth forward in the same way as did Orr.

Ed Snider

b. Washington, D.C.,
January 6, 1933

Ed Snider arrived in Philadelphia in 1964 as vice president of the Eagles football club, but in no time at all he decided that what the city really needed was a hockey team. It was primarily through his efforts that the city did, indeed, receive one of the six expansion spots in 1967, and it was under his leadership and guidance that the franchise became quickly the most successful of the new group of six. Just seven years after playing their first game, the Flyers won the Stanley Cup, in 1974, and the year after they repeated as champions. In the team's first 20 years, in fact, only Montreal had a better cumulative record in the NHL. Snider's devotion to amateur and minor hockey was evident in 1976 when he created Hockey Central, an organization devoted to youth hockey in the Delaware Valley area. Through his efforts, local participation in hockey tripled. In 1980, Snider received the Lester Patrick Trophy for his contributions to American hockey.

George Hayes

b. Montreal, Quebec, June 21, 1914
d. Beachville, Ontario, November 19, 1987

It was only a few months after Hayes passed away that he was accepted into the Hockey Hall of Fame, the first official to work in more than 1,000 NHL games. He started officiating in 1936 in the Ontario Minor Hockey Association and five years later joined the more senior Ontario Hockey Association. Within two years he was recruited by the American Hockey League until April 15, 1946 when he signed his first NHL contract. Up through 1965, when he retired, Hayes officiated 1,544 regular-season games and 149 more in the playoffs. Additionally, he worked in 11 All-Star Games. He earned the respect of his peers and the players through his ability to remain calm and controlled under even the most strenuous circumstances.

1989

October 3, 1989: International Heroes

There was great excitement surrounding the Hockey Hall of Fame in 1989, especially when the decision to move into a bigger space was followed by a deal that gave downtown Toronto's old Bank of Montreal to the Hall. Including space below the bank—inside the new BCE Place skyscraper—the Hall would occupy some 51,000 square feet, an enormous increase over the 6,800 at the Canadian National Exhibition. Hall president Scotty Morrison had to make a special petition to the City of Toronto to secure the building, but it was his intention, and that of the NHL, that the new home should remain in Toronto. The Selection Committee this year featured Danny Gallivan, Jean Béliveau, Alex Delvecchio, Bill Hay, Tommy Ivan, Keith Allen, Bud Poile, Milt Dunnell, Tim Moriarty, Fran Rosa, and Red Fisher. Gordon Juckes retired after many years on the Committee. There was a unique international scope to the inductees this year. Darryl Sittler, hero of the 1976 Canada Cup, was going in, as was Vladislav Tretiak, Soviet goalie who became the first non-NHLer of the modern era to be inducted. Father David Bauer was also honoured for his work with St. Mike's and the formation of Canada's first National Team, and super-agent Alan Eagleson was also inducted (though he later resigned from the Hall of Fame after serious legal problems damaged his reputation beyond salvation).

1989

Herbie Lewis

b. Calgary, Alberta, April 17, 1906
d. Indianapolis, Indiana,
    January 20, 1991

In an era when Howie Morenz was considered the fastest of them all, Herbie Lewis was considered just as fleet of foot. He was also a superb defensive player, and this combination made him a threat offensively but also made him perhaps the most complete player between the wars. Lewis played his entire career in Detroit, 11 seasons beginning in 1928. While he was a star on the team, he never won an individual award and was never voted to an All-Star Team. Nonetheless, his performance in the 1936 playoffs, which brought the Motor City its first Stanley Cup, has gone down in history as one of the great moments. Lewis played left wing on a line with Marty Barry at centre and Larry Aurie on the right side, and they led the team to the finals. Once there, Lewis smothered Toronto's great Charlie Conacher, while producing offensively himself. The Wings won again the year after. In 483 career games, Lewis had 148 goals and 309 points.

Darryl Sittler

b. Kitchener, Ontario, September 18, 1950

The Maple Leafs knew what they were doing on draft day 1970 when they chose Sittler eighth overall with their first selection. He made the team that fall and went on to become one of the greatest leaders the blue and white has known in an 11-and-a-half year career at Maple Leaf Gardens. He later played for Philadelphia and Detroit, but it was as a Leaf that he will always be remembered. Sittler had 12 successive seasons of at least 27 goals. Five times he passed the 40-goal mark, and in 1977–78 he set a Toronto record with 117 points, his second 100-point season. He was captain of the team from 1975 to 1981 and only once in his career did he fail to make the playoffs. He never won a Stanley Cup or an individual trophy, but Sittler played

in four All-Star Games and retired with Hall of Fame numbers: 1,096 games played, 484 goals and 1,121 total points. A fierce competitor, a leader, a gentleman off the ice, Sittler was everything a great player should be (pictured opposite, right).

1976: A Great Year

Few players have ever enjoyed the success in a calendar year that Sittler enjoyed in 1976. On February 7, he scored six goals and four assists—10 points!—in a single game to set a standard no one has yet to reach—not Gretzky or Lemieux, not Yzerman or Sakic. In the playoffs a few weeks later, on April 22, Sittler scored five goals against the Flyers to tie a record set by Maurice Richard back in 1944. Then, to complete the great hat trick of feats, Sittler scored the overtime winner on September 15 to give Canada a 5-4 win over Czechoslovakia and claim the first Canada Cup. It was a year for the ages and for the record book, and a series of feats only a Hall of Famer could perform.

He never made it to the NHL, but Tretiak's brilliance at the international level was so indisputable that induction into the Hockey Hall of Fame was fully deserved.

Vladislav Tretiak

b. Dmitrov, Soviet Union, April 25, 1952

The list of international successes of the greatest goalie never to play in the NHL is extraordinary. Tretiak first played as a 17-year-old at the 1970 World Championships, though he rose to greater prominence two years later during the historic Summit Series when he nearly defeated Team Canada. Until retiring in 1984, Tretiak won a record 10 World Championship gold medals and was four times named the best goalie. He also played in four Olympics, winning three gold (1972, 1976, 1984) and a silver (1980). He was drafted by the Montreal Canadiens in 1983 on the off chance the Soviets might release their great goalie, but that never happened and he retired without ever

having competed for an NHL team. Nonetheless, his abilities were unquestionably among the elite, and in 1989 he became the first European-trained player to be inducted into the Hockey Hall of Fame.

Father David Bauer

b. Waterloo, Ontario, November 2, 1924
d. Goderich, Ontario, November 9, 1988

There will only ever be one Father Bauer. He was ordained in 1953 and joined St. Michael's College in Toronto, coaching the students to a spiritually healthy way of life and coaching the hockey team to a Memorial Cup win in 1961. He pulled the team out of junior hockey at this time because he felt the hockey was outstripping learning at the school. But he also helped to organize a National Team to represent Canada at the World Championships and Olympics, a team composed of the best university students and available junior players from coast to coast. The program endured for eight years (1962–70) during which time Bauer created a philosophy that focused on the ice but extended well beyond. Good men make good players, he reasoned, and good men remain so long after their playing days are over. He believed representing Canada was a matter of integrity, and that victory came of pride, determination, and sporting conduct.

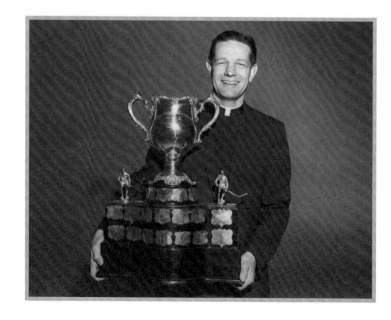

1990

September 24, 1990: The Flying Frenchman is Added

Dick Irvin hosted this year's induction dinner, held at the Westin Harbour Castle in Toronto. Louis Jannetta introduced Veteran Player Fern Flaman, and Builder Bud Poile was presented by his son, David. Bill Barber came on after remarks by Keith Allen and Joe Crozier introduced Gil Perreault. The Selection Committee included chairman Danny Gallivan, Keith Allen, Tommy Ivan, Gordon Juckes, Bud Poile, Milt Dunnell, Tim Moriarty, Fran Rosa, Red Fisher, Bill Hay, Jean Béliveau, and Alex Delvecchio.

1990

Bill Barber

b. Callander, Ontario, July 11, 1952

A knee injury forced Bill Barber to retire toward the end of the 1983–84 season, his 12th in the NHL, all with Philadelphia. But by this time he had established himself as one of the finest left wingers of the expansion era. He was called up to the Flyers in 1972 as an injury replacement, but once there he never left. As a rookie, Barber scored 30 goals, and in years two and three he had 34, the Flyers winning the Cup both seasons. He had his personal best year in 1975–76 when he scored 50 goals and 112 points, and another career highlight came the next fall when he scored a goal in the third period to give Canada a 4-4 tie with the Czechs to send the Canada Cup finals game into overtime (where Darryl Sittler scored the winner). Barber had five 40-goal seasons with the team, and although he never won an individual trophy, he did play in six All-Star Games. In just 903 career games, he scored 420 goals and had 883 points.

Fern Flaman

b. Dysart, Saskatchewan, January 25, 1927

This year's inductee in the recently-created Veteran Player category, Flaman was a defensive defenceman in the NHL for some 17 years, notably with Boston and Toronto. He began with  brief call-ups to the Bruins during the war years, making the team's blue line corps full-time in 1947. He was a devastating hitter playing on weak Boston teams at the time, but when he was traded to the Leafs early in the 1950–51 season his fortunes changed. Flaman won his only Cup that year with Toronto and in the summer of 1954 he was traded back to Boston where he closed out his NHL career. He went to the finals again in 1957 and 1958, losing both times to Montreal. In 910 career games, Flaman had 208 points and 1,370 penalty minutes, testament to the work he did inside his own blue line.

Gilbert Perreault

b. Victoriaville, Quebec, November 13, 1950

He played all his 17 seasons and 1,191 games with Buffalo, and during his time in the NHL there was no player who skated with as powerful and fluid a stride as the Sabres' premier centreman. He was the first overall draft choice by Buffalo in 1970, and after scoring 38 goals as a rookie he won the Calder Trophy. In ensuing years, he starred on one of the top lines in the league, the French Connection threesome also featuring Rick Martin and Rene Robert. Perreault led the Sabres to the Cup finals in 1975 and he never failed to score 20 goals in a full season in the league. He brought fans out of their seats with his great rushes, his brilliant moves one-on-one, and his superb finishing around the net. Perreault (pictured opposite) captained the team for the last six years of his career, and in 1,191 career games he scored 512 goals and 1,326 points. He had only 500 penalty minutes, and in 1972–73 was named winner of the Lady Byng Trophy for his gentlemanly play.

Norman "Bud" Poile

b. Fort William, Ontario, February 10, 1924

After 48 years in hockey, Poile might be considered not just a Builder but a super-Builder. He played seven years in the NHL in the years during and immediately after World War II, but his executive career began in earnest in 1955 when he coached Edmonton of the Western Hockey League and later San Francisco. In 1967, Poile became the inaugural general manager of the Philadelphia Flyers, developing a team that would soon win the Stanley Cup. Meanwhile, he went to Vancouver as general manager and then to the World Hockey Association as executive vice president. He was commissioner of the Central Hockey League for eight years (1976–84), the last of which he also served as president of the International Hockey League, and he continued as IHL president until 1989. It was under his leadership that the "I" became as important a developmental league as the American Hockey League, and he received the Lester Patrick Trophy for his service to hockey in the United States.

1991

September 23, 1991: Ottawa Hosts the Induction

There was a distinct Ottawa connection to this year's induction, and the Hockey Hall of Fame bestowed upon native Denis Potvin the honour of inducting him at the Congress Centre in his hometown. It was the last time the induction was held outside Toronto, and all proceeds from the $250-ticket affair went to the construction and renovation of the new home of the Hall in downtown Toronto. Distinguished guests included some of Ottawa's greatest athletes and the game's greatest players: Frank Finnigan, Maurice and Henri Richard, Guy Lafleur, Darryl Sittler, and Yvan Cournoyer. The Selection Committee this year included Danny Gallivan, Scotty Morrison, Keith Allen, Jean Béliveau, Ed Chynoweth, Red Fisher, Emile Francis, Bill Hay, Tommy Ivan, Tim Moriarty, Bud Poile, Fran Rosa, and Frank Selke, Jr.

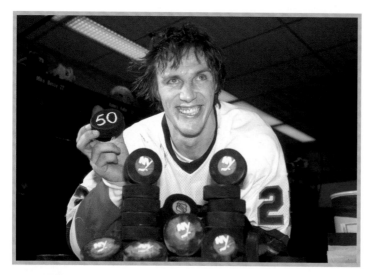

Mike Bossy

b. Montreal, Quebec, January 22, 1957

It was not only amazing that in four years of junior Bossy scored 70, 84, 79, and 75 goals, so much as that he kept that pace up throughout his NHL career. The right winger joined the Islanders in 1978 and in his first nine years he never failed to score 50 goals. His last, injury-ravaged season saw him score 38 times in just 63 games. In seven of those years Bossy also had more than 100 points. He twice led the league in goals (69 in 1978–79 and 68 in 1980–81) and was considered to have the quickest snap shot in the game. Bossy teamed with centreman Bryan Trottier to form one of the highest-scoring combinations in the NHL, leading the Islanders to four consecutive Stanley Cups from 1980 to 1983. His 53 goals as a rookie earned him the Calder Trophy and in 1982 he won the Conn Smythe Trophy. Bossy, a clean and fair player, also won the Lady Byng Trophy three times (1982–83, 1983–84, 1985–86). He was forced out of the game in 1987 because of a back injury, and despite playing in only 752 regular-season games, he scored 573 goals and 1,126 points, a points-per-game average of more than one and a half.

Denis Potvin

b. Ottawa, Ontario, October 29, 1953

"I shared four Stanley Cup rings with my teammates," defenceman Denis Potvin said at the induction dinner. "But this is the ring of all rings," he added. His induction capped a 15-year career in which he, like Bossy, played all his games with the New York Islanders. Potvin was the first overall draft choice in 1973 and started that fall with the young team as a 19-year-old. He won the Calder Trophy and went on to become the highest point-producing defenceman of all time, a rusher of the puck in the style of Bobby Orr. Potvin had nine seasons of at least 20 goals and three times reached 30. In 1978–79 he became only the second defenceman to reach 100 points after Orr, but it was the 1979–80 season that marked his greatest success. That year, the Islanders won their first of four straight Cups, and Potvin was team captain for all of them, from 1979 until he retired eight years later. He played 1,060 games and scored 310 goals (a record at the time), and he became the first blueliner to reach 1,000 points, finishing with 1,052. Potvin also played in the 1976 and 1981 Canada Cups, won three Norris Trophies, and played in nine All-Star Games.

Bob Pulford

b. Newton Robinson, Ontario, March 31, 1936

For 16 years Bob Pulford played his style of game, a determined and disciplined centreman who was a superb checker capable of scoring. In Toronto, the saying was, "As Pulford goes, so goes the Leafs." He won two Memorial Cups with the Marlies in 1955 and 1956 and joined Toronto the next year. He earned a regular spot in the lineup because of his tenacity, though he had 23 and 24 goals in his third and fourth season, respectively. Pulford stayed with the Leafs for 14 years, winning four Stanley Cups with the team in the 1960s. In 1964, he was given an assist on Bobby Baun's dramatic goal to force a game seven against Detroit, and in 1967 he scored in double overtime of game three against Montreal to propel the Leafs to victory. Off ice, Pulford devoted himself to education, and as a result he became the first president of the NHL Players' Association when it started in 1967. He finished his career as captain of Los Angeles for two years, by which time he had played 1,079 games. Pulford scored 281 goals and 643 points, and he also played in five All-Star Games.

More recently Bob Pulford has been associated with Chicago, but he spent most of his playing days with the Leafs in the 1950s and '60s, winning four Stanley Cups with the Blue and White.

Clint Smith

b. Assiniboia, Saskatchewan, December 12, 1913

Any player who makes Dave Keon look like a goon deserves a spot in the Hockey Hall of Fame on that merit alone! Keon, one of the least penalized players in NHL history, has to take his hat  off to Smith, a centreman who incurred only 24 penalty minutes in 483 games over 11 seasons of play. Three times he went a full season without getting a single penalty! He won two Lady Byng Trophies (1938–39 and 1943–44) and was runner-up three other times, but Smith was also a premier scorer in the game. He joined the Rangers toward the end of the 1936–37 season and was soon part of the Blueshirts' Cup victory in 1940. He went to Chicago in 1943, and in his first year he centred a line with wingers Bill Mosienko and Doug Bentley. Smith set an NHL record that year with 49 assists in the 50-game season, and the threesome set another record with 219 points as a unit. In all, Smith reached the 20-goal mark four times and retired in 1947 with 161 to his credit. He had 397 total points.

"Scotty" Bowman

b. Montreal, Quebec, September 18, 1933

By the time he was inducted into the Hockey Hall of Fame in 1991, Bowman had finished about two-thirds of his career, but just that was good enough to count among the most impressive careers of any coach. He learned the trade in the Montreal system, but he got his first taste of NHL bench bossing with the St. Louis Blues in 1967, their first year in the league. In three and a half seasons, he had a winning record and took the team to the Cup finals three years in a row, the beginning of a magnificent career. In 1971 he was offered the head coaching job in Montreal, and it was there he made his roots for the next eight

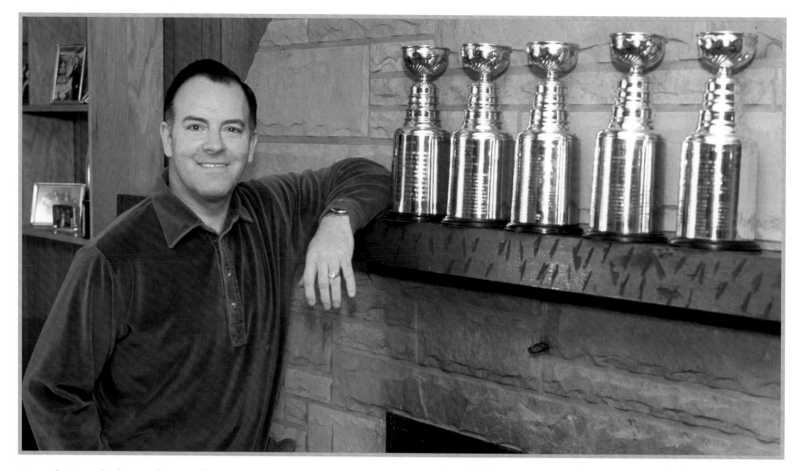

years, during which time he won five Stanley Cups. This period was highlighted by the 1976–77 season when the Canadiens posted an NHL-record 60 wins and just 8 losses (12 ties). Bowman moved to Buffalo to become coach and then general manager and he moved to Pittsburgh in an executive capacity afterward. The death of Penguins coach Bob Johnson pushed Bowman behind the bench for 1991–92, and the team won its second Cup. In 1993, he joined Detroit, beginning the final stage of his career, one that lasted nine years and three more Stanley Cups. His wins in 1996 and 1997 were remarkable for his use of a five-man Russian unit and his trap-style system which the Wings executed to perfection. By the time he retired in 2002, Bowman's numbers were staggering if not altogether unreachable: 30 years as a coach, more than 2,200 regular-season games and 350 in the playoffs, more than 1,200 victories, and nine Stanley Cups (to tie Toe Blake).

Neil Armstrong

b. Plympton Township, Ontario, December 29, 1932

Players might look to Doug Jarvis as an iron man, but officials look to Neil Armstrong, who never missed an assignment in 16 years calling games. He started officiating at age 15 and his rise to the NHL was meteoric. Armstrong never worked in the

minors, moving to the best league on November 16, 1957 at Maple Leaf Gardens to work a Toronto-Boston game. From then until his retirement in 1978, he was a fixture in the league, maintaining the highest integrity and standards that could be asked of any official. On October 16, 1973, in Detroit, he set a record for officials by working his 1,314th game, and by the time he took off his skates for the last time he had 1,744 games to his credit—in addition to another 208 in the playoffs, 48 of which came in Cup finals.

1992

September 21, 1992: Only the Best Get In

Roy Thomson Hall, a concert hall in Toronto and home to the Symphony, was the venue for this unique edition of the induction dinner. Billed as "A Stanley Cup Centennial Celebration," the dinner honoured seven new men, including three Players and one Veteran Player. The venue was chosen in preparation for next year's event, which would take place at the Hall's new home in BCE Place. Dick Irvin hosted the ceremony in the concert hall before more than 2,000 people. The post-induction party took place in the circular lobby of Roy Thomson Hall.

1992

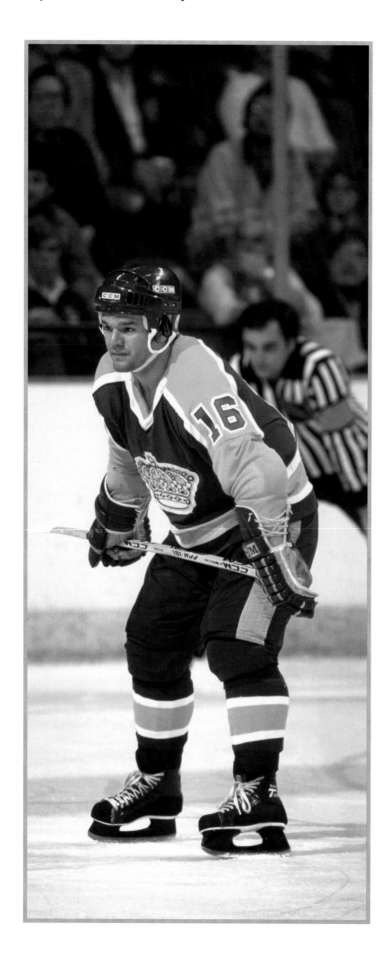

Marcel Dionne

b. Drummondville, Quebec, August 3, 1951

By the time the Little Beaver retired in 1989, only one man had scored more goals, assists, and points: Gordie Howe. Yet Dionne's achievements were eerily quiet by comparison, as they were achieved with a weak Detroit team in the early 1970s, an isolated Los Angeles team for a dozen years, and a Rangers team during the seeming twilight of his career. Dionne (left) scored 28 goals as a rookie and had 90 points in his second season. In 1974–75, his last season with the Wings, he captained the team and produced 121 points—but in four years in Detroit the team never once made the playoffs. Dionne signed with the Kings in 1975 as a free agent and had seven seasons of more than 100 points. Six times he had more than 50 goals, and in 1979–80 he won the scoring championship on a technicality. He and Wayne Gretzky both had 137 points, but Dionne had more goals and won the Art Ross Trophy. That year, he also won his second consecutive Lester B. Pearson Award. Dionne also won two Lady Byng Trophies, but he was most famous as the centreman for the Triple Crown Line with wingers Charlie Simmer and Dave Taylor (the highest-scoring line in the NHL for a time). Dionne never made it far in the playoffs, despite his quick shot and brilliant playmaking. He retired after 1,348 regular-season games, scoring 731 goals, 1,040 assists, and 1,771 total points, remarkable totals all.

Woody Dumart

b. Berlin (Kitchener), Ontario, December 23, 1916
d. Needham, Massachusetts, October 19, 2001

Left winger of the famed Kraut Line, Dumart helped Boston win two Stanley Cups in the three years prior to World War II. He played with Bobby Bauer and Milt Schmidt, first in Kitchener, then with the Bruins. Dumart was called up for a single game toward the end of the 1935–36 season and toward the end of the following season the Krauts were formed. Like his mates, Dumart played his whole career in Boston—16 years and 772 games, in his case. The three left the team after the 1941–42 season to enter the war, and three years later they were triumphantly reunited. Dumart scored 20 goals or more five times and 211 for his career, surpassing the once-magical, 200-goal plateau before retiring in 1954. He was also known as a superb checker, and while the line could score, it often played against the other team's best line to good effect (pictured below, far right).

Bob Gainey

b. Peterborough, Ontario, December 13, 1953

His statistics were more Original Six than post-expansion, but numbers did not tell the whole story of what Bob Gainey (right) brought to the ice. No finer compliment was paid a player than when Soviet hockey leader Anatoli Tarasov called Gainey technically the best player in the world, referring not specifically to a hard shot or scoring ability or checking but to overall play. True, Gainey scored 20 goals on four occasions, but this was during a scoring era. No, what separated him from the rest was his two-way play and leadership. He could check the very best offensive players in the world into the ice, and still score on his own merit. He broke in with Montreal in 1973 and over the next 16 seasons won five Stanley Cups. He captained the team from 1981 until he retired eight years later and he played in the 1976 and 1981 Canada Cups. Gainey was not flashy or spectacular, but when the NHL introduced the Frank Selke Trophy to honour the best defensive forward, it was as though Gainey had been in mind for it all along. He won the award its first four years in circulation (1977–1981) and also won the Conn Smythe Trophy in 1979 for his inspired play during that year's run to the Cup for the Habs. Gainey finished with 1,160 games played, 239 goals, and 501 points scored. He also played in four All-Star Games.

1992

Lanny McDonald

b. Hanna, Alberta, February 16, 1953

In his final NHL season, 1988–89 with Calgary, Lanny McDonald did it all: he recorded his 500th goal and 1,000th point; he won his first and only Stanley Cup, and he scored a goal in that Cup-winning game, his last in the league. It was a fitting end to a spectacular career for one of the good guys of the game. He turned pro with Toronto in 1973, and after two rough years he exploded for 37 goals in 1975–76, his trademark snap shot from the right wing doing most of the damage. He had three successive 40-goal seasons with the Leafs, and on his way to a fourth he was traded to Colorado, perhaps the most controversial deal in Maple Leafs history. McDonald ended in Calgary on November 25, 1981, and it was in his home province that he finished his career with a flourish. In 1982–83 he scored 66 goals and had a career high 98 points, and though his numbers diminished in succeeding years, his powers of leadership did not. No finer image of McDonald's career can be recalled than the teary-eyed 36-year-old holding the Stanley Cup high above his head the night he played his last game (below).

Keith Allen

b. Saskatoon, Saskatchewan, August 21, 1923

He was only a small part of the NHL as a player, appearing in parts of two seasons with Detroit during their glory years in the 1950s, but it was as a coach and general manager that Keith Allen left his mark on hockey. In 1956 he was named coach in Seattle, one of Detroit's farm teams, and over nine seasons his team never missed the playoffs save the last, when he was general manager, not coach. In 1966 he accepted the position of coach for the new Philadelphia franchise and three years later he moved up to general manager. As the man in control, Allen hired Fred Shero as coach and made numerous sage draft choices and trades, quickly building a team that won the Stanley Cup in 1974 and again the next year. The Flyers went on to reach the finals four more times, though in 1982 Allen moved from general manager to executive vice president. By the time he was inducted into the Hockey Hall of Fame, he had served with the Flyers for a quarter of a century and had made the team one of the strongest on ice and at the box office.

Bob Johnson

b. Minneapolis, Minnesota, March 4, 1931
d. Colorado Springs, Colorado, November 26, 1991

Coaching was a way of life for Bob Johnson (right). He took on a number of college and high school positions and won championships wherever he went. It was in 1966, though, that he started to make a greater name for himself when he was named coach of the University of Wisconsin Badgers, a team he led for 15 years and three national titles. "Badger Bob," as he came to be known, was effusive and energetic—to the game, to his players, to life. His motto was, "It's a great day for hockey," and he lived those words as passionately as he spoke them. In 1982, Calgary hired him to coach in the NHL, a job he held for five years until the opportunity to run USA Hockey was offered him. In 1991, he was hired by Pittsburgh and won a Cup the next spring. Unfortunately, poor health caused him to leave Team USA during the 1991 Canada Cup, and a few weeks later he passed away. His body may have gone, but his inspiration continued to touch all the players who had known him and played for him.

1992

Frank Mathers

b. Winnipeg, Manitoba, March 29, 1924

He may have been born in Winnipeg and played all his NHL career in Toronto, but the name Frank Mathers is synonymous with hockey success in Hershey, Pennsylvania. He was never a great success in the NHL, but in 1956 he went to Hershey to finish his career as a player and assume coaching duties as well. Mathers was considered an outstanding defenceman but also a fine student of the game. In his six years as playing coach, the Bears won three Calder Cups, and after retiring as a player in 1962, he continued to coach the team. In 1968, he added the title of general manager to his portfolio, and the team won another Calder Cup the next spring. In 1973 he continued to move up the executive ladder when he was named president and general manager. With him in that dual role, the team won three more championships, and by the time Mathers retired in 1991 he was a legend in Chocolatetown.

1993

November 16, 1993:
Moving into the Modern Era

Finally, the Hockey Hall of Fame had a home. The new Hall, the centrepiece of which was the old Bank of Montreal building at Front and Yonge Streets in downtown Toronto, featured 51,000 square feet of display and entertainment space, an archives and library, and rental and storage facilities that would take the museum into the 21st century. The Bell Great Hall featured the beautiful bank with a domed, stained-glass ceiling, which housed hockey's most prized trophies, among them the Stanley Cup, Art Ross, Hart, Norris, and other NHL trophies. The rest of the museum, built below the bank inside the magnificent BCE Place, featured expanded exhibits and interactive games, enhanced memorabilia displays, and ample room to accommodate thousands of visitors at any time.

The induction dinner this year was a black tie affair, hosted by Dick Irvin and Ron MacLean, and the three principal inductees—Guy Lapointe, Steve Shutt, Billy Smith—all represented concurrent dynasties from Montreal and Long Island. It was a remarkable opening for the Hall, and in its first year the museum attracted more visitors than any other tourist destination in the city.

1993

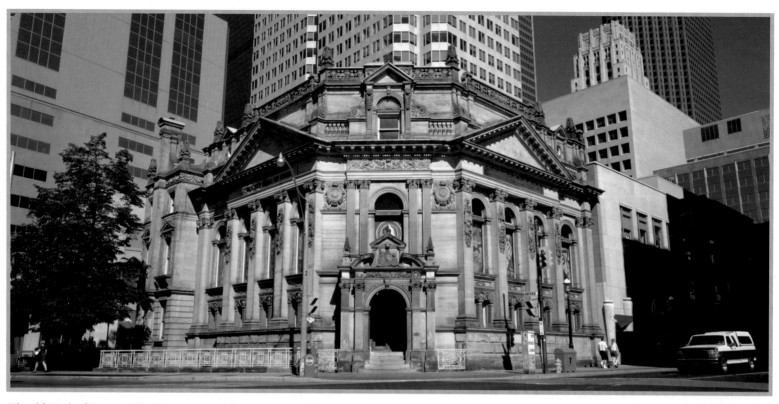

The old Bank of Montreal building at the northwest corner of Yonge and Front Streets in downtown Toronto is the heart and soul of the new Hockey Hall of Fame, opened to the public in 1993.

Guy Lapointe

b. Montreal, Quebec, March 18, 1948

Montreal won six Stanley Cups in the 1970s and Guy Lapointe anchored the defence for each and every one of them. He played a single game for the Habs toward the end of the 1968–69 season and after another year in the minors made the Habs for good in 1970. As a rookie, Lapointe scored 15 goals and had 107 penalty minutes, statistics that spoke of his offensive ability and his defensive toughness. He scored more than 20 goals three times and six times had more than 50 points in a season. Lapointe, Larry Robinson, and Serge Savard formed the so-called Big Three of the Montreal blue line corps, and Lapointe was runner-up in the Norris Trophy voting for 1972–73, the same year he joined Bobby Orr on the First All-Star Team. He played in the Summit Series, the 1976 Canada Cup, and the Challenge Cup in 1979. He finished his career with brief stops in St. Louis and Boston, by which time he had played 884 games and scored 171 goals and 622 total points. Lapointe also played in four All-Star Games.

Edgar Laprade

b. Port Arthur, Ontario, October 10, 1919

Edgar Laprade came to the NHL at a comparatively late time in life, joining the Rangers in 1945 at age 26. Up to that time, though, he had not been idle. Laprade skated for the Port Arthur Bearcats for many years. He was regularly the league's most valuable player and led the team to the 1940 Allan Cup—

the team that was going to represent Canada at the Olympics until they were cancelled because of the war. Laprade was in the army for two years and finally agreed to join the Rangers when they offered him a $5,000 bonus, which he put toward the mortgage on his house. Laprade had little difficulty proving

he belonged in the best league, winning the Calder Memorial Trophy in 1945–46. The hard-working centre played an even 10 years with the Blueshirts and was a gentleman from start to finish. He accrued just 42 penalty minutes in his career and won the Lady Byng Trophy in 1949–50. He played in the first four All-Star Games (1947–50) and retired with exactly 500 games under his belt. In that time, Laprade scored 108 goals and 280 points.

Steve Shutt

b. Toronto, Ontario, July 1, 1952

While playing junior for the Marlies, Steve Shutt was on the left wing on a line that featured Dave Gardner at centre and Billy Harris on the right side, a line that set all scoring records for Canadian junior hockey. Shutt (right) was drafted by Montreal, and after two seasons of apprenticeship, he made an impact in 1974–75 by scoring 30 goals and proving he had that un-coachable knack for finding the back of the net. He teamed with

Guy Lafleur and Pete Mahovlich and was the quiet star, the unsung hero who didn't seem to do much but at the end of the night had a goal and an assist somehow. Over the next two seasons, Shutt improved to 45 goals and then 60, a record for left wingers that stood for 16 years. During the 1970s, he won five Stanley Cups with the Habs. He played in the 1976 Canada Cup and the Challenge Cup in 1979 and had nine consecutive seasons of 30 goals or more. He finished his career in Los Angeles, but when he retired his accomplishments again went into the record books almost unnoticed. He scored 424 goals and had 817 points in 930 career games, 20th on the all-time scoring list, but goalies and opposing coaches still didn't know how he did it—only that he had.

1993

Billy Smith

b. Perth, Ontario, December 12, 1950

There are many things Billy Smith was famous for as a goalie for the New York Islanders, but the thing he would like to be remembered for most was his playoff record. In 132 appearances, he won 88 games and lost only 36, a win percentage not even many Hall of Famers can match. Smith (below, left) joined the Islanders in 1972 after being claimed in the Expansion Draft, and he quickly developed into an important piece of the team's Stanley Cup plans. Like Gerry Cheevers, he rarely had a spectacular goals-against average, but he kept the puck out of the net when it counted the most. On November 28, 1979 he made history by becoming the first goalie credited with a goal after he touched the puck last and Colorado put the puck into its own empty net on a delayed penalty. More infamously, Smith was known for using his stick on forwards who encroached upon his crease, but in the playoffs, he was scintillating. It was largely his timely saves that gave the Isles four successive Cups (1979–83). He won the Conn Smythe Trophy in the last of those victories. He also won a Vézina Trophy and shared the William Jennings Trophy with partner Rollie Melanson in 1982–83.

Seymour Knox III

b. Buffalo, New York, March 9, 1926

It was Seymour and brother Northrup who brought the NHL to Buffalo in 1970, a move that was five years in the making. They had applied in 1965 for one of the first six franchises, but when that was unsuccessful they tried to move the Oakland Seals to Buffalo. Seymour was a minority owner of that team and sat on the NHL's Board of Governors, and his insistence that a team would fare well in his hometown finally convinced the rest of the league to give him a team. Knox immediately hired Punch Imlach as coach, and the team's first-ever draft choice, Gilbert Perreault, launched the team to success that would take it to the Cup finals just five years later. Knox sat on the Board of Governors for 25 years and became director of the United States Hockey Hall of Fame in Eveleth, Minnesota.

Frank Griffiths

b. Burnaby, British Columbia, December 17, 1916
d. Vancouver, British Columbia, April 7, 1994

The strong business acumen of Frank Griffiths was a benefit to the NHL for a number of years, starting in 1974 when his company, Northwest Sports Enterprises Limited, bought the Vancouver Canucks. He became the team's representative with the NHL Board of Governors that year and guided his team to stability and growth on ice and off, solidifying finances and leading the team to the Cup finals in 1982. In 1979, Griffiths was made a member of the NHL's Audit Committee and helped stabilize other teams for the coming years. He was a credit to the Canucks and the NHL until he retired in 1987.

1993

Fred Page

b. Port Arthur, Ontario, September 29, 1915
d. Vancouver, British Columbia, December 23, 1997

Page began his association with hockey in Thunder Bay, first as a player, then a referee. In 1958, he had the whistle for the western Memorial Cup playdowns and the Allan Cup finals and he worked with the Thunder Bay Amateur Hockey Association as an executive from 1954 to 1962, serving as president the last four of those years. In 1958, Page also began his association with the Canadian Amateur Hockey Association. He served as a vice president from 1962 to 1964 and 1964 to 1966 and organized international tours for Canadian teams going to Europe. In 1964, he also became chairman of the Leadership Program Committee and then the Canadian National Team Committee. In 1966, Page was named president of the CAHA and helped establish ongoing and healthy relations between it, the U.S. counterpart, and the NHL. He also represented Canada at the International Ice Hockey Federation and was instrumental in arranging the World Championships to come to Canada in 1970 (though they were subsequently moved to Sweden when Canada boycotted all international competition). He also served on the IIHF Directorate for many years and helped organize the Pacific Coast Junior Hockey League.

John D'Amico

b. Toronto, Ontario, September 21, 1937

Once he had worked his final game as a linesman, on March 5, 1988, the last link to the Original Six had been severed. D'Amico officiated in the Toronto Hockey League in his youth and then in the Ontario Hockey Association for two years. After working an NHL exhibition game in Kitchener in 1963, he was discovered by Carl Voss, referee-in-chief, and signed to a contract. D'Amico's first game came at the Boston Garden on October 12, 1964. He started as a linesman, worked a few games as a referee, and moved back to the lines permanently in 1967. He went on to work 1,700 games and a further 20 Stanley Cup finals and seven All-Star Games. Such was his reputation that he was a constant in NHL-international competition. He officiated in four Canada Cups as well as the 1979 Challenge Cup and Rendez-vous '87.

1994

November 15, 1994: See It, Live It

The spectacular induction to inaugurate the new Hall location in 1993 gave way to a more serene 1994 induction in which two Veteran Players were added to the roster, one from between the wars (Lionel Conacher) and another from the post-war dynasty of the Leafs (Harry Watson). For the first time, the induction itself was broadcast live on TSN right across Canada, further evidence of the Hall of Fame's journey from museum to important cultural institution.

1994

Lionel Conacher

b. Toronto, Ontario, May 24, 1901
d. Ottawa, Ontario, May 26, 1954

He was named Canada's outstanding athlete of the first half of the 20th century, and—truth be told—hockey wasn't his best or favourite sport. Conacher was a better football player, a remarkable boxer, and a superb lacrosse player before he ever even put on a pair of skates, which he did for the first time at age 16. His natural athletic ability, though, was without compare, and soon enough he was playing defence in junior and senior hockey in Toronto. From there he moved to Pittsburgh in 1923 to play for the Yellowjackets, and when the franchise turned pro two years later, Conacher stayed on board. He later played for the Americans, Maroons, and Black Hawks, having his greatest success with the Hawks in 1933–34 and then Montreal the next year, becoming one of a select few to win consecutive Cups with different teams. Conacher was a pioneer on defence. He was famed for going down to one knee and sliding in front of the puck carrier to block shots or take away the pass. He was a First Team All-Star in 1933–34 and was twice runner-up in Hart Trophy voting, further testament to his reputation in the NHL.

Harry Watson

b. Saskatoon, Saskatchewan, May 6, 1923
d. Toronto, Ontario, November 21, 2002

At 6'1" and 205 pounds, Watson was head and shoulders above everyone else in the league during his heyday. But he was as gentlemanly as he was big and never played an intimidating style of hockey. Instead, he earned his respect through teamwork and leadership. He started with Brooklyn in 1941 and a year later wound up in Detroit after the Americans folded. In his first year, he won the Stanley Cup, but the year was 1943 and he left the league right after to join Canada's war effort. He returned in 1945 and a year later was traded to Toronto where he enjoyed his greatest successes. Watson won four Cups in the next five years,

scoring the Cup-winning goal in 1948 and assisting on Bill Barilko's overtime winner in 1951. He had four, 20-goal seasons with the Leafs playing left wing most notably on a line with Syl Apps and Bill Ezinicki, but in December 1954 Watson was sold to Chicago where he closed out his career. Although he never won an individual trophy, Watson (below, left) played in seven All-Star Games and retired in 1957 with his name on the Cup five times. He played 809 games and scored 236 goals and 443 points, the last total ranking 15th all-time at the time of his departure from the NHL.

Brian O'Neill

b. Montreal, Quebec, January 25, 1929

Brian O'Neill began his tenure in the NHL on April 1, 1966, when he was hired as the director of administration under league president Clarence Campbell. He helped oversee the 1967 Expansion Draft, and within four years he was promoted to executive director. In the summer of 1977, O'Neill again moved up, this time to executive vice president, and when Campbell retired it was left to O'Neill to take all disciplinary actions for the league. He was involved in all levels of the various drafts administered by the NHL on an annual basis and helped liaise between the league and European teams on the transfer of players. In 1992, he scaled back his activities and worked as a consultant for the league, though since 1988 he has had a far more important job—in name, at least—as trustee of the Stanley Cup.

1995

November 21, 1995: A Party Mix of Greatness

There was a little bit of everything this year for fans attending the induction dinner: one Veteran Player (Bun Cook), a Montreal dynasty defenceman (Larry Robinson), an Islanders dynasty Builder (Bill Torrey), and a champion of international hockey (Gunther Sabetzki). The ceremonies again took place in the Hockey Hall of Fame, and a back tie crowd of some 1,400 enjoyed the proceedings and broadcast.

Fred "Bun" Cook

b. Kingston, Ontario, September 18, 1903

d. Kingston, Ontario, March 19, 1988

The induction of Bun Cook completed the hat trick, the final member of the famed Bread Line to be inducted. Brother Bill and Frank Boucher had entered the Hall earlier, but Bun came in posthumously under the Veteran Players branch of selection. He played 10 of his 11 seasons with the Rangers and played his last season, in 1936–37, with Boston. It was thanks in large part to the Bread Line that the Blueshirts won the Cup in 1927–28, and Cook won a second Cup in 1933 with the team. He had won the Allan Cup in 1923 with Sault Ste. Marie before turning pro with New York in 1926 after a two-year stint out west. Cook was considered the innovator of the drop pass, a crafty manoeuvre which sprung the puck carrier free and presented the trailing man with a surprise opportunity to shoot or pass quickly.

Larry Robinson

b. Winchester, Ontario, June 2, 1951

In 20 seasons in the NHL, Larry Robinson set and maintained a standard of excellence that few defencemen before or since have equalled. Drafted 20th overall by Montreal in 1971, he turned pro with the Voyageurs but developed quickly into a player well beyond the limits of the American Hockey League. He was called up to the Habs midway through the 1972–73 season—and he never left. Big, gangly, and extremely strong, he provided a perfect balance of offence and defence. From the power play, his shots got through to the goalie, and his long strides were effective in moving the puck up ice. Inside his own blue line, he was tenacious and powerful enough to take his man and clear the front of the net. He won the Stanley Cup as a rookie, the first of six times he held the great trophy during his career. He never scored 20 goals in a season, but 10 times he had 50 points or more, testament to his passing and playmaking. Robinson won the Norris Trophy twice, in 1976–77 and 1979–80, and in the 1978 playoffs he won the Conn Smythe Trophy as the best player in the playoffs. He spent 17 of his years with the Canadiens, ending his NHL time with Los Angeles, for which he later coached. He won another Cup as head coach in New Jersey in 2000. In 1,384 career games, Robinson had 958 points. He also played in four Canada Cups, and perhaps most amazing of all, he never missed the playoffs as a player, appearing in 227 post-season games.

Gunther Sabetzki

b. Dusseldorf, Germany, June 4, 1915

The international hockey world changed in 1975 when Gunther Sabetzki was named president of the International Ice Hockey Federation. A dozen years earlier he had founded the German Ice Hockey Federation and in 1966 he was named to the IIHF Council. But from 1975 until his retirement some 19 years later, Sabetzki brought the IIHF into the modern world of sports. He increased membership from 31 countries to 50 and he brought Canada back into the fold by allowing pros to compete at the World Championships and assuring the NHL that the best Europeans would continue to play at the Canada Cup.

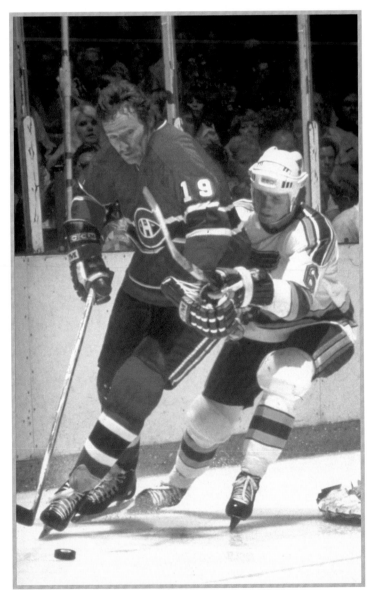

Larry Robinson (left) played 20 years in the NHL and his teams made the playoffs each and every season.

Bill Torrey

b. Montreal, Quebec, June 23, 1934

If there was a man who could most easily be identified as the builder of the New York Islanders dynasty of the 1980s, general manager Bill Torrey was it. He learned his craft over years of experience, starting in the American Hockey League with the Pittsburgh Hornets in the early 1960s. In 1968, Torrey was named executive vice president of the Oakland Seals, and on February 15, 1972 he joined the Islanders as general manager, a position he held for two decades. Along the way he also became president of the team and chairman of the board, but it was his work in building the team for which everyone will most remember him. He refused to trade his draft choices; he developed his young players in the farm system; he acquired veterans shrewdly and with purpose; and, he perfectly balanced youth with experience. From 1974 to 1988, the Islanders had a strong record of 14 consecutive winning seasons and produced a number of Hall of Famers, notably Bryan Trottier, Billy Smith, Denis Potvin, Mike Bossy, and Clark Gillies. In 1993, Torrey became president of the expansion Florida Panthers and three years later watched his new team play in the Cup finals before losing to Colorado.

1996

November 25, 1996: A European Pioneer Makes History

Of course, the contributions of Al Arbour and Bobby Bauer cannot and need not be called into question, but this induction had a special buzz to it because of Borje Salming. He was the first European-trained player to have such an outstanding career that he became an Honoured Member, and—as Scotty Bowman was assembling a Russian-based Detroit Red Wings team that was to win the Cup at the end of this season—his remarkable efforts highlighted the change in the NHL in just one generation. In a sense, Salming was to the Europeans what Lord Stanley was to Canadians.

1996

Bobby Bauer

b. Waterloo, Ontario, February 16, 1915
d. Kitchener, Ontario, September 16, 1964

In terms of games played, many other players rank ahead of Bobby Bauer. But, in accomplishments, that list is short indeed. He helped St. Mike's win the Memorial Cup in 1934 and two years later he was playing minor pro in Boston. At the end of the 1936–37 season he played a single game with the Bruins and scored a goal playing with future Hall of Fame linemates Milt Schmidt and Woody Dumart. Starting the following year, the Kraut Line tore up the league. Bauer scored 20 goals as a rookie and in five seasons before going off to war in 1942 he helped the Bruins win the Cup in 1939 and 1941. The three friends and mates then joined the army and were out of the NHL for three years, but when they returned, their skills were completely intact. Bauer retired after the 1946–47 season after scoring a career-high 30 goals and 54 points, though he returned five years later to play a final game with the Krauts. Amazingly, he scored a goal and an assist. In 327 regular-season games, Bauer scored 123 goals and 260 points. A gentleman on ice and off, he also won three Lady Byng Trophies during his career.

Borje Salming

b. Kiruna, Sweden, April 17, 1951

The first time Canadians encountered the name Salming occurred when Team Canada played a Swedish team between the four games in Canada and four in Moscow of the 1972 Summit Series. The second time came when Maple Leafs scout Gerry McNamara saw him play in the 1972–73 Swedish league system. And the third time was when he was dressed in a Leafs uniform to start the following season. He and teammate Inge Hammarstrom were the first Swedes to make the NHL since Thommie Bergman, but Salming (pictured, left) made an everlasting impression. He put up with taunts based on his heritage; he endured the physical intimidation of the Philadelphia Flyers; and, he showed the grace and force and skill of a superstar defenceman. Salming played 17

NHL seasons—the last with Detroit after some 1,099 games with Toronto. He became one of the most-loved players the Gardens has ever seen, and he teamed with Ian Turnbull to form one of the best tandems in the league. Salming was as fine a skater from the blue line as any in the league and his strength inside his own blue line was also admirable. He had four successive seasons of at least 70 points and his 768 points is a record for Toronto blueliners. Salming came close on two or three occasions to winning the Norris Trophy and he played in three All-Star Games. He also played in three Canada Cups and three World Championships, but his swan song came in 1992 when he played for Tre Kronor at the Olympics at age 40. Famed for his stamina, Salming paved the way for future Europeans to aspire to—rather than be afraid of—the NHL.

Al Arbour

b. Sudbury, Ontario, November 1, 1932

He was a bit player on four Stanley Cup teams in the 1950s and 1960s, but Arbour's accomplishments as a coach and general manager are what got him to the Hockey Hall of Fame. He split his final year as a player, 1970–71, doing some coaching in St. Louis, a part-time post he held for three years. In 1973, he was hired as bench boss of the new New York entry, the Islanders, and it was with that team he began a 20-year association that was second only to Scotty Bowman's in success. In his first year, the expansion team had a disappointing record of 19-41-18, but the next year it was 33-25-22, the first of 12 consecutive winning seasons under his guidance. Along the way, Arbour won 50 games in a year three times, but more importantly, he won four successive Cups, from the 1979–80 season to the 1982–1983 season. Arbour was a brilliant tactician who knew how each player fit into a team and a game plan. He used his resources to perfection and built a team that was a winner. As good a game coach as he was, he also knew how to replace players on a yearly basis, keeping the talent level consistently high. He retired in 1986 but returned three years later and stayed another six seasons. By the time he hung up his whistle in 1994, Arbour had coached 1,606 games, winning 781 times. He also coached 209 playoff games with a record of 123-86.

1997

November 17, 1997: Farewell Magnificent One... For Now

When Mario Lemieux played his last game, he was just 31 years old, but by then his name was synonymous with greatness. The Hockey Hall of Fame declared without hesitation to induct him right away, waiving the three-year waiting period for a man so clearly a part of hockey's greatest stars. Although he returned to the NHL three and a half years later Lemieux was hailed at this year's induction for his grace and strength, his perfect shot, and his masterful scoring touch.

1997

Mario Lemieux

b. Montreal, Quebec, October 5, 1965

In 1992–93, Mario Lemieux won the scoring title despite playing in only 60 games. The last time the NHL season was that short was 1948–49. Roy Conacher led the league in points that year with 68. In 1992–93, Lemieux had 160. When he announced his retirement in 1997, the Hockey Hall of Fame immediately announced he would be inducted that fall, a special dispensation given only a handful of the greatest of the greats. In his final year of junior with Laval, in 1983–84, he had 133 goals and 282 points in 70 games, an average of better than four points a game. On his first NHL shift with Pittsburgh the next fall, he scored, and in every full season he played up to 1997, he never scored fewer than 100 points. The hockey world has never seen a purer, more talented scorer, a player whose hands were smooth as silk and calm under all pressure. In his 10 full seasons, he averaged about 55 goals and he won the Art Ross Trophy six times. In 1988–89, he scored 199 points, the closest to 200 ever

recorded by a guy not named Gretzky. The heir apparent to Wayne Gretzky, it was the Great One himself who pushed Mario to super greatness during the Canada Cup in 1987, first advising him to demand more of himself, then setting up number 66 for the most famous goal in Canadian history since Paul Henderson's series winner in 1972. Lemieux led the Penguins to back-to-back Cups in 1991 and 1992, winning the Conn Smythe Trophy both years and establishing himself as one of the greatest players of all time. Along the way, though, his body was ravaged by debilitating injury, from Hodgkin's disease to a serious back problem. By the time he retired in 1997, he was tired and worn out, but a three and a half year absence lit a fire under his competitive desires and he returned to the game in December 2000. He continued to average nearly two points a game, and he reached a new high the year after when he captained Canada to a gold medal at the 2002 Olympics in Salt Lake City, despite missing most of the year with a serious groin injury. In 2002–03, healthy again, he led the league most of the year in scoring until fading down the stretch, again because of injury and a depleted roster. In 879 career games, Lemieux has scored an incredible 682 goals and 1,692 total points. He won three Hart Trophies, four Lester B. Pearson Awards, and, for his perseverance despite injury, he won the Bill Masterton Award in 1992–93. Had he played as many games as number 99, there might have been every chance he would have eclipsed the great, untouchable points record. As it is, Mario Lemieux goes down in history as one of the finest talents of all time.

Bryan Trottier

b. Val Marie, Saskatchewan, July 17, 1956

The argument can be made that in the modern era there was no more complete player than Bryan Trottier. He was routinely at or near the top of scoring leaders year in, year out. He was a master on faceoffs and a superb checker of opposing stars. He played the power play and killed penalties. The only thing he never got a chance to do was play goal. He joined the Islanders in 1975, and over the next 19 years he won six Stanley Cups. In his first year he recorded 95 points and won the Calder Trophy and by his third year he led the league in assists (77) and finished with 123 points, the first of five successive 100-point seasons. Trottier won four Cups with the Islanders dynasty (1979–83) and in 1978–79 won the Art Ross and Hart Trophies. Although he never captained the team, he was a born leader and his inspired play was key to the success of those teams. He also played in the 1981 and 1984 Canada Cups, and in 1990 he signed on with Pittsburgh as a veteran. He won two more Cups with that team in a supporting role to Mario Lemieux, his leadership taking some of the load from 66's shoulders. By the time he retired, Trottier had played 1,279 games and scored 524 goals and 1,425 points, Hall of Fame totals if ever there were any.

Captain Mario Lemieux proudly displays his Olympic gold medal in the dressing room after Canada beat the Unites States 5-2 to win gold at Salt Lake City, Utah in February 2002.

Glen Sather

b. High River, Alberta, September 2, 1943

Midway through the 1976–77 season with Edmonton in the World Hockey Association, gritty left winger Glen Sather was offered the job of coaching the team he was playing for. Thus started the end of a very pedestrian playing career and the beginning of one of the most successful coaching careers. Two and a half years later, the Oilers joined the NHL, and, under the forceful guidance of Sather, the fastest, highest-scoring team in league history changed the game forever. Sather preached goals, goals, and goals. He pioneered the art of killing a penalty, sending his scorers out and telling them to score more. He played Wayne Gretzky as often as possible, drove Mark Messier to play better and better and then better again, and he let goalie Grant Fuhr play until he could no longer stand. The Oilers set every conceivable team and individual scoring record, and won five Cups in seven years. Sather either coached or managed all these teams, blending speed with skill and youth with experience and the occasional reclamation project. He was father and taskmaster both to his players, a tough man and friend who wanted only to drive his players to great success and the maximum of their abilities.

1998

November 16, 1998: Two Great Nordiques Go in Together

The Quebec Nordiques never won a Stanley Cup, but in the 1980s the team provided the NHL with some of its greatest players. And the Montreal-Quebec rivalry was, without question, among the fiercest ever waged in sport. Two stars from those Nordiques teams, Peter Stastny and Michel Goulet, were the centre of attraction at this year's induction.

1998

Roy Conacher

b. Toronto, Ontario, October 5, 1916
d. Victoria, British Columbia, December 29, 1984

The main reason for the Veteran Player category was to ensure that a player who may have been overlooked at an earlier date could still receive his belated due, and Conacher is a case in point. He entered the NHL with Boston in 1938–39 and led the league in goals with 26, a feat not duplicated until 54 years later when Teemu Selanne did same. The Bruins won the Cup that year, and Conacher scored the winning goal. After dipping to 18 goals the year after, Conacher had two more seasons of 24 goals before going off to war. After an absence of almost four years he returned to the NHL, but Bruins general manager Art Ross decided no man could retain his skills after such a time out. He traded his star left winger to Detroit and Roy proved his boss wrong by scoring a career high 30 times. He was sold to Chicago at season's end, and proved himself again. In 1948–49, at age 33, he led the league in scoring with 68 points playing on a last place Hawks team, a miraculous accomplishment in hockey circles. He retired in 1952 having played 490 games. Conacher scored 226 goals and 426 points and was one of the highest scoring left wingers of all time.

Michel Goulet

b. Peribonka, Quebec, April 21, 1960

By the time Michel Goulet was forced to retire because of a head injury suffered in a game in March 1994, he was considered one of the best goal scorers of the 1980s. He started with the Quebec Nordiques in 1979 after a year in the World Hockey Association and started a streak of 14 straight 20-goal seasons. For four years (1982–86) he scored at least 53 in a season, and four times he eclipsed the 100-point mark in a year. He was a First or Second Team All-Star five times, and although he ended his career in Chicago, the people of Quebec City have always considered him an adopted son. Goulet also played on the champion Team Canada teams for the 1984 and 1987 Canada Cups. He retired having played 1,089 games, scoring 548 goals and 1,152 points, part of a select group of 1,000-gamers to average more than a point a game.

Peter Stastny

b. Bratislava, Czechoslovakia (Slovakia), September 18, 1956

Even if he never played in the NHL, Stastny had Hall of Fame credentials: five World Championships, two World Juniors, two Canada Cups, and two Olympics. He was a star in the Czech league before defecting to Canada in 1980, and in his first year in the NHL he had 109 points and won the Calder Trophy at age 24. Consider his first six years in the NHL: always at least 100 points, 32 goals, and 68 assists. In the 1980s, Wayne Gretzky, of course, was the points leader. Number two of the decade? Peter Stastny. In all, he played 977 NHL games, scoring 450 goals and 1,239 points. He ended his career playing in the B Pool of the World Championships for Slovakia, his tiny, new homeland finally autonomous from the Czechs, and under his leadership as player and later general manager the Slovaks won the gold at the Worlds in 2002. Without Stastny, it was a victory that would not have happened.

Monsignor
Pere Athol Murray

b. Toronto, Ontario, January 9, 1892
d. Regina, Saskatchewan, December 15, 1975

In 1914, a boy walked into a used bookstore, found a copy of St. Augustine's Confessions, and found his life forever altered. That boy was Pere Athol Murray, who was ordained four years later and moved west in the early 1920s. He became parish priest in Wilcox, Saskatchewan, and when the Depression hit he opened a small schoolhouse to help children of poor farmers get an education. Over time, the school expanded and Murray introduced sports into the curriculum. In time, the school became a place where many parents wanted to send their children for the combination of education and hockey. Murray made men out of boys and players out of schoolchildren, sending countless of these on to the NHL imbued with values that helped make them pros and then develop them further at the pro level. Outside of St. Mike's in Toronto, no single school in Canada has done more for hockey than what is now called Athol Murray College of Notre Dame. He sent men on to the NHL, but he sent many more on to success in the business world. The Hounds are one of the most recognized team names in the country, and everyone who has ever attended the college thanks the legacy of "Pere" for his success.

1999

November 22, 1999: The Greatest Honour

With the induction of Wayne Gretzky, the Hockey Hall of Fame also started a new tradition, a new way to connect to the current NHL and to join past and present. The Hockey Hall of Fame Game was to feature the Leafs and a visiting team at the Air Canada Centre on Saturday night of the induction weekend. For the inaugural event the Rangers, Gretzky's last team, came to town. In a pre-game ceremony, the newest Honoured Members walked out to centre ice with a select group of previous inductees to be acknowledged and to perform the ceremonial faceoff. At the game's conclusion, rather than the traditional Three Stars, teams lined up at their respective blue lines and MVPs from each team were announced.

For the first time, the Hall put on a spectacular parade of inductees attending the dinner. All Honoured Members were introduced in a parade of greats, much to the delight and applause of the more than 3,000 fans in attendance. Further, because of the overwhelming popularity of Gretzky, the Hall of Fame expanded the induction into the galleria of BCE Place proper to double the accommodation. Stompin' Tom provided the entertainment, including his singular rendition of "The Good Old Hockey Game."

1999

Wayne Gretzky

b. Brantford, Ontario, January 26, 1961

The statistics are staggering and the numbers overwhelming. Consider this: if a player were to break Wayne Gretzky's record for career points, he would have to produce 100 points for 29 seasons. Or, he would have to record 15 seasons of 200 points each year. Say no more. From the second he entered the NHL, and many years before, Gretzky was the best player around. In his first year with Edmonton, 1979–80, he tied for the scoring lead with Marcel Dionne but lost the Art Ross Trophy on goals scored. No matter—Gretzky led the league outright for the next eight years, sometimes earning

more assists than the second-place man had total points. He was the first player other than Bobby Orr to have 100 assists in a season. He was the first to record a 200-point season (which he did four times). He scored 50 goals in his 39th game in 1981–82, the year he scored 92 goals in all. He captained the Oilers to four Stanley Cups and took Los Angeles to its first-ever finals in 1993. He was a First Team All-Star eight times, won five Lester B. Pearson Awards and a like number of Lady Byng Trophies. He won the Conn Smythe Trophy twice and was named All-Star Game MVP three times with three different teams.

From the time he was a child skating on the backyard rink built by father, Walter, Gretzky showed a passion for the game that remains unmatched. He was a brilliant skater by the time he was six, and by 15 he was playing junior in the Ontario Hockey League. He turned pro at 17 in the World Hockey Association and a year later was in the NHL. For the next 20 seasons, he was the best player in the world, a record setter on ice and an indefatigable promoter of the game and of Canadian hockey off it. He played in the All-Star Game every year there was one, and

internationally he was the most involved skater in the history of the NHL. He never said no to an invitation. When the Oilers were eliminated from the 1982 playoffs, he was on an overnight plane to Finland and 24 hours later scored a goal for Canada in a World Championships game. He played in all four Canada Cups that took place during his lifetime (1981, 1984, 1987, and 1991), setting up Mario Lemieux for the dramatic winner in game three of the 1987 finals against the Soviets. He played in Rendez-vous '87 and the World Cup in 1996. He played in the 1998 Olympics in Nagano and was general manager of the gold medal team four years later in Salt Lake City. Within the context of the NHL, he played the game with competitive fire and with an unquenchable thirst for success. He gave his heart and soul to Edmonton, but when he was traded to Los Angeles in the summer of 1988 he became a promoter of the Kings and hockey on the west coast. Thanks to his Hollywood-star personality he brought expansion to California, both at the NHL level, the minor pros, and the grassroots level. The Kings became a hotter ticket than the basketball Lakers, and the NHL turned into a glitzy league from Original Six heartland in the east to Gretzky's Kings in the west. He ended his career on Broadway, going from one American cultural extreme to the other, but all along playing with a pride that spoke to his father and that tiny rink in Brantford, Ontario, where it all began.

Wayne Gretzky stands behind the net at Madison Square Garden during his final career game, the ice in "Gretzky's Office" adorned with his number 99 to honour his career.

It didn't take long for Gretzky to achieve great success in his post-playing career, winning gold with Canada as general manager of the 2002 Olympics team and presenting Hall of Fame curator Phil Pritchard with the "Lucky Loonie" that was buried at centre ice during the tournament.

The Records

The current NHL Official Guide & Record Book is filled with records Gretzky continues to hold. Some might fall with time; others are here for decades. Here are the cream of the crop: Most goals, career (894); Most assists, career (1,963); Most points, career (2,857); Most goals, season (92); Most assists, season (163); Most points, season (215); Fastest to 50 goals (39 games); Most 100-plus–point seasons (15); Most hat tricks, career (50); Most hat tricks, season (10, twice); Longest point streak (51 games); Fastest to 500 goals (575 games); Most Art Ross Trophies (10); Most Hart Trophies (9); Most goals, one period, All-Star Game (4); Most points, career, All-Star Game (25); Most goals, playoffs, career (122); Most assists, playoffs, career (260); Most points, playoffs, career (382); Most assists, playoffs, one year (31); Most points, playoffs, one year (47); Most points in one finals series (13); Most hat tricks, playoffs, career (10); Not a record exactly but amazing all the same, Gretzky led the NHL in assists 16 times, something no player has come close to duplicating.

Scotty Morrison

b. Montreal, Quebec, April 22, 1930

A life of more than forty years passed quickly for Scotty Morrison who began his career humbly in the Quebec leagues as a referee. In 1952, he moved to the Western Hockey League and within two years his work so impressed NHL boss Carl Voss that

Morrison was in the best league as an official at the ripe old age of 24. He remained in the league for just two years before going into private business, but his love for the game didn't diminish and in 1965 he was offered Voss's position as NHL referee-in-chief when Voss retired. Morrison was at the helm of the league's officials for

16 years until being named an officer of the league and the vice president of officiating. In 1986, he took on an even bigger job when NHL president John Ziegler appointed Morrison vice president, project development as well as president of the Hockey Hall of Fame. Morrison's mandate was clear: find a new and expanded home for the Hall of Fame, which was quickly outgrowing its space at the Canadian National Exhibition. In October 1991, Morrison was named chairman of the Hall and two years later, under his auspices, the new Hall opened at BCE Place.

Andy Van Hellemond

b. Winnipeg, Manitoba, February 16, 1948

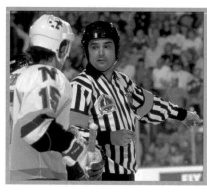

Like any hockey-loving kid, Van Hellemond played the game, going as far as junior before deciding on a career with the whistle rather than the stick. He worked in the Western Hockey League and in 1970 signed a minor-league contract with the NHL, getting into his first game in 1972–73 as a 23-year-old fill-in for the injured Bruce Hood. For the next quarter-century, "Andy Van" was a fixture in the NHL, ranked the number-one man for an incredible 14 consecutive seasons. When he retired after the 1996 playoffs, he was the record holder for games (1,475), playoff games (227), and finals appearances (19 seasons). He also refereed two All-Star Games and Rendez-vous '87 and served as president of the NHL Officials' Association. He later became senior vice president of the East Coast Hockey League.

2000

November 13, 2000: An American Miracle Takes His Place

This year's Hockey Hall of Fame induction weekend got off to a great start on Friday afternoon as the Hall unveiled a new sculpture outside the building to commemorate Team Canada 1972, voted by The Canadian Press as the country's team of the century. On Saturday night, in honour of Denis Savard, the Leafs and Blackhawks played to a 3-3 tie in the Hall of Fame Game. During the induction dinner itself, the Hall repeated its hugely popular parade of inductees as all hockey greats in attendance were introduced to the appreciative crowd. Music featured a performance by two members of Blue Rodeo, Jim Cuddy and Greg Keelor.

2000

Joe Mullen

b. New York, New York, February 26, 1957

The journey from the streets of Hell's Kitchen, New York to the podium of the Hockey Hall of Fame in Toronto is such a difficult one that only one man has ever made it. Joe and brother Brian Mullen grew up in survival mode. Hockey came later and hard, and that they both made it to the NHL was a testament to their skill and fortitude. Joe Mullen may have been the first American-born player to reach the 1,000-point mark, but his achievements in the game need no national qualification. He joined St. Louis as a rookie in the 1980 playoffs and over the next couple of years worked himself into the lineup on a regular basis. In 1981–82,

he became the first pro to score 20 goals in both the minors (Salt Lake of the Central Hockey League) and the NHL (with the Blues) in the same season. He then posted six consecutive years of 40 goals or more with the Blues and Flames. His peak year came in Calgary in 1988–89 when he scored 51 goals and 110 points and led the team to the Stanley Cup. Soon after he was traded to Pittsburgh, and playing on Mario Lemieux's team Mullen won two more Cups. He won the Lady Byng Trophy twice and played in three All-Star Games, and by the time he retired he had dressed for 1,062 games. Mullen had 502 goals and 1,063 total points in his 17-year career.

Joe Mullen (left) epitomized hard work and determination during his 1,062 NHL games, qualities he first learned while growing up in New York City.

Denis Savard played for Tampa Bay toward the end of his career, though he'll always be remembered first and foremost as a star with the Chicago Blackhawks.

Denis Savard

b. Pointe Gatineau, Quebec, February 4, 1961

Because he played centre in the era of Gretzky and Lemieux, Savard never won any individual trophies. He was, however, an exciting player to watch, a man who perfected the spin-o-rama move to avoid defencemen and give himself time to pass or shoot. Savard was drafted third overall by Chicago in 1980 and joined the Hawks that fall as a 19-year-old rookie. He scored 28 goals in that first year and became a fan favourite for his skating and ability to deke at top speed, and for the next six years his goal production increased each year, peaking at 47 in 1985–86. He had five seasons of 100 points or more and in his first 13 seasons in the league, his teams never missed the playoffs. The Hawks traded him to Montreal in 1990, and three years later he was part of his first and only Cup team with the unheralded Canadiens. He then went to Tampa Bay and finished his career back in the Windy City. In 1,196 career games, Savard scored 473 goals and had 1,338 total points.

Walter Bush

b. Minneapolis, Minnesota, September 25, 1929

His 22 years of playing hockey at various levels were admirable accomplishments, but not the stuff of the Hockey Hall of Fame. For that honour, Walter Bush had to make his contributions off the ice. In 1955, he helped form the Central Hockey League and was the league's first president. Four years later he was named director of the Amateur Hockey Association of the United States and was integral in Minnesota's successful bid for an NHL team in 1967. Bush has worked with the Hockey Hall of Fame as a member of the Selection Committee and Board of Directors, and in 1986 he became director of USA Hockey, successor in name to the Amateur Hockey Association of the United States. In 1986, he was elected to the International Ice Hockey Federation Council and eight years later became that group's vice president. Bush has devoted his life to hockey, at the American and international levels, for decades.

2001

November 12, 2001: From Soviet Russia to NHL Stardom

This year, in honour of Slava Fetisov, the Hall of Fame Game on Saturday night at the Air Canada Centre featured the Leafs and the New Jersey Devils in a fiercely played 1-1 tie. The induction dinner was graced by Mario Lemieux and most members of the Penguins—their presence was considered a terrific gesture of support for the Penguins general manager Craig Patrick, who was one in a succession of Patricks to be inducted into the hall of fame and the man credited with building the Pittsburgh Cup champions of 1991 and 1992.

Slava Fetisov

b. Moscow, Soviet Union (Russia), April 20, 1958

There are few players, indeed, who had two distinct Hall of Fame careers as a player, and only one who was drafted twice, five years apart. Fetisov was selected by Montreal in 1978 around the same time the Habs chose Vladislav Tretiak, using a low choice to ensure that if—just if—the Soviets released players, the Canadiens would get two of the best. In 1983, New Jersey re-selected him for the same reason, but it wasn't until 1989 that he made his way to the NHL. No matter. Fetisov's career began as a 17-year-old back in Moscow in 1975, and his 14 years with various national and international teams led to his being called the Bobby Orr of the Soviet Union. The list of victories was staggering. Fetisov won a gold with the World Juniors. He played in 11 World Championships, winning gold six times and being named to the tournament all-star team nine times. He won two gold and a silver at the Olympics. He played in the 1981 and 1987 Canada Cups. And then, he played in the NHL! By then, he was 31 and a bit slower from 14 years of fierce hockey, but he was still a remarkable force on the blue line, first for New Jersey and then more famously for Detroit. Fetisov won Cups with the Wings in 1997 and 1998, the only years he also played in the All-Star Game. He retired in 1998 at age 40, his reputation long ago having earned him a spot in the Hall of Fame.

Few players endured as much to get to the NHL as Slava Fetisov, who started a pro career in the Soviet Union at age 17 and didn't get to North America until some 14 years later.

Mike Gartner

b. Ottawa, Ontario, October 29, 1959

Perhaps owning any career scoring record not held by Wayne Gretzky is rightful enough achievement to make a player an Honoured Member for the Hockey Hall of Fame. Mike Gartner holds a unique record in that he scored 30 goals or more for 15 successive seasons, and 17 overall. His streak was stopped only in 1994–95 by the owners' lockout. Gartner had turned pro in the World Hockey Association as an 18-year-old and joined the NHL with Washington a year later, in 1979. He scored 36 goals as a rookie and thus began a remarkable streak of consistently high performance even though his teams made the playoffs only sporadically. He played 10 years with the Caps and later moved to Minnesota, the Rangers, Toronto, and Phoenix, and at every stop along the way there was one common fact: 30-plus goals. He reached a high of 50 scores and 102 points in 1984–85 with the Caps, a year that began with a victorious run for Team Canada at the Canada Cup. Gartner also played in the 1987 edition of that tournament. The right winger played in seven All-Star Games and retired in 1998 with some phenomenal statistics:

1,432 games played, 708 goals, 627 assists, 1,335 total points. Only Wayne Gretzky, Marcel Dionne, Gordie Howe, and Phil Esposito had more goals than "Garts" when he skated his last.

Dale Hawerchuk

b. Toronto, Ontario, April 4, 1963

He may not have been inducted in his first year of eligibility, but there was every reason to induct him later than never. Hawerchuk burst into the NHL in 1981 with Winnipeg and scored 45 goals and 103 points as a rookie, winning the Calder Trophy and heralding a new respect for the Jets around the league. In six of his first seven years he eclipsed the 100-point mark, peaking in 1984–85 with 53 goals and 130 points. But for every tremendous regular-season performance, Hawerchuk and the team simply could not beat the perennial giants Edmonton in the playoffs, and for every amazing season the centreman had on a personal level, he could never win a major trophy playing behind Wayne Gretzky and Mario Lemieux. Yet Hawerchuk was not only talented, he was also consistent. He played 16 seasons and scored 1,409 points, an average of nearly 100 points a season. This was done in 1,188 games, an average well above a point a game for such a lengthy time. His points came in the form of 518 goals and 891 assists, and when he was inducted this year into the Hall of Fame, every hockey voice applauded the career of a gentleman and competitor who achieved such great success.

Dale Hawerchuk averaged nearly 100 points a year during his 16 years in the NHL, a number that spoke to his skill and justified his induction into the Hall of Fame in 2001.

Jari Kurri

b. Helsinki, Finland, May 18, 1960

By the time Jari Kurri came to the NHL at the age of 20 in 1980 he had already been a pro in Finland for three years, competed in two World Junior Championships, played for the National Team, and represented Suomi at the 1980 Olympics in Lake Placid. When he joined the Oilers, he played right wing to Wayne Gretzky and went on to record 10 seasons of 30 goals or more. A true sportsman with a great shot, Kurri scored 32 goals as a rookie. By his third year he scored 45 goals and 104 points, his first of five successive 100-point seasons. In 1984–85 and 1985–86 he had 71 and 68 goals (the latter a league-leading total) and 135 and 131 points, respectively. In his prime, he was on the team that won five Cups during these dynastic 1980s and four times during these years he led the playoffs in goals scored.

He was the first great Finn to play in the league for any duration, and by the time he retired in 1998 he had played 17 years in the NHL. Additionally, Kurri played in the 1998 Olympics, the 1996 World Cup, four World Championships, and three Canada Cups. He played a total of 1,251 games with Edmonton, Los Angeles, Anaheim, Colorado, and the Rangers, scoring 601 goals and 1,398 points, a career worthy of the Hockey Hall of Fame in every way.

Craig Patrick

b. Detroit, Michigan, May 20, 1946

Patrick had a pedestrian playing career to precede his exceptional executive career in the NHL—but like a good Patrick he made his way to the Hockey Hall of Fame. Brother Glenn played in the NHL as did father Lynn, grandfather Lester, and granduncle Muzz. Craig retired as a player in 1979 and by the next year was an assistant general manager with the Rangers. Just a year later he became general manager, a position he held for the next five seasons until returning to his alma mater, the University of Denver, to work in a similar capacity. In 1989, Patrick was offered the job of general manager in Pittsburgh, and he jumped at the chance to build a contending team with a centrepiece named Mario Lemieux. Two years later, he was in the team's dressing room drinking champagne from the Stanley Cup, a celebration he repeated the next spring. Patrick continues to work as general manager for the Penguins; he is the longest-serving general manager in the league after Lou Lamorielllo in New Jersey.

2002

November 4, 2002: An Unlikely Group

This year's Hockey Hall of Fame Game featured a classic Canadian battle as Montreal beat Toronto 5-2. The induction dinner that followed was one of the liveliest ever, largely due to Roger Neilson's roasting of Harold Ballard and the Leafs of Neilson's era, the late 1970s. The three Player inductees all fit into one category: unlikely heroes. Their inclusion was clear example of what separated hockey's Hall from that of other sports where exclusion, rather than inclusion, is the norm. All three had outstanding careers, with varying degrees of team success, and all had made a contribution to the game. That was enough for the Selection Committee to vote these three men into the pantheon of greats.

2002

Bernie Federko

b. Foam Lake, Saskatchewan, May 12, 1956

By the time he was inducted in 2002, Federko remained the only member of the 1,000-point club not in the Hockey Hall of Fame. His being overlooked earlier likely had to do with the fact that he played 13 of his 14 years in St. Louis, far from public attention. Yet Federko was the first player in the game's history to record 10 successive 50-assist seasons. He had seven seasons of 30 goals or more, and 11 successive seasons of at least 20 goals. It was his playmaking, though, more than his scoring that set him apart. Four times he had more than 100 points in a season, but his highest goal total was 41. In 10 straight seasons he led the Blues to the playoffs, though he never won a Cup with the Blues or Detroit, the team he finished his career with in 1989–90. A centre, Federko was drafted seventh overall by the Blues in 1976 and made his debut with the team later that year. He never won an individual trophy and played in just two All-Star Games, but never in the history of the game has centre been so strong a position as when Federko was in his prime, the 1980s. He retired having played exactly 1,000 games, scoring 369 goals and 761 assists for 1,130 points, better than a point-per-game average.

Bernie Federko (centre, #24) retired in 1990 and had to wait longer than many players for his induction, but there were nothing but compliments for him once he made it into hockey's most select company.

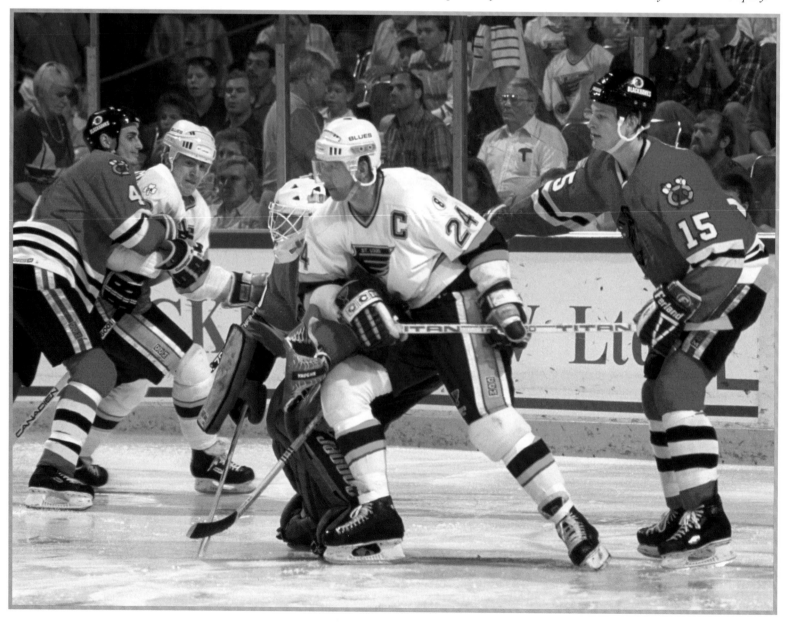

Clark Gillies

b. Moose Jaw, Saskatchewan, April 7, 1954

Perhaps a less obvious selection to the Hockey Hall of Fame, Gillies made more than a passing contribution to the Islanders dynasty of the early 1980s. He won four Stanley Cups playing on a line with Bryan Trottier and Mike Bossy, two of the game's premier players of the day. Gillies was a large left winger whose job was to go into the corners and come out with the puck. Yet while he was effective in this role, he also managed to produce six seasons of at least 33 goals, proving as capable of finishing a play as creating one. He joined the Isles in 1974 after a junior career in Regina and scored 25 goals as a rookie. The next year, 1975–76, he began a string of four straight 30-goal seasons and helped bring the team respect and results. He played 14 seasons in the NHL, 12 with New York and the final two with Buffalo. Gillies was a First Team All-Star in 1977–78 and 1978–79. He played in 958 games and scored 319 goals and 697 points. In 164 playoff games, he had 47 goals and assists, 94 points. An even 12 of those goals were game winners.

Rod Langway

b. Maag, Formosa, May 3, 1957

Born on a military base in Taiwan, Langway actually grew up in Massachusetts and attended the University of New Hampshire on a football scholarship. But it was his hockey skills that shone brighter and Montreal drafted him in 1977. He spent a year in the World Hockey Association and then joined the Canadiens during their Stanley Cup drive in 1978–79. After three years he was traded to Washington, where he spent the rest of his career. He was no offensive star, no end-to-end rusher like Bobby Orr. He did his best work inside his own blue line, preventing goals, which he did better than anyone. He captained the Caps for 11 years, led them into the playoffs every year, and became the first American-born player to win the Norris Trophy, which he did twice (in 1982–83 and 1983–84). He played in six straight All-Star Games (1981–86) and played for Team USA in three Canada Cup tournaments, as well as Rendez-vous '87. By the time he retired in 1993, he had redefined the term defensive defenceman—or at least typified it better than anyone.

2002

Roger Neilson

b. Toronto, Ontario, June 16, 1934
d. Peterborough, Ontario, June 21, 2003

It is not often that the measure of a successful coach is how many teams he worked for, but Neilson's peripatetic longevity speaks volumes about how well loved and respected he was during his quarter-century in the NHL (after a decade in junior hockey). With Peterborough, he interpreted and revised the rule book, and in the NHL with Toronto in 1977, he was known as Captain Video for his use of tapes to break down opponents' tendencies and analyze the game. For the rest of his career, he was hired by expansion teams (Florida), hired to take a bad situation and make it stable (Vancouver, Philadelphia), and hired to take a winning team to the top (the Rangers). In all, he coached for seven teams and worked as an assistant coach for four others, though really the stats page will show he coached an eighth team as well. At the end of the 2001–02 season, he had 998 games to his credit while in Ottawa, so Jacques Martin relinquished the reins for two games to make it an even 1,000 for Neilson. In winters, Neilson devoted every minute of every day to helping his team, and in the summers he did the same with kids and coaching clinics, trying to improve the game with every breath he took. That was what made Neilson a Hall of Famer.

2003

November 3, 2003: 10th Anniversary Celebrations

On June 11, 2003 the Hockey Hall of Fame Selection Committee met in the Founder's Room at the Hall to vote on its newest eligible Players and Builders. The Committee now boasted the presence of Scotty Bowman, who was named to the group on April 2, 2003—to replace the outgoing Cliff Fletcher. Along with Bowman and chairman Jim Gregory, the Committee included 16 others: Al Arbour, Ed Chynoweth, John Davidson, Mike Emrick, Red Fisher, Emile Francis, Dick Irvin, Stan Mikita, Richard M. Patrick, Marty Pavelich, Pat Quinn, Bertrand Raymond, Serge Savard, Frank Selke, Harry Sinden, and Frank Udvari. In selecting Grant Fuhr and Pat LaFontaine, the Committee acknowledged two great players of the 1980s and first half of the 1990s, players who represented the high-scoring NHL of the day (with LaFontaine as a scorer, and Fuhr as a preventer of scores!).

Grant Fuhr

b. Spruce Grove, Alberta, September 28, 1962

In his first six seasons in the NHL (1981–87), Grant Fuhr had a grand total of just two shutouts in 255 games, hardly a statistic that would lead one to the Hockey Hall of Fame. However, he won three Stanley Cups during those years, and he tended goal for the highest-scoring team in NHL history: the Edmonton Oilers that included Wayne Gretzky, Mark Messier, Jari Kurri, Paul Coffey, and Glenn Anderson. Fuhr was the last line of defence—some jokingly said the only line of defence!—and his teammates credited him first and foremost for their great success. The Oilers knew what they were doing right from the get-go, drafting him eighth overall in 1981, one of the highest selections used for a goalie to date. As a rookie, he set a record by going undefeated in 23 games, and in succeeding years he became the league's number-one goalie and its busiest. Fuhr was in net for all five Oilers Cup wins during their dynastic 1980s, and he later played for five other teams during a 19-year career that spanned 868 regular-season games. In 1995–96, he set another record by appearing in 79 games, but it was his playoff performances that made his reputation. He won 92 games in the playoffs—second only to Patrick Roy—and he won Canada Cups with Team Canada in 1984 and 1987, again facts that are often forgotten because of the high-scoring teams of the day. Fuhr was also the best puckhandling goalie, setting another record with 14 assists during the 1983–1984 season. By the time he retired, he was only the sixth man to reach the 400-win mark (403), and although his shutouts and goals-against average were nothing to boast about compared to today's game, five Stanley Cups is plenty to be impressed by for any goalie of any era.

Pat LaFontaine

b. St. Louis, Missouri, February 22, 1965

Although he had to retire early because of a series of head injuries, Pat LaFontaine left his mark on the game as a player and a man to such a degree that the Selection Committee deemed him worthy of membership to hockey's most exclusive family. He was an extraordinary scorer with Verdun in the Quebec league as a junior, starting as a rookie when he scored a record 104 goals. He was named the top player in the Canadian Hockey League for 1982–83, and that summer the Islanders drafted him third overall. LaFontaine played the next year with the U.S. National Team, including the 1984 Olympics, but finished that season in the NHL with the Isles where he began a remarkable career. In 1985–86, he began a string of eight successive seasons of 30 goals or more, culminating with 1992–1993 when he had 53 goals and 148 points with Buffalo. In all, he averaged better than a point a game and became the 54th player to reach the magical 1,000-point mark. In addition to his NHL career, LaFontaine represented the United States at the 1987 and 1991 Canada Cups and the 1996 World Cup. He also played at the 1989 World Championships and the 1998 Olympics in Nagano.

Brian Kilrea

b. Ottawa, Ontario, October 21, 1934

Few men are as loved in the hockey world as Brian Kilrea, and his unparalleled success with the Ottawa 67's in the Canadian junior system is such that he becomes the first Builder to be inducted into the Hockey Hall of Fame whose achievements rest primarily as a coach in the Ontario Hockey League. He played briefly in the NHL, as had his uncles Hec, Wally, and Ken, but in 1974 he was hired to be general manager and coach of the 67's. He's been there ever since, with a two-year exception (1984–86) when he was an assistant coach with the New York Islanders. He has won two Memorial Cups (1984 and 1997), been named OHL coach of the year four times, and in 2002–03 won his 1,000th game, a Canadian Hockey League record. He has 10 division titles to his credit. He is the living stuff of legend. The CHL's coach of the year trophy is now named after him, and he has an arena named after him as well. Kilrea is the most beloved and respected man in junior hockey, but perhaps the finest testament to his abilities and contributions come from the thousands of players who have developed under him—both as people and players—during their late teens. Not one has ever had anything but great things to say about they man they call "Killer."

Mike Ilitch

b. Bitola, Macedonia, July 20, 1929

When Mike Ilitch bought the Detroit Red Wings from the Norris family on June 22, 1982 for the princely sum of $8 million, he was acquiring an Original Six franchise that had missed the playoffs in 14 of the previous 16 seasons. It was a team rooted deeply in tradition and successes, but in 1982 it had a season ticket base of just 2,100. Under Ilitch, the team became a Stanley Cup champion again, though the trek was long and patience necessary. The team missed the playoffs in two of the first four seasons, but it had a young talent and captain named Steve Yzerman that gave Ilitch and fans hope the likes of which they hadn't had since the Gordie Howe days. Slowly but surely, Ilitch developed a solid farm team, put together a scouting staff second to none, and combined smart dealing with a willingness to spend money to build a winner. Today, the Wings have won nine division championships under his ownership and, more importantly, three Cups: in 1996–97, 1997–98, and 2001–02. Ilitch, owner of Little Caesar's, has also been awarded the Lester Patrick Trophy (in 1991) for his contributions to the game in the United States, and he has brought in many family members to help run the team, namely his wife, Marian, and his children Ron, Lisa, Denise, Mike Jr., Chris, Atanas, and Carole.

Mike Ilitch (far right) and his wife (beside him) celebrate Steve Yzerman's Conn Smythe Trophy win following Detroit's run to the Stanley Cup in 1998.

International Ice Hockey Federation Hall of Fame Inductees

1997

John "Bunny" Ahearne (Great Britain)
Father David Bauer (Canada)
Vsevolod Bobrov (Russia)
Walter Brown (USA)
Vlastimil Bubnik (Czech Republic)
Bill Cleary (USA)
Gerry Cosby (USA)
Jaroslav Drobny (Czech Republic)
Arne Grunander (Sweden)
Anders Hedberg (Sweden)
Vladimir Kostka (Czech Republic)
Erich Kuhnhackl (Germany)
Bob LeBel (Canada)
Vic Lindquist (Canada)
Seth Martin (Canada)
Louis Magnus (France)
John Mayasich (USA)
Vaclav Nedomansky (Czech Republic)
Alexander Ragulin (Russia)
Gunther Sabetzki (Germany)
Harry Sinden (Canada)
Andrei Starovoitov (Russia)
Anatoli Tarasov (Russia)
Richard "Bibi" Torriani (Switzerland)
Vladislav Tretiak (Russia)
Sven Tumba (Sweden)
Walter Wasservogel (Austria)
Urpo Ylonen (Finland)
Vladimir Zabrodsky (Czech Republic)

1998

Helmut Balderis (Latvia)
Lars Bjorn (Sweden)
Ferdinand Cattini (Switzerland)
Hans Cattini (Switzerland)
Bill Christian (USA)
Vladimir Dzurilla (Slovakia)
Carl Erhardt (Great Britain)
Anatoli Firsov (Russia)
Josef Golonka (Slovakia)
Karel Gut (Czech Republic)
Jiri Holecek (Czech Republic)
Gustav Jaenecke (Germany)
Marshall Johnston (Canada)
Valeri Kharlamov (Russia)
Jacques Lacarriere (France)
Paul Loicq (Belgium)
Hakan Loob (Sweden)
Cesar Luthi (Switzerland)
Pekka Marjamaki (Finland)
Jack McCartan (USA)
Terry O'Malley (Canada)
Eduard Pana (Romania)
Bob Ridder (USA)
Jack Riley (USA)
Borje Salming (Sweden)
Arne Stromberg (Sweden)
Viktor Tikhonov (Russia)
Xaver Unsinn (Germany)
Valeri Vasiliev (Russia)
Harry Watson (Canada)

Sven Bergqvist (Sweden)

Roger Bourbonnais (Canada)

Herb Brooks (USA)

Enrico Calcaterra (Italy)

Arkady Chernyshev (Russia)

Jim Craig (USA)

Mike Curran (USA)

Rudolf Eklow (Sweden)

Jiri Holik (Czech Republic)

Derek Holmes (Canada)

Leif Holmqvist (Sweden)

Fran Huck (Canada)

Tore Johannessen (Norway)

Mark Johnson (USA)

1999 Harry Lindbld (Finland)

Machac Oldrich (Czech Republic)

Alexandwer Maltsev (Russia)

Boris Mayorov (Russia)

Jackie McLeod (Canada)

Barry MacKenzie (Canada)

Lasse Oksanen (Finland)

Frantisek Pospisil (Czech Republic)

Sepp Puschnig (Austria)

Jan Starsi (Slovakia)

Roland Stoltz (Sweden)

Hal Trumble (USA)

Yoshiaki Tsutsumi (Japan)

Jorma Valtonen (Finland)

Joachim Ziesche (Germany)

2000

Wayne Gretzky (Canada)

Tomas Jonsson (Sweden)

Udo Kiessling (Germany)

Jari Kurri (Finland)

Boris Mikhailov (Russia)

Peter Stastny (Slovakia)

Goran Stubb (Finland)

2001

Dave King (Canada)

Sergei Makarov (Russia)

Vladimir Martinec (Czech Republic)

Gyorgy Pasztor (Hungary)

Hans Rampf (Germany)

Ulf Sterner (Sweden)

2002

Ernerst Aljancic, Sr. (Slovakia)

Ivan Hlinka (Czech Republic)

Matti Keinone (Finland)

Nisse Nilsson (Sweden)

Peter Patton Bethune Minet (Great Britain)

Gord Renwick (Canada)

Thayer Tutt (USA)

Vladimir Yurzinov (Russia)

2003

Gustafsson, Bengt-Ake

b. Karlskoga, Sweden, March 23, 1958

In 1973 at the age of 15, Gustafsson was already playing second division hockey for his KB Karlskoga club, and at 19 he was ready for action with nearby Farjestads BK. One year later, in 1978, Bengt-Ake made his international debut with the "Tre Kronor." After the successful 1979 IIHF World Championship in Moscow, Gustafsson signed with the WHA's Edmonton Oilers and played briefly with the club before the league folded. He was immediately claimed by the Washington Capitals where he spent nine NHL seasons in which he played 629 regular season games and accumulated 196 goals and added 359 assists. Despite playing abroad, Gustafsson always made himself available for the Swedish national team. His 117 games included two Canada Cups, the 1992 Olympic Winter Games, and five IIHF World Championips, which earned him two gold, a silver, and a bronze medal. In 1989, Gustafsson returned to Farjestad and the Elitserien. After retiring in 1999 at age 41, he coached the Swiss club Langnau and was also the assistant coach of the Swiss national team between 1999 and 2002. In his first season as head coach Farjestads BK, Gustafsson captured the 2002 national championship.

Jutila, Timo

b. Tampere, Finland, December 24, 1963

Timo Jutila's playing career lasted from 1980 until 1999, during which time he played for Tappara Tampere in the Finnish Hockey League, the NHL's Buffalo Sabres, the Rochester Americans in the AHL, Lulea Hockey in Sweden and SC Bern in Switzerland. An outstanding career in Finland was highlighted with five national championship titles. He was a five time all-star and in 1988 was voted the league's best defenseman. Jutila also represented Finland in two IIHF World Junior Championships, earning a silver and a bronze medal in 1981 and 1982 respectively, and three Olympic Winter Games—1984, 1992, and 1994—where he took home a bronze medal. During his eight IIHF World Championship tournaments, Jutila won two silver medals, but, more importantly, he was an instrumental part of

Finland's first ever IIHF World Championship gold medal winning team in 1995. In his 246 national team games which also included two Canada Cup appearances, Jutila served as the team captain for much of his career.

Malecek, Josef

b. Prague, Czech Republic, June 18, 1903

Malecek was a major part of the early development of ice hockey in Czechoslovakia, first honing his skills with in the AC Sparta Praha club, and later becoming a legend with LTC Praha. He spent 16 seasons with LTC between 1927 and 1943, taking 12 national titles out of 13 times and four Spengler Cup titles. Toward the end of his career, Malecek suited up for Slovan Bratislava and lastly as a playing coach with HC Davos. Malecek already represented his national team at age 17, and starred in 17 different IIHF events from 1922 to 1939, including the Olympic tournaments in 1924, 1928, and 1936. Aside from the two World Championship bronze medals, Malecek helped Czechoslovakia earn four gold, four silver, and four bronze medals as part of the European Championships.

Yakushev, Alexander

b. January 2, 1947

Alexander Yakushev starred for Spartak Moscow from 1963 to 1980 during which time he scored 339 goals in 568 Soviet League games and won the national title on three occasions—1967, 1969, and 1976—to go along with a 1976 Soviet League All-Star Team selection. He finished his impressive playing career after three seasons in Kapfenberg, Austria in 1983. Internationally, Yakushev represented the former Soviet Union during 218 national team games, including two Olympic Winter Games, the 1972 event in Sapporo and 1976 in Innsbruck winning the gold medal in both. His 10 IIHF World Championship appearances produced seven gold medals, two silver, and a bronze. His performance during the 1972 Summit Series between the Soviet Union and Team Canada (where he led the Soviet team in scoring with seven goals and four assists in eight games) led many to view Yakushev as the first modern Soviet superstar.

Berglund, Curt

b. Stockholm, Sweden, August 30, 1923

In 1972, Swedish Ice Hockey Association elected Curt Berglund to its Board of Directors. That same year, Berglund also became a Board Member with the prestigious Stockholm club AIK where he served as chairman and treasurer. Berglund's knowledge, hard work, and attention to detail were soon extended beyond his native Sweden. Just three years later, in 1975, the IIHF recruited Berglund for similar duties. Berglund spent the next 15 years as the IIHF's Minister of Finance before retiring in 1990, but not before helping the IIHF further establish itself economically for the future. For these efforts and others, Curt Berglund was made an IIHF Honorary Member in 1990 and more recently handled Tournament Chairman duties at the 2001 IIHF World Championship Division I that was held in Ljubljana, Slovenia.

Henschel, Heinz

b. Berlin, Germany, January 27, 1920

During a playing career which lasted 24 seasons (1932-56), Heinz Henschel represented Berliner EV 1898, LTTC Rot-Weiss Berlin, Berliner SC (where he won two national championship titles), and SC Brandenburg. After his retirement as a player, he remained in the game, becoming an official not only domestically but internationally as well. Henschel was a founding member of the Berlin Ice Sport Federation, the Berlin Regional Sport Federation, the German Ice Sport Federation, and, finally, in 1963, the German Ice Hockey Federation – the DEB. His work with the the German Ice Hockey Federation covered more than 25 years during which time he served as the delegation leader of the national teams in eight Olympic Winter Games as well as 27 IIHF World Championships events. Henschel was also President of the German Ice Sport Federation, a member of the National Olympic Committee and Chef de Mission to the 1984 Olympic Winter Games in Sarajevo.

Kompalla, Josef

b. Katowice, Poland, March 13, 1936

Josef Kompalla's first involvement with ice hockey began as a player, beginning with Gwardia Katowice in 1951 and later

Gornik Katowice (where he won a Polish championship) before leaving for the German Federal Republic in 1958 to play for Preussen Krefeld where he retired after 13 seasons in 1970. After his playing career, Kompalla began his magnificent career as a referee, which saw him officiate some 2,019 international and national league games. His international career included three Olympic Winter Games in 1976, 1980, and 1984, nine IIHF World Championships, three IIHF World Championship Pool B tournaments, and two IIHF World U20 Championships. He totalled 157 international games as referee. Kompalla refereed the famous 1972 Summit Series between the former Soviet Union and Team Canada as well as 1974 series between the former Soviet Union and the WHA Team Canada. More recently, Kompalla was member of the IIHF Referee Committee from 1994 to 1998, and has been assigned Referee-in-Chief duties during numerous IIHF championship tournaments.

Wiitala, Unto

b. Kuolemajarvi, Finland, July 5, 1925

Unto Wiitala began his playing career in the Finnish League in 1946 with Karhu-Kissat Helsinki and retired as a player in 1959 with Tarmo Hameenlinna. Aside from winning the Best Goalkeeper Award three times, he also earned one silver and one bronze medal in the Finnish National Championships. Internationally, Wiitala played in the 1952 Olympic Winter Games in Oslo, Norway and represented Finland in five IIHF World Championship tournaments. Immediately upon retirement as a player, Wiitala made a quick transition to a referee which spanned 15 seasons, including selection as Best Referee on four occasions in the Finnish League. During that time, he also officiated at two Olympic Winter Games and three IIHF World Championships. Later, Wiitala became a valuable member of the IIHF Referee Committee member and served for many years as Referee-in-Chief for the Finnish Hockey League and until recently, as Chairman of the Board to Finland's Hockey Hall of Fame Museum, where he was himself inducted back in 1985.